"Victor Hugo once said, 'There is one thing stronger than all the armies in the world, and that is an idea whose time has come.' I believe *The Oz Principle* is that idea which will transform corporate America and prepare us for the twenty-first century."

—Michael L. Eagle,
Vice President, Global Manufacturing,
Eli Lilly and Company

"*The Oz Principle* is a thoughtful and straightforward approach to the complex subject of accountability. This book lays out the method and approach for building greater accountability to maximize the impact of every organizational initiative. It has been my experience that implementation of the concepts found in *The Oz Principle* will improve individual and companywide results."

—Ed Vanyo,
General Manager, Can Operations,
Nestlé Purina

"We tried for several years to make some basic changes in our Global Manufacturing Group and just couldn't get there. We finally internalized the concept of the accountability process as defined in *The Oz Principle*. It has really turned us around in the direction we wanted and we're now making the progress we've been trying to make for years."

—Bill Smith,
Vice President,
Global Corporation Manufacturing Services,
Eli Lilly

"*The Oz Principle* has inspired our people at every level to rally around an easy-to-understand approach for creating accountability throughout our organization. Simply put, *The Oz Principle* has helped us get even better at 'doing what we say we are going to do,' with a measurable impact on results!"

—Michael E. Woods, Senior Vice President, and
Eric Houseman, Vice President of Operations,
Red Robin Gourmet Burgers

"*The Oz Principle* has really made accountability very easy to understand and has improved our effectiveness in obvious ways. Our entire organization has not only embraced the concept but has also made it our culture to operate *Above The Line*. Most important, *The Oz Principle* made it very easy for a new representative joining the organization to quickly understand what Pfizer Pratt Pharmaceuticals is all about, both in terms of our culture and how we operate as a group."

—Dick Reggio,
Senior Vice President,
Training and Development,
Pratt Pharmaceuticals,
A Division of Pfizer, Inc.

"*The Oz Principle* is very easy reading and practical in its content. The message is so straightforward that it is many times overlooked. . . . We are totally accountable for making things happen. It was extremely well received."

—David Grimes,
Vice President, Sales, AT&T

"The concepts in the book are practical and are the things we are living day to day. It is well written; in plain talk like face-to-face discussion. Less theory and more examples and approaches that are immediately usable. We have applied *The Oz Principle* concepts and empowered the people in our whole facility toward the objectives we need to accomplish. The concepts have really served as motivation tools and closed the gap between management and the line workers."

—Vincente Trellis,
Vice President, Surgical Operations, Allergan

"Our success rests in our strong culture developed over the years. Our recent addition of new cultural language, i.e., '*Above The Line, Below The Line*' from *The Oz Principle Accountability Training,* has enabled our company to be more aligned and riveted us on the targeted results."

—Richard Methany,
Vice President, International Human Resources,
Carlson Restaurants Worldwide

"It will help you to approach any new idea or problem and impact your ability to be successful. . . . *The Oz Principle* hit the punch line early and then supported it. It introduces a global concept right away, and then the components of each chapter give you a better understanding of that global concept. After our clients' reorganization, we had the worst month we've ever had leading into January (typically a low recruiting month in our industry). We required everyone to submit an Accountability Plan and we beat our projected hires by 20 percent— a direct result of implementing *The Oz Principle* in our organization."

—Mark Wortley,
President,
Beverly Care Alliance

"*The Oz Principle* unlocks your potential and helps you think differently about the way you approach both your personal and your professional life. The language is easily adopted and you can readily identify with the stories and the principles that are taught. If you embrace *The Oz Principle* and you really apply the points that are made, you will change your behavior and become more successful in achieving the results you want."

—Kelli Fitten,
Vice President, Human Resources,
Brinker International,
On the Border Cafes Division

"*The Oz Principle* shows how to create a sense of urgency and accountability for change that unleashes a power that only comes when each employee, at every level, fulfills his obligation and realizes the opportunity to participate in creating solutions."

—Ginger Graham,
President and CEO,
Amylin Pharmaceuticals, Inc.

"The language introduced in *The Oz Principle* is powerful. The principles are time tested and when implemented the impact is immediate. The learning we acquired from this book is universally applicable."

—Chuck Rink,
COO, El Torito Restaurants

"From the way we give and receive feedback to how we conduct our weekly staff meetings to basic performance management, we have begun the journey of bringing *The Oz Principle* to life within our organization. *The Oz Principle* provides powerful concepts and a common language, which we rely on daily to remind one another that we can't afford to wallow '*Below The Line*' and substitute excuses for results."

—Fred Wolfe,
President and CEO,
El Torito Acapulco Restaurants

"It has made a lasting impression on my career and in my personal life. *The Oz Principle* has made a very positive impact on the way I try to interact with individuals and deal with myself and my interactions, both professionally and personally."

—Dennis Antinori,
Senior Vice President,
Corporate Accounts/Sales Operation,
Guidant Corporation

"All year long we struggled to show some increase in store sales with no real success. However, after applying *The Oz Principle Accountability Training*, store sales climbed and continued to climb for the next eleven weeks thereafter. Numerous obstacles presented themselves throughout the year, but the team remained *Above The Line* and nailed our year-end budget."

—Kenneth White,
President,
Smith's Food and Drug

"A penetratingly insightful book that exposes and examines the essence of personal and corporate success."

—Joseph A. Cannon,
Chairman and CEO,
Geneva Steel

"Simply shatters shopworn 'I'm the victim' excuses with a yellow brick. A lucid assessment and on-target plan for restoring accountability, personal success, and organizational vitality."

—Paul R. Trimm, Ph.D.,
Professor of Organizational Leadership and Strategy,
Brigham Young University

"We had a history of entrepreneurial success, but we weren't satisfied with staying in place. In order to step up to the next level, we needed to be more results oriented. *The Oz Principle* was the cornerstone to achieving this objective."

—Paul J. Byrne,
President,
Precor, Inc.

"*The Oz Principle* eloquently captures the secret to overcoming obstacles and achieving success. It is filled with practical insights essential to the personal and organizational journey of getting results. The book explains an enduring principle that will long outlive the supposed wizardry of the many management fads that melt away with time. I would personally recommend this book to everyone who has tired of wizards and who is eager to get results."

—Dorothy Browning of Kansas

The Oz Principle

PORTFOLIO

The Oz Principle

Getting Results Through Individual
and Organizational Accountability

ROGER CONNORS • TOM SMITH

CRAIG HICKMAN

PORTFOLIO

PORTFOLIO

Published by the Penguin Group
Penguin Group (USA) Inc., 375 Hudson Street, New York, New York 10014, U.S.A.
Penguin Books Ltd, 80 Strand, London WC2R 0RL, England
Penguin Books Australia Ltd, 250 Camberwell Road, Camberwell,
Victoria 3124, Australia
Penguin Books Canada Ltd, 10 Alcorn Avenue, Toronto, Ontario, Canada M4V 3B2
Penguin Books India (P) Ltd, 11 Community Centre, Panchsheel Park,
New Delhi–110 017, India
Penguin Books (N.Z.) Ltd, Cnr Rosedale and Airborne Roads, Albany,
Auckland, New Zealand
Penguin Books (South Africa) (Pty) Ltd, 24 Sturdee Avenue, Rosebank,
Johannesburg 2196, South Africa

Penguin Books Ltd, Registered Offices:
80 Strand, London WC2R 0RL, England

This edition published in 2004 by Portfolio, a member of Penguin Group (USA) Inc.

20 19 18 17

Selected quotations were taken from the book *The Wonderful Wizard of Oz* by L. Frank
Baum (1899). The authors of *The Oz Principle* have no affiliation with or connection
to the producers or owners of the motion picture *The Wizard of Oz*.

CIP data available

ISBN 1-59184-024-4

This book is printed on acid-free paper ∞

Printed in the United States of America
Set in Minion
Designed by Erin Benach

PREFACE

We think that most people would agree that the need for more accountable organizations, teams, and individuals has done nothing but grow since *The Oz Principle*® was first published ten years ago. Who can deny the business case for making accountability a core ingredient in any corporate culture? People who take accountability and operate *Above The Line*® always make things happen in organizations. With a company full of accountable people, extraordinary things, even the entirely unexpected, tend to happen.

We have been gratified to see and experience the impact of *The Oz Principle* over the last ten years. Time and time again, we have been reminded that accountability produces results as we have added up the shareholder value, increased profits, decreased costs, and productivity gains from clients and others who have successfully implemented greater accountability in their organizations. In addition to increased financial performance we have also witnessed improved morale as people come to love their jobs more, learn to cope more capably with daily obstacles, and get the results they want.

The way *The Oz Principle* has influenced the personal lives of our readers and clients has moved us deeply. Their unsolicited testimonials demonstrate that *The Oz Principle* works as much magic in our personal life as in our business life. While greater accountability may not cure all the world's ills, it does provide a sturdy foundation on which you can build long-lasting solutions.

Businesses all over the world have moved to new ground—downsizing, flattening, empowering, team working, liberating, knowledge basing, networking, quality imbuing, continuously improving, process mapping, transforming, and reengineering. For some companies the gains have proved remarkable. For many others, however, the bewildering array of current success formulas, both theoretical and practical, seem overwhelming or foolish as they fail to accomplish the promised results. To our minds, what all the fads and bandwagon programs fail to address is that one essential ingredient is missing from the mix: the fact that results come from people who accept accountability for achieving them. Accountability. Without it, no program can succeed; with it, any program can accomplish even more than its promoters promise.

We've seen it over and over again. Whether it is a company on the most-admired list or an organization languishing and on the brink of failure, performance invariably improves when people take greater accountability and ownership for results. Why do they do it? We believe people *want* to be accountable. Accountability makes them feel better. It empowers them to get amazing results. That is why so many people around the world have so enthusiastically embraced *The Oz Principle*.

Only when people in organizations escape the deadly trap of victimization and begin to ascend the steps to individual accountability can they claim their own destinies and the future of their enterprises.

We wrote *The Oz Principle* to help people become more accountable for their thoughts, feelings, actions, and results; and so that they can move their organizations to even greater heights. And, as they move along this always difficult and often frightening path, we hope that they, like Dorothy and her companions, discover that they really do possess the skills they need to do whatever their hearts desire.

Please join us on this new journey through Oz.

Roger Connors
Thomas Smith
Craig Hickman

ACKNOWLEDGMENTS

This ten-year anniversary edition of *The Oz Principle* owes a huge debt of gratitude to the hundreds of thousands of readers who have found the book useful both in their lives and in their organizations. We deeply appreciate all the enthusiastic readers who have helped to propel the success of this book through the years. We also find ourselves indebted to L. Frank Baum, the author of *The Wizard of Oz,* for so imaginatively capturing the journey to personal accountability. The Oz metaphor has served as a useful tool for helping people in many nations throughout the world realize the benefits of greater accountability. To this end, we wish to thank Pat Snell for her breakthrough suggestion that we use Dorothy and her companions to illustrate the arduous journey we must all take before we can click our heels and get the results we want.

We also wish to acknowledge all of the people we have encountered on our journey into organizations around the world who have helped shape our deeper understanding of one of the most powerful principles of success. These influences include the examples of our parents, the profound questions clients ask during an engagement, the lessons taught by fellow workers, the principles learned through our faith, and the experiences gained working to create greater accountability in organizations.

Our work with clients over the last two decades has increased our appreciation of how *The Oz Principle* applies in businesses of all types and sizes. We wish particularly to thank Mike Eagle, Dave Schlotterbeck, Jay Graf, Dick Nordquest, Ginger Graham, and Joe Cannon for teaching us even more about what it means to act *Above The Line.*

We also wish to thank our collaborator and agent Michael Snell for his thoughtful suggestions, editorial expertise, and encouragement throughout this process. He also offers an example of someone who lives *Above The Line,* always helping the team get greater results.

We also appreciate all the feedback we received from the many people who reviewed the original book and the revised manuscript: Aubree Pinheiro, Brad Starr, John Grover, Adrienne Sigman, Tracy Skousen, and the *Partners In Leadership®* team. We also wish to thank Chris Crall, John Fink, Dr. Michael Geurts,

Tom Kasper, Ran Jones, Dave Pliler, Robert Skaggs, and Tom Power of Prentice Hall. We also value the meticulous review of our work by our fathers Craig Connors, Fred Smith, and Winston Hickman. To these individuals we express our appreciation for their input and for their constant encouragement and continued enthusiasm for this project.

We thank our editor, Adrian Zackheim, who provided strong encouragement and support to publish this ten-year anniversary edition of *The Oz Principle*.

Most of all we would like to acknowledge the helpful input, candid feedback, and never-ending encouragement of Gwen, Becky, and Laura. We say thank you, we could not have done this, again, without your support and your participation.

CONTENTS

The Oz Principle

Part I

The Oz Principle:
Getting Results Through Accountability

Individual and organizational results of people improve dramatically when people overcome the deceptive traps of the victim cycle and take the **Steps To Accountability®.** *In Part One we illustrate how the attitude of victimization has captured businesses everywhere in a choking stranglehold. We explain why people in organizations must avoid the debilitating effects of the victim cycle in order to get results. Finally, we reveal the* **Steps To Accountability** *as the key to obtaining what you desire, for yourself, your team, and your organization.*

Chapter 1

OFF TO SEE THE WIZARD: SEARCHING FOR GREATER ACCOUNTABILITY IN BUSINESS

"Who are you?" asked the Scarecrow when he had stretched himself and yawned, "and where are you going?"

"My name is Dorothy," said the girl, "and I am going to the Emerald City, to ask the great Oz to send me back to Kansas."

"Where is the Emerald City?" he inquired; "and who is Oz?"

"Why, don't you know?" she returned, in surprise.

"No, indeed; I don't know anything. You see, I am stuffed, so I have no brains at all," he answered sadly.

"Oh," said Dorothy; "I'm awfully sorry for you."

"Do you think," he asked, "if I go to the Emerald City with you that Oz would give me some brains?"

"I cannot tell," she returned; "but you may come with me, if you like. If Oz will not give you any brains you will be no worse off than you are now."

"That is true," said the Scarecrow.

—*The Wizard of Oz,*
L. Frank Baum

Like all powerful literature, *The Wizard of Oz* continues to enthrall audiences because its plot strikes a nerve. The book recounts a journey toward awareness; and from the beginning of their journey, the story's main characters gradually learn that they possess the power within themselves to get the results they want. Until the end, they think of themselves as victims of circumstance, skipping down the yellow brick road to the Emerald City where the supposedly all-powerful Wizard will grant them the courage, heart, wisdom, and means to succeed. The journey itself empowers them, and even Dorothy, who could have clicked her red slippers and returned home at any time, must travel the yellow brick road to gain full awareness that only she herself can achieve her desires. People relate to the theme of a journey from ignorance to knowledge, from fear to courage, from paralysis to powerfulness, from victimization to accountability, because everyone has taken this same journey himself. Unfortunately, even the most ardent admirers of the story often fail to learn its simple lessons: Don't get stuck on the yellow brick road; don't blame others for your circumstances; don't wait for wizards to wave their magic wands; and never expect all your problems to disappear. In today's complex environment, the temptation to feel and act like victims has become so pervasive that it has created a very real crisis.

BUSINESS CHARACTER IN CRISIS

Most companies fail because of managerial error, but not many CEOs and senior executives involved will admit that fact. Instead of taking responsibility for shortfalls and failures, far too many of today's business leaders offer every conceivable excuse from a shortage of resources to inept staff to competitor sabotage. From presidents in the Oval Office to entrepreneurs in the garage, no one wants to take responsibility for their misjudgments and mistakes. Yes, shortfalls and failures occur every day. This is a natural part of business and life, part of the human experience, but attempting to duck responsibility for such shortfalls and failures serves only to prolong suffering, retard correction, and prevent learning. Only acceptance of greater accountability for results can get a person, a team, or an organization back on the path to success.

Unfortunately, no one wants to hear the brutal facts associated with bad news, especially Wall Street. No wonder the public's confidence in the economy, the stock market, business in general, and CEOs in particular, has plummeted to new lows. After Lucent's stock price dropped in value by more than 80 percent, CEO Rich McGinn was replaced because he had listened and responded to Wall Street rather than to his own company's scientists and salespeople. Lucent scientists were telling him that the company was losing its position in new optical technology; his salespeople were telling him that sales were being propped up by deep discounting. But that wasn't the sort of news that Wall Street wanted to hear, and McGinn knew it. McGinn had gotten very good at delivering unwavering growth, and stock analysts loved it. As a result, Wall Street glorified McGinn and his executive team. McGinn and Wall Street, it was a match made in economic heaven. Sadly, however, it was a fool's match made in a temporary heaven. Lucent's scientists and salespeople were eventually proven right. Competitor Nortel eclipsed Lucent by introducing improved voice and data transmission technology with huge market success, leaving Lucent lagging far behind, and the deep discounting eventually devastated the bottom line. McGinn was finally replaced by Henry Schacht, who spent his first few months on the job reminding Lucent shareholders and the rest of the world that a company's stock price is a byproduct, not a driver, of success. When the entire global economic system seems to favor rhetoric and excuses over results and accountability, the problem threatens us all.

It threatened Xerox, even though Xerox CEO Anne Mulcahy finally faced reality and told Wall Street analysts that the company had an "unsustainable business model." Her acceptance of that reality came too late, as Xerox teetered on the brink of bankruptcy. For years, Xerox executives had been blaming the company's poor performance on everything from international politics to economic fluctuations to market upheavals, never facing the bad news of the company's deeply flawed business model. Management wizard Jim Collins, best-selling author of *Good to Great* and *Built to Last*, argues that what must glaringly separate great companies from mediocre ones is the latter's tendency "to explain away the brutal facts rather than to confront the brutal facts head-on." Companies such as Lucent and Xerox sank into mediocrity because they attempted to avoid accountability for the underlying causes of their bad news. They're not alone. The list of well-known companies that encounter problems, fail to face bad news and deal with it, and waste time justifying and explaining inadequate performance continues to grow. Enron, Arthur Andersen, Global Crossing, Kmart, Sunbeam, Tyco, WorldCom, AT&T, Polaroid, and Qwest all became slaves to Wall Street, turned a deaf ear to bad news, oversold their strategies, dumbed down their cultures, glorified their bosses, and made count-less other mistakes that destroyed value.

Even though Wall Street sends its share of wrong messages and certainly needs revamping, that's no excuse for any company to sit back and wait for the government to fix the system, or to blame others or circumstances beyond their control for poor results. When bad things unexpectedly happen, as they always do, or when serious errors in judgment occur, as they do more often than most of us wish to admit, accountable companies and their executives take action to control the damage and set a new course for achieving results. Much of Intel's current success dates back to a pivotal moment of accountability almost two decades ago. Japanese companies were pushing Intel's main line of business, memory chips, into the realm of cheap commodities. In a now famous inter-change that still guides Intel's culture, CEO Andy Grove asked COO Gordon Moore, "If we got kicked out and the board brought in a new CEO, what do you think he would do?" They answered that question by acknowledging the hard facts, facing reality, and taking decisive action. They got out of the memory chip business and into microprocessors. After that, they did what they had to do to redirect the company, and that has made all the difference. Andy Grove's and Gordon Moore's decision to face some harsh realities and take their com-pany in a whole new direction showed their employees, shareholders, and those on Wall Street who were willing to face reality that accountability pays, and pays handsomely, if you can only muster the necessary courage, heart, and wisdom to accept it.

Most people in organizations today, when confronted with poor perfor-mance or unsatisfactory results, immediately begin to formulate excuses, ratio-nalizations, and arguments for why they should not be held accountable, or at least, not fully accountable for an organization's problems. Such cultures of failed accountability or victimization have weakened business character, stress-ing ease over difficulty, feeling good over being good, appearance over sub-stance, saving face over solving problems, and illusion over reality. This trend toward victimization will only further weaken business character, deluding business leaders into providing quick fixes over long-term solutions, immedi-ate gains over enduring progress, and process over results. If left uncorrected in an organization, victim attitudes can erode productivity, competitiveness, morale, and trust to the point that correction becomes so difficult and expensive that the organization can never fully heal itself or its people.

CAN THE WIZARDS HELP?

Global business leaders have long been searching for management wizards who will magically bestow greater productivity, lower costs, expanded market shares, world-class competitiveness, swifter speed to market, continuous improvement, and instant innovation. With great excitement and fanfare, these wizards have taken the world's largest corporations on breathtaking adventures down attractive, but imaginary, paths to Oz, where the leaders eventually discover more make believe than make it happen. When you pull back the curtains you discover the incontrovertible fact, as did Dorothy and her companions, that success springs not from some new-fangled fad, paradigm, process, or program but from the willingness of an organization's people to embrace full accountability for the results they seek.

Do all the new management solutions bring an organization great success and force its competitors to their knees? Hardly. Such solutions fall by the wayside in a year or two in favor of the next wave of management wizardry, bringing with it the hope of undiscovered improvements, profits, and growth. Moving from one illusion of what it takes to achieve organizational effectiveness to another, executives never stop long enough to discover the truth, that when you strip away all the trappings, gimmicks, tricks, techniques, methods, and philosophies of the latest management fads, you find one clear and compelling fact: The results you seek depend on shouldering greater accountability for those results. Regardless of the shape and texture of your organization's structure, the scope and sophistication of its systems, or the completeness and profoundness of its latest strategy or revitalized culture, your organization will not succeed in the long run unless people assume accountability for achieving desired results. Unless executives stop fooling around with the symptoms of organizational malaise, abandon their preoccupation with new-fangled philosophies that emerge each season, and start uncovering and putting to work the fundamental cause of success, they will simply continue to wallow in one distraction after another.

In our view, the quest for greater results has, for too many business organizations, culminated in little more than a series of smokescreens and mirrors because it has failed to follow *The Oz Principle*. Like Dorothy and the Scarecrow and the Lion and the Tin Man, the power and ability to rise above your circumstances and achieve the results you desire resides within you. It may be a long journey of self-discovery, but in the end, you'll find you possessed that power all along. In this book, we want to go beyond current management and leadership fads, trends, and philosophies by focusing on the very heart of what it takes to attain success in business. This anniversary edition of *The Oz Principle* will draw upon more than a decade of experience at *Partners In Leadership* implementing the concepts and ideas presented in this book in hundreds of organizations. We will draw upon the experiences of thousands of individuals and hundreds of teams from a wide variety of both established and emerging companies whose stories will, we hope, strike a nerve the same way *The Wizard of Oz* has for generations.

For instance, you'll meet an executive who tells how he and his associates consciously ignored the eroding competitiveness of their company's products and marketing programs over the years, pretending that things would get better without investing a huge amount of effort. He describes in his own words how the company finally came to face reality and began fighting for its life, the first step toward getting the results it once took for granted. Many of the best-run, most-admired corporations succumb from time to time to attitudes of victimization, failing to understand and apply the basic principles and attitudes that get results. Even the brilliant Jack Welch, Chief Executive Officer of General Electric for twenty years and font of wisdom for many American executives, failed more often than many people realize, but, like all truly accountable people, he accepted responsibility for overcoming any setback.

You'll also hear from people at lower levels in their organizations, who, while experiencing genuine obstacles to performance, allowed themselves to get stuck in attitudes of victimization when only they themselves possessed the power to break the pattern and get results. For example, you'll meet a man who claims he can't advance within his company because his boss won't provide the coaching he needs; a director of financial analysis who worries that she's been taken off the fast track because she's a woman and needs more time with her children; a cake decorator who becomes distressed when her boss tells her to "get the lead out" and "get yourself into high gear," prompting her to sue the company; a marketing manager who blames R&D's late product introduction for his division's loss of market share and his own flagging performance; a CEO who argues that too much shareholder oversight has stifled the risk-taking of companies like his; and a department store buyer who fumes daily because it's just too hard to get anything done in a bureaucracy totally tangled up in red tape.

Then you'll meet people with attitudes of accountability who work hard to hold themselves and others responsible for achieving the results they want. For example, at AES, the builder and operator of electricity-producing cogeneration plants, CEO Roger Sant implemented a "they busters" campaign with all the necessary buttons, posters, and flyers to help workers stop blaming the elusive "they" who always seem to stifle results. "They" represent all the finger-pointing, denying, ignoring, pretending, and waiting habits that grow up in organizations and keep people from taking charge of their own destinies. It worked, and AES's productivity has been climbing ever since. It's hard work. Even in this era of high-performance teams, people at super-companies such as General Electric, Rubbermaid, and Microsoft may on occasion point the finger at "them," blaming their own teams for chewing up time, thwarting career advancement, and making it difficult to get the "real" job done.

The latest, most up-to-date management concepts and techniques won't help if you've neglected the basic principles that empower people and organizations to turn in exceptional performances. With humor, satire, and war stories so close to home they'll shock you with recognition, this book explores the very foundation of every organization's productivity woes, providing insight into the undernourished business character and presenting a proven program for rebuilding business from the bottom up. In addition to its case studies, you'll find valuable lists (such as *Twenty Tried and Tested Excuses*), self-tests, salient tips, and one-on-one feedback exercises all designed to keep you off the road of victim thinking and on the path toward full accountability. First, however, you must recognize and appreciate the basic difference between victimization and accountability.

THE DESTRUCTIVE FORCE OF VICTIMIZATION

The world's societies suffer from the current cult of victimization because its subtle dogma holds that circumstances and other people prevent you from achieving your goals. Such an attitude prevents a person from growing and developing. In Charles Sykes's book on American society, *A Nation of Victims,* he says,

> A society that insists on stressing self-expression over self-control generally gets exactly what it deserves. The sulking teenager who insists, "It's not fair!" is not referring to a standard of equity and justice that any ethi-

cist would recognize. He is, instead, giving voice to the vaguely conceived but firmly held conviction that the world in general and his family in particular serve no legitimate function except to supply his immediate needs and desires. In a culture that celebrates self-absorption and instant gratification, however, this selfishness quickly becomes a dominant and persistent theme. No wonder, then, that the range of the external victim—majority and minority, male and female, "abled" and "disabled"— is so often expressed in the plaintive cry of disappointed adolescence. When I refer to America's youth culture, I do not mean merely one that worships the young. I mean a culture that refuses to grow up.

A thin line separates success from failure, the great companies from the ordinary ones. Below that line lies excuse making, blaming others, confusion, and an attitude of helplessness, while above that line we find a sense of reality, ownership, commitment, solutions to problems, and determined action. While losers languish *Below The Line®*, preparing stories that explain why past efforts went awry, winners reside *Above The Line®*, powered by commitment and hard work. The Accountability Chart on page 11 will help you visualize the difference between *Below The Line* victimization and *Above The Line* accountability.

People and organizations find themselves thinking and behaving *Below The Line* whenever they consciously or unconsciously avoid accountability for individual or collective results. Stuck in what we call the victim cycle or the blame game, they begin to lose their spirit and resolve, until, eventually, they feel completely powerless. Only by moving *Above The Line* and climbing the *Steps To Accountability®* can they become powerful again. When individuals, teams, or entire organizations remain *Below The Line*, unaware or unconscious of reality, things get worse, not better, without anyone knowing why. Rather than face reality, sufferers of this malady oftentimes begin ignoring or pretending not to know about their accountability, denying their responsibility, blaming others for their predicament, citing confusion as a reason for inaction, asking others to tell them what to do, claiming that they can't do it, or just waiting to see if the situation will miraculously resolve itself.

The crucial element of personal and corporate accountability should be woven into the very fabric of the business character, process, and culture of organizational life. At Enron, Arthur Andersen, WorldCom, any number of dot-

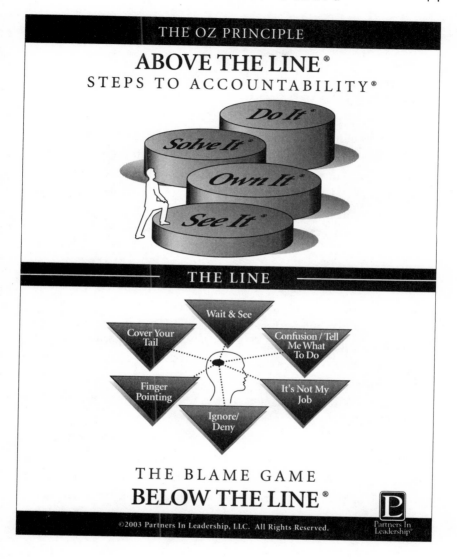

THE OZ PRINCIPLE

ABOVE THE LINE®
STEPS TO ACCOUNTABILITY®

Do It®
Solve It®
Own It®
See It®

THE LINE

Wait & See
Cover Your Tail
Confusion / Tell Me What To Do
Finger Pointing
It's Not My Job
Ignore/Deny

THE BLAME GAME
BELOW THE LINE®

coms, or anywhere *Below The Line* behavior exists, you will find victims—and victims of victims. In business, the descent *Below The Line* usually begins with creating an environment where no one acknowledges the truth and people don't speak up. In their article, "Why Companies Fail," Ram Charan and Jerry Useem offer a description of one company's demise:

The descent occurred because of what one analyst calls "an incremen-
tal descent into poor judgement." A "success-oriented" culture, mind-
numbing complexity, and unrealistic performance goals all mixed
until the violation of standards became the standard. Nothing looked
amiss from the outside until boom. It was all over. It sounds a lot like
Enron, but the description actually refers to NASA in 1986, the year of
the space shuttle *Challenger* explosion. We pull this switch not to
conflate the two episodes—one, after all, involves the death of seven
astronauts—but to make a point about failures: even the most dramatic tend to be years in the making. At NASA, engineers noticed
damage to the crucial O-rings on previous shuttle flights yet repeatedly convinced themselves the damage was acceptable.

Charan and Useem go on to say, "Companies fail the way Ernest Heming-
way wrote about going broke in *The Sun Also Rises*: gradually, and then suddenly."
Nonaccountability can creep into any organization. First it may come unan-
nounced as a reasonable excuse; then it may escalate into the more aggressive blame-oriented accusation; then, finally, it just becomes the way we do
things around here. The price paid by such inaction does not become clear until you see its opposite: accountable people getting results. Then, you can actually calculate the value of accountability in terms of profit gains and market
share expansion.

Cisco Systems provides another example of the cost of living *Below The
Line* in the victim cycle. Cisco Systems, by no means a failing company, suffered
a market-value drop of nearly 90 percent. After forty straight quarters of
growth, the company's managers got soft and neglectful; success often does that
to people. Evidence of customers going bankrupt, declining demand, and rising
inventories wasn't enough to cause CEO John Chambers and his executive
team to change their rosy assumptions and projections. The company had
never worried about what might happen if its assumption of growth ever fal-
tered. When the signs of slowing growth began to emerge, Cisco's managers
stayed *Below The Line*, ignoring and denying the problem. Forced to face reality,
the company finally had to write down $2.5 billion in excess inventory and lay
off 8,500 people. Cisco shares lost 90 percent of their value almost overnight. To
its credit, the company has now begun modeling what might happen when

growth assumptions show initial signs of faltering. Sometimes, getting *Above The Line* means anticipating and preparing for worst-case scenarios.

To get *Above The Line,* and out of the blame game, you must climb the *Steps To Accountability* by adopting *See It, Own It, Solve It, Do It®* attitudes. The first step—*See It®*—involves recognizing and acknowledging the full reality of a situation. As you'll soon see, this step poses the greatest hurdle because it's so hard for most of us to undertake an honest self-appraisal and acknowledge that we can do more to get results. The second step—*Own It®*—means accepting responsibility for the experiences and realities you create for yourself and others. With this step, you pave the road to action. The third step—*Solve It®*—entails changing reality by finding and implementing solutions to problems that you may not have thought of before, while avoiding the trap of falling back *Below The Line* when obstacles present themselves. And fourth, the *Do It®* step entails mustering the commitment and courage to follow through with the solutions you have identified, even if those solutions involve a lot of risk. Happily, these four steps make enormously good sense—common sense. Ultimately, your common sense can propel you *Above The Line.*

THE TRANSFORMING POWER OF ACCOUNTABILITY

However much we may try to ignore the fact or try to shake it off, we all know that we remain on the line for results. We know our responsibilities and that we must accept them and perform at expected levels. While we all have our bad days, when we feel down or sick, we still know intuitively that our work in this world must still get done. Much of the work that gets done in this world gets done by those who don't feel well. Down deep, we know that we shouldn't blame others when we make mistakes or "drop the ball." And we know ever so poignantly that, ultimately, we alone determine the course of our lives and the measure of happiness we achieve. In our own work, we have spent years studying, writing about, and struggling to improve the ways individuals and organizations get results. Since the first edition of *The Oz Principle,* we have witnessed countless organizations create greater accountability by applying the lessons of *The Oz Principle* to move from *Below The Line* to *Above The Line* and thereby produce such results as a 200 percent increase in pace-setting profit margins, a 50 percent reduction in customer handling time, a 900 percent increase in stock price, and an 80 percent reduction in quality-control complaints. We have followed, even more closely in recent years, all the major developments in management thought, from innovative business models to the essence of team leadership. Although we've continued to learn something from each new trend, adding to them a few twists of our own, we've concluded that success in business boils down to one simple principle: You can either get stuck or get results. Period. Case closed.

Accountability for results rests at the very core of the continuous improvement, innovation, customer satisfaction, team performance, talent development, and corporate governance movements so popular today. Interestingly, the essence of these programs boils down to getting people to rise above their circumstances and do whatever it takes (of course, within the bounds of ethical behavior) to get the results they want. If creating this individual accountability was one of the top managerial and leadership challenges facing organizations ten years ago, it's become number one today. However, while many people and organizations recognize the pervasive and urgent need for accountability, few know how to obtain it or maintain it, as evidenced by the vast number of creative excuses promulgated every day for why affairs have deteriorated to such a sorry state. Unfortunately, even when well-documented, legally defensible or logically compelling excuses let people off the hook for poor results, those responsibility duckers do nothing but reinforce a habit of side-stepping problems rather than facing up to and solving them.

All of us, at one time or another, succumb to the urge to take ourselves off the hook with one excuse or another: "I didn't have enough time," "If we only had the resources," "The schedule is too tight," "That's not my job," "It's the boss's fault," "I didn't know," "The competition outsmarted us," "The whole economy's in trouble," "Things will get better tomorrow." Whatever the wording, all our justifications for failure focus on "why it can't be done," rather than on "what else I can do." To be sure, people really do fall victim every day to manipulating bosses, unscrupulous competitors, conniving colleagues, economic calamities, and all manner of liars, cheats, and villains. Things do happen to people over which they have little or no control. Sometimes, people do not deserve what happens to them because they did not contribute to it nor are they legitimately accountable for it. But even in the worst of such circumstances, people can't move forward if they just sit around feeling powerless and blaming others for their misery. Regardless of the situation, you cannot even begin to turn things around until you take charge of your circumstances and accept your own responsibility for better results in the future. You must get *Above The Line.*

Thankfully, over the ten years since the publication of *The Oz Principle,* we have seen and continue to see substantial progress in the attitudes of CEOs and senior executives regarding accountability. According to recent surveys conducted by the Conference Board and *Business 2.0* magazine, today's CEOs worry most about acquiring and developing talent that can produce results consistently and with continuous improvements. Attracting and retaining talented people who demonstrate ownership for achieving results has become so indispensable for success in today's competitive business environment that most CEOs refer to it as their number one priority. Why? Because the other topics that CEOs worry about most—stock market value, competitive threats and new product innovation—depend entirely on talented people who can accelerate and facilitate the delivery of results. They are the business leaders who increase market value, hit their numbers, beat the competition, constantly innovate, and steadfastly teach and guide their people to thrive on assuming accountability for results. That's why we've revised *The Oz Principle:* Senior executives, managers, business leaders, and self-improving workers everywhere desire, now more than ever, to find ways to create even greater accountability for results.

Further, the increasing size, complexity, and adaptability of business enterprises both globally and locally have made accountability for results not only the number one leadership issue, but also the most urgent organizational issue. Forty years ago, in his seminal work *The Effective Executive,* Peter Drucker identified a single, universal question that, if continually asked, could help guide business leaders and workers everywhere to bring success to their organizations: "What can I contribute that will significantly affect the performance and the results of the institution I serve?" Finally, four decades later, most CEOs and business leaders recognize the need to create organizational cultures that produce a strong sense of personal accountability that keeps them asking and acting on Drucker's question.

In his recent bestseller *Good to Great: Why Some Companies Make the Leap . . . and Others Don't,* Jim Collins describes superior work environments this way: "When you combine a culture of discipline with an ethic of entrepreneurship, you get the magical alchemy of great results." We agree, wholeheartedly, but we would argue that cultures of discipline with ethics of entrepreneurship are results in and of themselves, results that spring from workers and teams who continually ask the accountability question posed by *The Oz Principle:* "What else can I do to operate *Above The Line* and achieve the desired results?" When people do that, they learn the secret to getting better results, faster and more cost-effectively. And that's even more important in today's business environment than it was ten years ago. As the performance and expectation bar continues to rise so does the effort it takes to clear the bar.

It's worth repeating: An attitude of accountability lies at the core of any effort to improve quality, satisfy customers, empower people, build teams, create new products, maximize effectiveness, and get results. Simple? Yes and no. It's a simple message, but it takes a tremendous investment of time and courage to make accountability an integral part of an organization. Whether you confront your own self-diminishing attitudes in your small start-up enterprise or in the management ranks of a *Fortune* 500 firm, you cannot expect to create a better future unless you begin to take the time and find the courage to get *Above The Line.*

THE JOURNEY BEGINS

Part One of this book explores *The Oz Principle,* revealing how many business people and organizations the world over share the same feelings of anxiety and helplessness that beset Dorothy, the Scarecrow, the Lion, and the Tin Man on their trek down the yellow brick road to Oz. In these early chapters we show how people who use their victimization to justify inaction, excuse ineffectiveness, or rationalize poor performance unwittingly stifle their own progress, while in later chapters we demonstrate how people who accept accountability for making things better move beyond their victimization to overcome obstacles, deal with setbacks, and rise to new heights. By the end of the journey, you will not only have learned how to become more accountable for results, you will know how to create organizational cultures that develop and reward the sort of accountability needed to rebuild business character and culture in every job and at every level.

An understanding of the seriousness of the current character crisis will help you travel the real path to results and prepare you to discern the subtle, often obscure, line between victimization and accountability. Once you come to distinguish *Below The Line* attitudes and behavior from *Above The Line* performance, you'll find yourself so much more able to tap the transforming power of accountability for yourself, your team and your organization, the subjects of Parts Two and Three.

The book's broad mix of examples will detail exactly how people and organizations, armed with attitudes of accountability, can overcome the obstacles, excuses, and biases that keep them from getting the results they want. Drawing from the sometimes startling and always eye-opening experiences of individuals and groups in a wide array of organizations, we hope to show how people and organizations can overcome victim attitudes and behavior and step *Above The Line* to attain superior performance. Our aim is to transcend the conventional literature on innovation, leadership, productivity, customer service, quality, and team performance by striking at the core of what causes people to get results in all their endeavors, something so desperately needed in today's organizations. By focusing on the fundamental cause of poor leadership, low productivity, unacceptable quality, customer dissatisfaction, inadequate innovation, wasted talent, dysfunctional teams, or a general lack of accountability, we hope to move you beyond explaining why you didn't or can't do better to what you can do to make your future brighter.

Chapter 2

THE YELLOW BRICK ROAD: GETTING STUCK IN THE VICTIM CYCLE

The next morning the sun was behind a cloud, but they started on, as if they were quite sure which way they were going.

"If we walk far enough," said Dorothy, "we shall sometime come to some place, I am sure."

But day by day passed away, and they still saw nothing before them but the scarlet fields. The Scarecrow began to grumble a bit. "We have surely lost our way," he said, "and unless we find it again in time to reach the Emerald City I shall never get my brains."

"Nor I my heart," declared the Tin Woodsman. "It seems to me I can scarcely wait till I get to Oz, and you must admit this is a very long journey."

"You see," said the Cowardly Lion, with a whimper, "I haven't the courage to keep tramping forever, without getting anywhere at all."

Then Dorothy lost heart. She sat down on the grass and looked at her companions, and they sat down and looked at her, and Toto found that for the first time in his life he was too tired to chase a butterfly that flew past his head; so he put out his tongue and panted and looked at Dorothy as if to ask what they should do next.

—*The Wizard of Oz,*
L. Frank Baum

Victimization has infected so much of our world, from small, inconsequential acts to life-destroying abuses, that it affects us all each and every day. To be sure, the suffering a person inflicts on another poses one of the greatest dilemmas of modern life, yet the shelter of victimization can render the sufferer completely ineffective. Even the most successful people and organizations can fall prey to the virus of victimization.

Why do all of us, even the most virtuous, fall so easily *Below The Line* from time to time? Of course, making excuses is so much easier than accepting responsibility. Consider all the excuse-invoking jokes you've heard about arriving late to work, missing a deadline, neglecting an assignment, forgetting an appointment, losing a document, blowing an opportunity, or just plain failing. Here's a list of actual excuses given to the IRS by tardy tax-return filers, captured by the southern California newspaper, *The Press Enterprise*:

"I didn't know today was the deadline."

"I didn't realize it was April."

"I lost the paperwork."

"I hate numbers. If I can't balance my checkbooks, what makes anyone think I can correctly file a tax return?"

"It's too complicated."

"I was too tired."

"I had no time to read the forms and instructions."

"I'm afraid of owing money."

"I don't want to know how much I made because I don't know where I spent it."

"I was afraid going to a tax professional would be worse than going to the dentist."

"My husband and my tax return have been misplaced. Can you please send me replacements?"

"As I was getting the tax forms out of the box, I was bitten by a black widow spider and I have been too sick since then to complete the return. I am not really accusing your office of sending the spider with the forms, but let's face it, fellas—I didn't put it there. Can I get some extra time to do my taxes?"

"I'm recently divorced and I was lucky to get out with my life, much less my tax records."

These wacky, yet all too true, excuses make us laugh and cry at the same time because we have all made our own foolish and justified excuses, trying to duck away from the full weight of our responsibility. Ironically, there is usually a kernel of truth in our excuses—mitigating circumstances that warrant consideration or genuine reasons for our failing—but whenever we use our excuses to stay *Below The Line,* we abandon the opportunity to rise above ourselves, our circumstances and our limitations, no matter who bears the blame.

The victim cycle can ensnare even the most admired corporations, as General Electric discovered a few years ago. *Fortune* magazine's survey of the most admired companies in America consistently ranks General Electric among the top ten and many business people consider the company the epitome of continuous corporate transformation. More than one hundred years ago, on January 1, 1900, *The Wall Street Journal* identified GE as one of America's top twelve companies. Today, only it remains from that original list of twelve. However, GE is far from perfect.

Several years ago the company felt pressure to increase the market share and profits of its appliance division. To get the ball rolling, it hired consultant Ira Magaziner to analyze GE's refrigerator business. As part of his recommendations, Magaziner suggested that GE either buy refrigerator compressors abroad or figure out how to make better ones at home. Opting for the latter course, GE assigned its chief design engineer, John Truscott, the task of assembling a team to design a new rotary compressor. After Truscott and another engineer, Tom Blunt, and division head Roger Schipke presented the results to Jack Welch, chairman and CEO of the company, Welch authorized the construction of a $120 million factory to produce the new compressors. The board of directors gave its full approval to the decision. Within a few months, twenty senior executives met to review test data on the new compressor before initiating production. Finding no faults, they decided to go forward. Full-scale production began in the new Tennessee plant, where a new rotary compressor came off the assembly line every six seconds (compared to the sixty-five minutes it took to produce the old compressor).

One year later, the first compressor failure occurred in Philadelphia, followed shortly thereafter by thousands more. Eventually, engineers found the problem: the use of powdered metal instead of hardened steel or cast iron in the manufacture of the compressors. Ironically, GE had tried powdered metal parts in its air conditioners a decade earlier and had found the material unacceptable. At this point, Schipke decided to drop the new compressor in favor of foreign models, causing GE to report a $450 million pretax charge for resolving the fiasco.

A closer examination of this situation reveals how GE went through every stage of the victim cycle. Executives overlooked earlier problems with rotary compressor technology. Although Japanese companies had already experienced severe difficulties with rotary compressors, no one at GE could recall that fact. Ditto with problems involving powdered metal parts.

All the hints that rotary compressors might not work were denied. Even early reports of excessive heat, worn bearing surfaces, and the breakdown of the sealed lubricating oil fell on deaf ears up and down the line.

Once the failure of the compressor became a stark reality, fingers began pointing in every direction. Senior executives, division management, design engineers, consultants, and manufacturers all took turns blaming others for the problem. Engineers, initially concerned that the new compressor wasn't getting enough field testing, set aside their worries by doing what they were told to do, namely, keeping the project on schedule. When concerns became more widespread, people seemed to think, "We can't tell Jack the bad news" and "We can't let the schedule slip."

Finally, everyone in the appliance division determined that the best course of action was to wait and see if things would get better on their own. Many people thought that perhaps things would never really get that bad; after all, this was General Electric, one of the most effective organizations on earth.

Even one of the most effective organizations on earth can fall *Below The Line* on occasion. Whenever it does, the bill comes due sooner or later. In GE's case, the price tag for their dip *Below The Line* accumulated an estimated $450 million in direct expenditures and eight years of lost opportunity.

In this chapter we want to deepen your understanding of the dangers inherent in all victimization attitudes, particularly those that relate to business and management situations, because our experience has taught us that no one can easily climb the *Steps To Accountability* without fully understanding how and why people get stuck *Below The Line.*

THE LINE BETWEEN VICTIMIZATION
AND ACCOUNTABILITY

Imagine a line between accountability and victimization that separates rising above your circumstances to get the results you want and falling into the victim cycle where you can easily get stuck. Neither individuals nor organizations can stay on the line between these two realms because events will inexorably work to push them *Below The Line*. While both people and organizations can exhibit accountability in some situations, yet manifest victim behavior in others, some issue or circumstance will prompt them to think and act either *Above The Line* or *Below The Line*.

But drawing the line between victimization and accountability isn't easy, especially in our complex society. Most people consider the recent lawsuits blaming McDonald's, Burger King, KFC, and Wendy's for children's obesity to be utter nonsense because everyone, whether for themselves or for their children, should take responsibility for their eating habits. Right? Well, consider Caesar Barber's case. This maintenance worker from the Bronx has filed suit against four major fast food companies for deceptive marketing practices that promote obesity. At fifty-six, Barber is 5 foot 10 inches, weighs 272 pounds, has had two heart attacks, and suffers from diabetes. His attorney, Samuel Hirsch, thinks Barber and millions of others like him deserve compensation. Why? Because they've been eating food high in fat, salt, sugar, and cholesterol without sufficient warning. In Barber's case, he admits to eating fast food for thirty years because he can't cook. He claims he didn't know that fast food was bad for his health until he suffered two heart attacks and his doctor told him to stop eating fast food. In an MSNBC interview Barber said, "It was 100 percent beef and that to me said it was good. I never knew about the saturated fat, the sodium content, the sugar content, none of that." Negligent ignorance or innocent naïveté? You decide, just as all must decide, many times every day, exactly where to draw the line between victimization and accountability.

Even the strongest commitment to accountability will not prevent you from falling *Below The Line* at one time or another. Nobody's perfect. Everyone, even the highest achievers in our complex interrelated society, can get stuck in the victim cycle on occasion, but those who believe in accountability never remain there for long.

People and organizations operating *Below The Line* consciously or unconsciously avoid accountability for results. Languishing in the victim cycle, they begin to lose their spirit and will, until eventually they feel powerless, just as Dorothy and her friends did. If they choose to continue feeling victimized, they will move through predictable stages in an unending cycle that thwarts individual and organizational productivity: ignoring or pretending not to know about their accountability, claiming it's not their job, ducking their responsibility, blaming others for their predicament, citing confusion as an excuse for inaction, asking others to tell them what to do, claiming that they can't do it, developing their story for why they are not at fault, and finally waiting to see if some hoped-for miracle will be bestowed by an imaginary wizard.

HOW TO RECOGNIZE WHEN YOU'RE *BELOW THE LINE*®

Whenever you get stuck in the victim cycle, you can't get unstuck until you first acknowledge that you're functioning *Below The Line* and paying a high price for it. Only with that acknowledgment can you begin assuming a *See It* attitude that gives you the perspective you need to get *Above The Line*. Oftentimes, unable to overcome the inertia of the victim cycle on your own, you need feedback from an objective person such as a friend or spouse, or as in the case of GE, a customer in Philadelphia with a failed refrigerator compressor. However, you can greatly improve your ability to recognize your predicament by looking for one or more of the following telltale clues:

- You feel held captive by your circumstances.
- You feel you lack any control over your present circumstances.
- You don't listen when others tell you, directly or indirectly, that they think you could have done more to achieve better results.
- You find yourself blaming others and pointing fingers.
- Your discussions of problems focus more on what you cannot do, rather than on what you can do.
- You fail to confront the toughest issues you face.
- You find yourself being sought out by others so they can tell you what someone else did to them this time.

• You resist asking probing questions about your own accountability.

• You feel you are being treated unfairly and you don't think you can do anything about it.

• You repeatedly find yourself in a defensive posture.

• You spend a lot of time talking about things you cannot change (e.g., your boss, shareholders, the economy's performance, government regulations).

• You cite your confusion as a reason for not taking action.

• You avoid the people, the meetings, and the situations that require you to report on your responsibilities.

• You find yourself saying:

"It's not my job."

"There's nothing I can do about it."

"Someone ought to tell him."

"All we can do is wait and see."

"Just tell me what you want me to do."

"If it were me, I'd do it differently."

• You frequently waste time and energy "boss or colleague bashing."

• You spend valuable time crafting a compelling story detailing why you were not at fault.

• You repeatedly tell the same old story about how someone took advantage of you.

• You view the world with a pessimistic attitude.

If you detect any of these signs in yourself, your team, or your organization, act immediately to help yourself or someone else recognize those excuses for what they are: impediments to accountability and results. Once this recognition occurs, you and others can begin to understand the nuances and subtleties of the victim cycle, just as Dorothy and her companions ultimately did.

COMMON STAGES OF THE VICTIM CYCLE

While the victim cycle can be bafflingly complex, we have identified six basic stages common to most people and organizations. As you consider the following descriptions, ask yourself if you see any of your own or your organization's behavior in them.

1. Ignore/Deny. A typical beginning point for those who become ensnared in the victim cycle is the ignore or deny stage where people pretend not to know that there is a problem, remain unaware that the problem affects them, or choose to deny the problem altogether.

For instance, many of us have witnessed this stage of the victim cycle play itself out over the past few decades as entire companies and industries in denial have fallen prey to smart competitors. First, the American steel industry denied the need to change and procrastinated its efforts to be more competitive, thus losing its predominance in the marketplace to the more advanced technology of foreign competitors. Then the American automakers paid a terrible price for ignoring customers who wanted higher-quality, more fuel-efficient cars. Denying the changes in consumer preferences, Detroit continued to believe that "customers will drive whatever we build for them." Japanese automakers, on the other hand, operating from *Above The Line,* designed cars better suited to the world's customers.

How many industries will fall victim to their own denial by continuing to pretend not to know what will one day appear obvious? This stage in the victim cycle can prove devastatingly costly. People and companies, unwilling and unable to see what is really going on around them, court calamity and only begin to recognize the extent of their problems after the damage has been done.

As a so-called superpower and leader among nations, you'd think America would have learned more from its *Below The Line* experiences over the past three decades. However, the challenge continues as seen in the results of the Adult Literacy in America surveys released by the Department of Education. One four-year survey concluded that nearly half of the adults in the United States lack the literacy necessary for dealing effectively with modern life. A *Time* magazine article on the subject reports that "roughly 90 million Americans over age 16—almost half that category's total population—are, as far as most workplaces are concerned, basically unfit for employment. Who is included in that definition? Those who can sign a credit-card receipt, but are incapable of writing a letter when they think their bill is wrong; those who can pay the correct change at the supermarket, but have difficulty calculating the difference between regular and sale prices; those who can scan a newspaper story, but cannot paraphrase its contents." What price does American business pay for this lack of literacy? What is the price America will pay in the future for the inability to compete with other nations that have come to recognize their most important national resource: an educated people? The article continues, ". . . Perhaps the worst news from the survey was the hubris expressed by those who were tested: when asked if they read well or very well, 71 percent of those in the bottom grade said yes. If these surveys are accurate, the U.S. is not only significantly populated by people unprepared for current and advancing technologies, but most of them do not know that they do not know."

At the other end of the educational spectrum, consider the studies that show 70 to 80 percent of graduating MBAs leaving their first job within the first twelve months out of school. Why do they leave? Not because they lack technical competence, but because they cannot function effectively in a real world work environment, get along with people, and fit into a company's culture. Both graduating MBAs and business schools continue to deny the reality that it's not just what you do or what you know, but how you do it that determines success in business. When confronted with this reality, most business schools, management professors, and MBAs claim to appreciate the problem. But do they really?

Some CEOs aren't as smart as they think they are, either. When Enron CEO Jeffrey Skilling finally broke his silence about the company's demise, he denied any responsibility or wrongdoing. "We're all trying to figure out what happened," he told a *New York Times* reporter. "This was a tragedy. I had no idea the company was in anything but excellent shape." Tragedy, indeed. Enron had made every Wall Street analyst's and business reporter's list from Goldman Sachs to *Fortune* magazine as one of the world's most outstanding, futuristic companies. Now the company lay in ruins, with its former CEO claiming both innocence and ignorance. Obviously, Skilling was not a victim of adult illiteracy; he had just gotten stuck in the victim cycle. According to *The New York Times,* "One financing arrangement that undermined Enron was a provision that required $3.9 billion in debts not on the balance sheet to be paid if the stock price dropped below certain levels and Enron lost its investment-grade credit rating. Mr. Skilling said, 'I did not know about that.'" You be the judge.

And some are too smart for their own good. *The Wall Street Journal* reported that the Chambers Development Company, an acclaimed waste management firm, had overstated its profits by $362 million and had perpetuated many other accounting errors for several years after going public. Reporter Gabriella Stern characterized John G. Rangos, Sr., the company's sixty-three-year-old founder and CEO, as a man "obsessed with making his garbage company a star and insistent on managers meeting his lofty profit goals," leading to an "environment in which manipulating numbers was tolerated." After one executive told Rangos that his company would fall short of projected profits, Rangos told the executive to "Go find the rest of it." However, when auditors Grant Thornton refused to continue signing off on Chambers's numbers, the company's bright track record dimmed. In a report submitted by the accounting firm Deloitte & Touche, auditors revealed that Chambers Development "covered its losses by grossly understating expenses and in the process violated generally accepted accounting principles." In response, John G. Rangos, Jr., denied "that his family in any way encouraged subordinates to manipulate earnings figures or use inappropriate accounting practices." Chambers Development Company and its CEO obviously ducked its accountability and denied their involvement in any wrongdoing.

Mark Twain captured the challenge of the ignore/deny stage of the victim cycle when he said, "It's not what you don't know, it's what you know that just ain't so." Pretending not to know or ignoring a problem will keep you *Below The Line* and impair your ability to get results.

2. It's Not My Job. How many times have we heard, and perhaps even spoken, the words, "It's not my job?" This age-old excuse is a well-worn phrase that has been used in countless discussions to excuse inaction, to redirect blame, and to avoid responsibility. This stage reflects an awareness that something needs to be done to get the result, coupled with an acute avoidance of getting involved. People assuming this victim attitude seek shelter from what they perceive to be additional effort without sufficient reward, from personal sacrifice without benefit. Why take on this *added* responsibility? "It's not my job" gained legitimacy in a past era of job descriptions that set boundaries across which no worker dared step, of performance expectations that focused on individuals' ability to do their jobs rather than on their ability to contribute to getting the result, and of organizations that assumed it was okay for departments to fight for what they needed instead of working for what would best benefit the company.

No matter where you look, at work or at home, you will see examples of this stage of the victim cycle every day. For instance, can you recall a time when you were on the other side of "it's not my job?" Imagine the following scenario. You walk into a store seeking help. Encouraged by the company's heavily advertised slogan, which reads "We do what it takes to make you happy," you are shocked to hear, "I'm sorry, but I can't help you; that's not my job." Nothing infuriates most people more than becoming a pawn in an endless cycle of "it's not my job," as you bounce from one person to the next, finding no one willing to take responsibility. The price of such *Below The Line* behavior becomes onerous when you must pay it, which is precisely the point. Whenever people use this phrase to duck responsibility, avoiding the opportunity to play a role in getting results, someone pays the price. It may be an indirect price, it may even be difficult to trace, but ultimately someone pays a price. Perhaps the price includes how others perceive you, perhaps it involves how the company's performance ultimately affects your pay, or perhaps it will accumulate until you lose your job or your company goes out of business. In the end, "It's not my job" means "don't blame me, it's not my fault."

3. Finger-Pointing. In this well-practiced stage of the victim cycle people deny their own responsibility for poor results and seek to shift the blame to others. "Don't blame me" becomes the catch phrase for transferring fault to the other guy. For instance, the chief operating officer of a leading health care company publicly admitted that a problem with its polyurethane extrusion process was "perplexing everyone in the company." As soon as company employees became aware of the COO's admission, they began using the "extrusion process" excuse for all sorts of product defects, schedule delays, and inefficiencies. Productivity and profitability plummeted as hundreds of employees pointed their fingers in every direction but at themselves.

Blaming can take many forms, and it occurs in even the best of companies. Herman Miller, the furniture manufacturer widely respected as one of the best managed American companies, engaged in a bit of finger-pointing itself. The company's marketing copywriters, keeping in mind the company's heralded commitment to customer satisfaction as outlined in the best-selling book, *Leadership Is an Art* by CEO Max DuPree, pasted the following statement for placement on all Herman Miller shipping cartons:

This furniture has been carefully inspected before being packed for shipment. It was in perfect condition when packed and received by the transportation company for shipment and delivery to you. If, when you open this crate or carton, you find that the piece of furniture has been damaged, hold shipment intact and call the transportation company immediately, requesting that they send an agent to supply you with an inspection report. This report is necessary, along with the original freight bill, to support a claim. Damage received during transit is the responsibility of the transportation company. If the above instructions are followed, we will be glad to assist in handling claims. Herman Miller, Inc.

That disclaimer lays the groundwork for Herman Miller to point the finger at the transportation company if anything goes wrong, and it reveals a *Below The Line* attitude toward customer satisfaction. To Herman Miller's credit, the company's vice president of corporate quality issued the following statement in response to customer feedback: "The notice as it now stands communicates a feeling of 'we did our jobs; if it's wrong it must be the other guy's fault.'" Not desiring to play the victim game by blaming or appearing to blame others, the company changed the label to read:

This furniture has been crafted with pride and care and reflects our commitment to supply you with the best products available in the world. If, when you open this crate or carton, you notice that the piece of furniture has been damaged, hold the shipment and the original freight bill intact and call your Herman Miller dealer immediately. The transportation company should send an agent to supply you with an inspection report. This report is necessary, along with the original freight bill, to support a damage claim. We are fully committed to your complete satisfaction and ask only that you follow the above procedure in the event of product damage during shipment.

Unfortunately, many other companies keep indulging in blame games: marketing blames R & D for designing products or features that marketing doesn't need instead of the ones marketing knows the customer wants; sales attacks marketing for such inadequate support as ill-conceived brochures or mis-targeted commercials; manufacturing accuses sales of signing off on poor forecasts that cause either too many back-orders or too much inventory; R & D points the finger at manufacturing for not resolving manufacturability problems on the factory floor; vice presidents heap scorn on directors for not taking more responsibility, while directors chide vice presidents for either not providing sufficient guidelines or not letting go. Around and around it goes, a merry-go-round of accusations that do nothing to solve an organization's problems.

4. Confusion/Tell Me What to Do. At this more subtle stage of the victim cycle people cite confusion as a way of alleviating themselves of their accountability. If they don't understand the problem or the situation, surely they can't be expected to do anything about it. For example, a quality assurance manager at a major chemical company received from his superiors comprehensive and confidential feedback about his department's poor performance. After he had thoroughly researched the problem himself, however, he heard so many conflicting reasons for it that he felt completely baffled. Approaching his boss, he confessed his confusion, saying, "Given all these mixed signals, how can you hold me responsible for this mess?"

Another manager at a large food processing company received a mixed review from her boss during a performance appraisal session: "You do some things well, other things not so well." Given the mixed review, the boss asked the manager to think about the feedback and respond to it within a week. The manager, befuddled by the appraisal, complained to her husband, her peers, and her subordinates during the week that her boss's evaluation made no sense: "He just doesn't understand me." Rather than seek clarification, the manager opted to remain confused and resentful. When she met with her boss to discuss her reactions, she complained that he had sent her such mixed signals that she couldn't possibly initiate any changes in her approach to her job. "I don't think that's wise," cautioned her boss. "What about the negative feedback I gave you? That was pretty clear."

"Well, it wasn't to me," she replied.

"I expected the review session to stimulate some changes that would further your growth and development with the company," her boss countered.

"You just don't understand me," was the employee's response.

"You're right, I don't," was the boss's answer.

Within a few months the manager left the company to take another job. Unfortunately, she allowed herself to remain as confused as ever, hoping somehow that a change of scenery would clarify things. It didn't. It seldom does.

Out of the finger-pointing and confusion stages naturally grows the response: "Just tell me exactly what you want me to do, and I'll do it." Unfortunately, such a plea, while seeming to indicate a willingness to change behavior, simply transfers accountability to a superior or someone else. Too many bosses perpetuate such an attitude by telling their people *exactly* what to do in difficult situations. Asking someone else to tell you exactly what to do represents nothing more than an advanced form of excuse making because it stems from the victim's desire to prepare his or her excuse before ever taking action.

In the view of codependency expert Abe Wagner, author of *The Transactional Manager,* people display three ego states of the child: the natural child, the compliant child, and the rebellious child. The natural child refers to the part of the personality that someone inherits at birth, and it characterizes an individual's inherent needs, wants, and feelings. When children or adults display their natural child, they do what they want to do and don't do what they don't want to do. Such behavior can be natural and positive. However, the behavior of both the compliant and rebellious child reflect codependent relationships with respect to mother's wishes. Each of these codependent postures illustrates the *Below The Line* "tell me what to do" stage of the victim cycle because they depend on someone else assuming responsibility. Compliant children do what a mother or boss tells them to do, then transfer to mothers or bosses the consequences of the children's actions. Rebellious children find out what mothers or bosses want them to do, then they defy it, all the while blaming mothers or bosses for all negative consequences. Whether codependents comply or rebel, their behavior depends on what a superior tells them to do. They never assume their own accountability. Unfortunately, far too many people in organizations act like compliant or rebellious children.

Most of us have probably found ourselves in a similar endless circular pattern of "tell me what do to." It plays itself out in business every day, as people try to shift accountability by refusing to take responsibility for their future actions.

Corporate cultures of the past that relied heavily on a command and control model provided a paternalistic approach to employee involvement that promoted this stage of the victim cycle: "You just do what you are told, do it well, and we will take care of you for the rest of your life." Some people still depict their organizations as places where you begin work in the morning by "checking your brain at the front door." However, most organizations today are fleeing from this "tell me what to do" model in an effort to create an environment that attracts, develops, and retains the best and the brightest people. As accountability deepens and people move *Above The Line* within the organization, a shift occurs from "tell me what to do," to "here is what I am going to do, what do you think?"—a truly profound and empowering approach to getting results.

5. Cover Your Tail. The penultimate stage of the victim cycle is cover your tail, where people continue to seek imagined protection *Below The Line* by crafting elaborate and precise stories as to why they couldn't possibly be blamed for something that might go wrong. These stories usually got fabricated after the fact. However, as amazing as it may seem, many excuse makers prepare these stories before the results come in, or are even known, just in case an eventual problem or potential failure should occur.

Cover your tail comes in many forms, ranging from documenting everything in writing to sending back-up E-mail messages that can be used as later proof of innocence. Most of us have experienced someone coming to substantiate a sequence of events or a series of conversations in order to substantiate an alibi.

Sometimes the cover-your-tail stage of the victim cycle plays itself out more subtly. We have witnessed individuals who actually run and hide in order to disassociate themselves from situations that could erupt into potential problems. They avoid meetings where they might be put on the line, or they fail to open mail that they know might bear some anticipated bad news. We remember hearing of one such example where a particular company, at a critical juncture of its development and growth, was preparing for an upcoming government inspection that would either make or break the company. Mere days before the inspection, the president of the company announced that he would be going on vacation and would not be available for any communication or decision making during the inspection. Immediately, people felt the burden of potential problems totally shift to them, leaving the president seemingly in the clear. They scrambled to avoid the fallout. The effort expended to cover your tail almost always produces little more than reasons and justifications for why people are not responsible, not to blame, and not accountable for things that go wrong. While some situations may warrant such behavior, such as when you must defend yourself against unscrupulous people set on taking advantage of you, even then cover-your-tail behavior drains both the time and resources of all involved.

6. Wait and See. Initially, people remain mired in the victim cycle when they choose to wait and see if things will get better. In such a climate, however, problems can only get worse. For example, the senior management team of a $300 million personal care products manufacturer and marketer found themselves struggling over the introduction of a new product line. Because the company had grown so rapidly, it lacked clear precedents for such an introduction. After hours of fruitless debate, company officials decided to wait and see if the right approach might emerge naturally from the product management group after everyone's emotions cooled down. As months of indecision slipped by, a smaller competitor beat them to the punch, making the whole product introduction problem moot. The wait-and-see stage of the victim cycle often becomes a sinkhole where possible solutions get swallowed up in a swamp of inaction.

In an amusing example of this phenomenon, *The Wall Street Journal* reported that bird droppings have been piling up for years in the Amherst, Massachusetts, Town Hall attic, posing an increasing health risk to occupants. The Amherst Select Board voted to allocate $125,000 to clean up the mess, but according to contractors, the job could cost as much as $260,000. Enter a local hero, David Keenan, an Amherst real estate broker, who offered to organize a volunteer group called the pigeon busters, which would clean up the estimated fifty-five gallons of bird droppings for free. However, one of the Select Board members pointed out that such an effort would require insurance covering each of the volunteers, a far too expensive proposition. After listening to a lot of discussion, Keenan exclaimed in frustration, "Anyone who would volunteer would gladly sign a waiver. It's not a liability issue. The problem with the Amherst government is they won't roll up their sleeves and shovel the poop." When the community leaders hired lawyers to study the liability issue, the lawyers concluded, "regardless of who does the cleanup, the town could still be sued." In the meantime the bird dung keeps piling, with the people who come to Town Hall on business hoping they don't get psittacosis, a viral disease that can be transmitted from bird to man and develop into pneumonia. As a final resort, Keenan and his pigeon busters suggested that the select board allot enough money to fix the hole in the window frame through which the pigeons have been entering.

STUCK IN THE VICTIM CYCLE: THE PLIGHT OF MIKE EAGLE

People tend to remain in the victim cycle because they find a certain amount of at least temporary comfort *Below The Line.* They think, "I don't have to admit I

was wrong," "I won't lose face," "I don't have to do anything differently in the future," and "I can justify my lack of performance and growth." For whatever reasons a person remains in the victim cycle, the comfort proves illusionary, since
they will never get out of it and move toward results until they learn to recognize the trap. Let's see how one CEO learned to spot the traps.

We appreciate Mike Eagle (whom we rank today at the very top of those executives we know who model *Above The Line* leadership) for allowing us to
share this story, because it sheds strong light on the inner struggles of executives
today as they attempt to get and stay *Above The Line.*

Mike Eagle had racked up a string of successes in his last corporate assignment as vice president of a manufacturing facility, and his advancements had
impressed the higher-ups in his corporation. Everyone above him agreed that
Mike would enjoy a spectacular future, probably at the top of the corporation's
executive ranks. To further his career development, his superiors proposed a
move to running a subsidiary company where he could bring his talents to bear
on reenergizing a poorly performing organization.

As Mike approached the end of his first year managing the company, however, he was feeling frustrated at the lack of improvement in its overall performance. Nothing he had tried seemed to be working, and for the first time in his
career he feared that he might fail in an assignment.

With the performance issue continuing to frustrate him, Mike decided to
explore the feelings of key people in the organization. During his investigation
he invited one of the supervisors to lunch, where he asked for candid feedback
about people's perceptions of his impact on the company over the past year.
Seemingly taken aback by this request, the supervisor asked Mike if he really
wanted to hear the truth. When Mike insisted he did, the supervisor opened up,
detailing how most people attributed lack of improvement to his own behavior.
Mike couldn't believe what he was hearing:

> "Eagle's in over his head."
>
> "He's a manufacturing guy, and we need someone who knows our
> work."
>
> "Mike hasn't made any difference at all."
>
> "He's trying to run new product development the way he ran
> manufacturing."
>
> "Mike's not doing anything to increase quality."

"He's not communicating clearly."

"He's ignoring significant personality conflicts on his own team."

"Eagle doesn't seem capable of making tough decisions."

Although shocked by this realization of people's negative feelings about his management skills, Mike expressed appreciation for the candor of those observations. While he really did appreciate the feedback, he also found himself sorely aggravated by it. After all, when he headed up the manufacturing facility in his last job he constantly heard people complaining: "All we need is for R & D to quit throwing products over the wall before it has solved the design problems that make quality manufacturing impossible." This memory prompted Mike to chalk up the feedback as "just so many sour grapes." Why couldn't the company accept the blame for its own flaws?

The following Saturday he went biking up the California coast with a former colleague and trusted friend whom we shall call Pete Sanders. Pete had started his own business just as Mike took on his new assignment. It didn't take long after beginning the ride for Mike and Pete to start reminiscing about the good times they'd spent together over the years. As the casual conversation unfolded, Pete asked Mike how things were going, and since Mike trusted Pete, he told him that the situation had turned into a nightmare. Before long he was venting all his pent-up frustrations to his friend: "Pete, I've inherited a basket case. And it really upsets me that people expect me to do something to solve their problems. I didn't create the mess! They did. When I decided to take this position twelve months ago I had no idea what I was getting myself into. No one on the board told me how bad it really was. I'm between a rock and a hard place. Managers at every level deny responsibility, and so does corporate management. Morale has sunk to a new low. At least three lower-level people quit every week, no matter what I do. And I've tried everything! But no one communicates with anyone else, and everyone blames everyone else for their problems. It seems like the CEO before me let things get completely out of control. The volume of new product introduction is pitiful, and the products that we do get from new product development aren't ready when we get them. I can't solve all these problems myself. I'm all alone out there. Corporate management doesn't provide any useful direction. They just assume that I'll do the right thing."

For his part, Pete could not believe this was his old friend talking. Back at the plant, Mike had acted with supreme confidence, a take-charge guy who felt he could solve any problem thrown his way. Now he was sounding desperate, with his reasoning looping around in circles. He blamed the corporate management team for putting him in this untenable situation, he blamed his own senior team for not owning up to their problems, but he blamed himself for getting blindsided by a set of circumstances over which he felt no control whatsoever.

Although Pete sympathized with Mike, saying he knew there must be plenty of good reasons for why he was feeling the way he did, he also observed that continuing to feel victimized would not help him move an inch toward the results he wanted. Pete concluded, "You know, Mike, I attended an interesting accountability workshop a few weeks ago, and, based on what I learned there, I'd say you're stuck in what the workshop leaders call the victim cycle. That's the bad news. The good news is that you can do something about it."

GETTING UNSTUCK: MIKE EAGLE'S RECOGNITION

As Mike and Pete rode up the coast, Pete continued his explanation: "In this workshop I learned that everyone falls into the victim cycle from time to time. It's nothing to feel ashamed about. In fact, if you can only learn to see when you're falling into it, you can start getting out of it. Victims never accomplish anything unless they start taking control over their own futures. The key is accountability, but you can't climb what they called the *Steps To Accountability* without first developing a full understanding of the victim cycle. Think about it. Have you been claiming to be unaware of certain circumstances, pretending not to know what's really going on, denying that it's your responsibility, blaming others, attempting to get someone else to take you off the hook and tell you what to do, arguing that you can't do anything, or waiting for things to get better tomorrow?"

These words seemed to strike a nerve in his friend, so Pete continued gently yet forcefully to help Mike see himself and his behavior more objectively. "Mike, I really respect you. Remember, getting stuck in the victim cycle is not bad, it's just not effective. It keeps you from getting results. Now I can see hundreds of times when I was in the victim cycle, and that's good, Mike! The more quickly I can recognize the trap, the more quickly I can get out of it and start working more productively toward my goals. The problems you face in the company are real. I saw it myself. But given those problems, try asking yourself what else you can do to rise above those circumstances and get the results you want. When you described your situation, I didn't hear many words expressing your ownership for what's happened over the past year. You talk as if the managers aren't really your managers, as if the company's problems are something you inherited, that you had no choice in the matter. Did you ever really, completely leave your old job for this new position? Have you really shown up to make it happen here?"

Mike thought about all that, and the more he thought about it, the madder he got. "You make it sound like I'm to blame for everybody else's problems. I don't buy that!" When Pete remained silent, Mike took a deep breath, then apologized for his tirade. "I'm sorry. I guess if I were totally honest with myself I would have to acknowledge that I haven't really brought my best efforts to bear on the situation. The only fun I have lately is when I think about the good old days in manufacturing. Things went so smoothly then. Improvements were so visible. It all comes back when I review the weekly update report on my old projects that I still get. I always call my old friends to congratulate them and give them advice."

At this point Pete interrupted Mike by saying, "Do you remember the story about Alexander the Great? When Alexander's army reached the coast of what is now called India, he ordered his men to burn their ships. When the men hesitated at such a shocking order, Alexander responded, 'We're either going home in their ships or we're not going home at all.' In other words, burning the ships would cement his army's commitment to conquest because retreat would cease to be an option. Now, victory could become the sole objective." Pete continued by suggesting that it looked to him as if Mike had kept a boat handy for retreat or escape and thus had never completely committed to winning his battle. When he asked Mike if that were the case, Mike confided, with a certain level of pride, that he had several escape plans. He'd already hinted to his superiors that he might like to move back to his old job, and he had even interviewed for a job with a competitor. Now, however, he could see that he had been operating with one eye on the exit, while his situation demanded that he keep both eyes on the job at hand. Finally, he was able to see that he really was stuck in an unproductive cycle playing the victim when he should be taking decisive steps to improve conditions in the organization. Could he focus his full attention on the problem?

As he did so, Mike came to realize that he needed to create a more cohesive team with his managers before any meaningful change could occur. To his regret, he had done little over the past year to foster a close team spirit between himself and the managers who reported to him. Instead, he had simply gone around the managers to the supervisors, getting together with them in early morning meetings to obtain their input and to give them direction. Mike acknowledged that he had essentially skirted his managers, and, in effect, disempowered them as a management team.

Strangely enough, Mike's recognition of his own accountability for the company's poor performance no longer made him feel angry or depressed but increasingly exhilarated. Wanting to feed the feeling, Mike told Pete, "You know, I really have been getting in my own way and waiting for someone else to solve these problems. While it's true there are a lot of things that have happened that I had nothing to do with, I've allowed those things to distract me from focusing on the positive action I can take. And, worst of all, my acting like a victim has given everyone else permission to do the same. Thinking about it now, I can even see that a lot of people throughout the organization are stuck the same way, ignoring problems, denying responsibilities, and blaming others. And, as for me, I think I have let myself become so paralyzed by it all that even if I start acting differently, even if I start accepting full accountability for the company's performance, I could still fail. That scares me."

Mike's realization took time and effort to accomplish; but with it he, just like Dorothy in *The Wizard of Oz,* began to see his way home. He understood that it's okay to fall into the victim cycle from time to time because it's only human to do so, and it's also okay to feel a little scared of the possibility of failure. But the accountable person learns to overcome that fear by recognizing that success can only come from getting *Above The Line* and working hard to get better results. In Mike's case, his ownership became infectious, and his team rose to the occasion. With determination and some outstanding leadership, Mike led the company to record sales and profits. A couple of years into this endeavor, Mike was recognized by the president of the parent company with an award for achieving results that even they thought impossible. Mike ultimately became a member of the senior executive management team of this parent organization. The message: Sometimes you must be willing to burn all your other ships and grasp the helm of the one under your command. Doing so can stimulate the conviction and create the ownership necessary to get started on a new program of action that will help you rise above your circumstances. The shoes are on your feet. Now, all you have to do is click your heels.

THE VITAL LESSON:
DETECTING SIGNS OF THE VICTIM CYCLE

Over the years, we've worked through a Mike Eagle type of truth-telling, soul-searching session with hundreds of executives, professionals, friends, and family. Every situation is different, every person is unique, but everyone reaches a critical moment when he or she recognizes having been stuck in the victim cycle. Take a minute to think about what happened to Mike Eagle. For twelve months he honestly believed he could not control his circumstances. Dwelling upon the bleakness of the situation, he chose to think he couldn't do anything about it, that no one could expect him to fix all the company's long-standing problems overnight. As a result, Mike had languished, unhappily and unproductively, until he recognized he was ducking responsibility by blaming former CEOs and other managers, asking the parent corporate management team to tell him what to do, claiming that he couldn't do anything more than what he was already doing, and waiting to see if things would get better on their own. Fortunately, when he finally saw how he'd become stuck in the victim cycle, he could commit himself fully to helping everyone in the organization solve their problems and obtain better results.

Like Mike Eagle, every human being can fall *Below The Line* from time to time, but whenever you do so, you can't get back on track until you first acknowledge that you're incurring a high cost for functioning *Below The Line.* That's when you begin assuming a *See It* attitude that gives you the perspective you need to get *Above The Line* and start climbing the accountability ladder. You'll begin reading about the *See It* rung on the *Steps To Accountability* in the next chapter, but before you do, you might pause here to ask yourself a few penetrating questions. The next page will help you spot *Below The Line* attitudes. Take a few minutes to examine your questions in the Victim Cycle Self-Examination.

If the scenario in a given question has ever happened to you, check either yes or no in the appropriate spaces. As you read each question, ask yourself "Has this ever happened to me?" or "Have I ever felt this way?" Try to play your own best friend, answering the question as frankly as possible.

VICTIM CYCLE
Self-Examination

ONE	Were you ever surprised by negative feedback from someone else when you thought all along you were doing your very best to solve a problem?	YES ☐ NO ☐
TWO	Have you ever spent time blaming others and pointing fingers when things did not go the way you wanted them to go?	YES ☐ NO ☐
THREE	Did you ever suspect something would become a problem for someone else or for your organization but did nothing about it?	YES ☐ NO ☐
FOUR	Have you ever spent time covering your tail just in case things went wrong?	YES ☐ NO ☐
FIVE	Have you ever said, "It's not my job" and expected someone else to solve a problem?	YES ☐ NO ☐
SIX	Did you ever feel totally powerless, with no control over your circumstances or situation?	YES ☐ NO ☐
SEVEN	Have you ever found yourself waiting to see if a situation would miraculously resolve itself?	YES ☐ NO ☐
EIGHT	Have you ever said, "Just tell me what you want me to do and I'll do it"?	YES ☐ NO ☐
NINE	Have you ever felt that you would have done things differently if it was your own company?	YES ☐ NO ☐
TEN	Do you ever tell stories about how someone took advantage of you (a boss, a friend, a contractor, a salesperson, etc.)?	YES ☐ NO ☐

Once you have completed the Victim Cycle Self-Examination, total up your scores. Give yourself one point for every yes response and no points for every no response. After totaling your points, compare your total to the scoring table that follows.

VICTIM CYCLE
Self-Examination Scoring

If you scored 0 points: You are not being honest with yourself. Go back and try it again, but this time sit in a closet so no one can see your results.
If you scored only 1 point: You know you are capable of falling *Below The Line*, but you probably do so more often than you're willing to admit.

If you scored 2–4 points: You should take some satisfaction from the fact that you're only human.

If you scored 5–7 points: You realize that you can easily fall *Below The Line*.

If you scored 8–10 points: You are very honest, quite normal, and should find the rest of this book extremely useful!

Your actual score matters less than the recognition that, as a normal human being, you can be tempted at almost any time to avoid accountability for the false security and imagined safety of the victim cycle, where it's always someone else's fault that you're not getting results. The recognition that you can fall *Below The Line* sets the stage for you to experience *The Oz Principle:* to rise above your circumstances and achieve the results you desire.

MOVING OUT OF THE VICTIM CYCLE

Throughout this chapter you have seen examples of *Below The Line* attitudes and behavior that should help you more fully appreciate the difference between victimization and accountability. However, just as Dorothy discovered on the yellow brick road to the Emerald City, you will have to work hard to spot victimization attitudes and behavior in your own life and in the operations of your organization. In the next chapter you'll begin seeing accountability in a whole new light as you prepare yourself to climb the four steps to greater accountability.

Chapter 3

THERE'S NO PLACE LIKE HOME: FOCUSING ON RESULTS

"But you have not yet told me how to get back to Kansas."

"Your Silver Shoes will carry you over the desert," replied Glinda. "If you had known their power you could have gone back to your Aunt Em the very first day you came to this country."

"But then I should not have had my wonderful brains!" cried the Scarecrow. "I might have passed my whole life in the farmer's cornfield."

"And I should not have had my lovely heart," said the Tin Woodsman. "I might have stood and rusted in the forest till the end of the world."

"And I should have lived a coward forever," declared the Lion, "and no beast in all the forest would have had a good word to say to me."

"This is all true," said Dorothy, "and I am glad I was of use to these good friends. But now that each of them has had what he most desired, and each is happy in having a kingdom to rule beside, I think I should like to go back to Kansas."

—*The Wizard of Oz,*
L. Frank Baum

Citigroup, a world leader in global finance, earned more than $16 billion in profits in 2002, but did the company earn the money honestly? Citi and its Salomon Smith Barney unit have generated a lot of news because they allegedly helped Enron keep its debt off the balance sheet, marketed questionable World-Com debt, promoted Winstar when it was going down the tubes, rewarded Telecom executives with IPOs, and raised AT&T's market rating to win its business. Time to quit, run, or hide? Not Citi's CEO Sandy Weill. He told the business press, "I'm embarrassed." He admitted that Citi made mistakes while he was CEO and he accepted personal accountability, saying, "I'm part of those mistakes." He told his board that he would make it his top priority to make sure Citigroup operates more ethically and honestly. Is it all confessional rhetoric designed to appease an enraged public by admitting wrongdoing? Only time will tell. Yes, many other companies in the investment banking industry have pursued practices similar to Citi's and Salomon's, but that's no longer an acceptable excuse. What will Citigroup executives think and feel and do behind the scenes? We'll find out soon enough. To Weill's credit, he has made some impressive moves: firing star analyst Jack Grubman, releasing Salomon's top boss, and expensing stock options. Still, many observers chalk up what happened at Citigroup as a massive management failure. Will Weill's confessions and concessions help bring Citigroup back to respectability and keep it from faltering? That will depend on how much accountability for real results Sandy Weill and his executive team can muster over the next five to ten years.

ACCOUNTABILITY POORLY DEFINED

Over a decade of experience working with thousands of managers, leaders, and team members has shown us that most people view accountability as something that happens to them when performance wanes, problems develop, or results fail to materialize. In fact, many think accountability only crops up when something goes wrong or when someone else wants to pinpoint the cause of the problem, all for the sake of pinning blame and pointing the finger. When things are sailing along smoothly and failure has not yet sunk the ship, people rarely ask, "Who is accountable for this success?" It seems that only when the hull springs a leak does anyone start looking around for the responsible party.

Not surprisingly, most dictionaries present a definition of accountability that promotes this somewhat negative view. Consider Webster's definition: "subject to having to report, explain, or justify; being answerable, responsible." Notice how the definition begins with the words, *subject to,* implying little choice in the matter. This confession-oriented and powerless definition suggests what we all have observed—accountability viewed as a consequence for poor performance, a principle you should fear because it can only end up hurting you. Since most people experience accountability this way, it's no wonder they spend so much time shunning it and explaining and justifying poor results.

We have learned over the years that when a leader announces that he or she has embarked on a campaign to create greater accountability in the organization, people often first respond with a moan, "not more of that!" Fearing the worst, they await more scrutiny to identify the culprits responsible for failed results. No wonder the blame game is so rampant and played so well, and so creatively! However, we have learned through firsthand experience that a more positive and powerful definition of accountability can do more to achieve outstanding results than all the finger pointing and blaming in the world.

Take, for instance, Sandy Weill's case. We honor his willingness to stand up and take the blame, but did he do so only because things had gone so terribly wrong and the time had finally come to determine fault? Whether through blame or self-admission, we must come to understand that *accountability is more than a confession.* If we are not careful, we may even confuse the act of taking responsibility for failure as some sort of compensation for a lack of success. This fear-inducing approach to accountability has caused millions of people, in thousands of organizations, to expend their valuable time and energy justifying their lack of performance with such tired excuses as "we were over budget, overextended, overloaded, underinformed, underfunded, and underutilized." Justification then becomes the aim, damaging or replacing a conscientious focus on what else can be done to achieve results. One leader, intently focused on improving the performance of his people, suggested that his organization could save a lot of time and energy by handing out a list of tried and tested excuses, so that employees would need only recite a number when explaining failure:

TWENTY TRIED AND TESTED EXCUSES

1. "That's the way we've always done it."
2. "It's not my job."
3. "I didn't know you needed it right away."
4. "It wasn't my fault that it's late."
5. "That's not my department."
6. "No one told me what to do."
7. "I'm waiting for approval."
8. "Someone should have told me not to do that."
9. "Don't blame me. It was the boss's idea."
10. "I didn't know."
11. "I forgot."
12. "If you had told me it was that important, I would have done it."
13. "I'm too busy to do it."
14. "Someone told me to do the wrong thing."
15. "I thought I told you."
16. "Why didn't you ask me?"
17. "No one invited me to the meeting—I didn't get the memo."
18. "My people dropped the ball."
19. "Nobody's followed up on me; it can't be that important."
20. "I told someone else to take care of this."

This list sounds pretty silly, doesn't it? Yet in some way or another, people weave these excuses so deeply into the fabric of their lives that they resort to them without really thinking about what they're really saying. To overcome that impulse, people must abandon the past-oriented, blame-centered who-done-it definition of accountability. Almost without exception, when things go wrong, people start playing the who-done-it game, a not-so-subtle variation of the blame game, as they immediately begin identifying the person in the group most responsible for the failure. All too often the who-done-it game excludes any intention of rectifying the situation. Instead, in an effort to avoid the career-limiting consequences of failure, those who play the game seek only to make sure the spotlight shifts to someone else while they themselves dive for the shelter of excuses, explanations, justifications, and disassociations.

A tragic example of the who-done-it game received national attention when it was reported that contaminated meat in hamburgers sold at Jack in the Box restaurants caused the death of two children and severe sickness in scores of others. Jack in the Box quickly prepared its explanation, pointing the finger at the supplier of the meat, Vons grocery stores, which, of course, had already prepared its own explanation, blaming the meat inspector, the U.S. Department of Agriculture, which, in turn, explained that insufficient funds made it impossible to employ enough meat inspectors. So who's at fault? The taxpayers, who don't want more taxes for more inspectors. However, the taxpayers had prepared their own explanation: "If the federal bureaucracy were only more efficient, it wouldn't cost so much to get the services we need." And the game goes on and on, further robbing organizations up and down the line of a means to get better results: genuine and positive accountability.

As the downward spiral continues, fueled by a wrong-headed definition of accountability, more and more people are learning to become adept at playing the who-done-it game. When a major project commences, people at all levels of the organization begin taking copious notes about the unfolding progress, not to document success, but to justify the lack of results if and when the project fails. The amount of wasted time and energy, even in the most quality conscious organizational environments, continues to rise as the who-done-it game turns into the craft-your-story game, which allows its players to build a handy excuse, regardless of the outcome. Sadly, people have learned that they live in a litigious society that loves to place blame and fix accountability on someone else so that party can pay for the mistake. In such a society, winning the game of life equals covering your tail.

By defining accountability in this way, people perpetuate a powerless, reactive view of it, one obsessed with the past and blissfully ignorant of the future.

Consumed with dotting the i's and crossing the t's of their elaborate explanations for why they're not responsible, people today are robbing themselves of the power of accountability—a power that *The Oz Principle* defines as the key to a successful future.

A POWERFUL DEFINITION OF ACCOUNTABILITY

The Oz Principle's definition of accountability can help revitalize the business character, strengthen the global competitiveness of corporations, heighten innovation, improve the quality of products and services produced by companies worldwide, and increase the responsiveness of organizations to the needs and wants of customers and constituents.

Consider the following new definition of accountability, one that embodies the essence of *The Oz Principle:*

Accountability: "A personal choice to rise above one's circumstances and demonstrate the ownership necessary for achieving desired results—to *See It, Own It, Solve It,* and *Do It.*"

This definition includes a mind-set or attitude of continually asking, "What else can I do to rise above my circumstances and achieve the results I desire?" It involves a process of seeing it, owning it, solving it, and doing it, and requires a level of ownership that includes making, keeping, and answering for personal commitments. Such a perspective embraces both current and future efforts rather than reactive and historical explanations. Armed with this new definition of accountability, you can help yourself and others do everything possible to both overcome difficult circumstances and achieve desired results.

The contemporary view of accountability tends to emphasize past actions as opposed to current or future efforts. Just as W. Edwards Deming has been telling businesspeople for decades, most organizations operate on the assumption that the fear of failure will cause people to succeed. To the contrary, we feel such an assumption only causes people to prepare their explanations of history before the fact.

Rather than focusing on powerful accountability, which stresses what you can do *now* to get better results, the customary definition impels people to account for what they have done in the past. This after-the-fact view of account-ability prevents a before-it's-too-late approach. It should come as no surprise that the real value and benefit of accountability stems from a person's or an organization's ability to influence events and outcomes before they happen. The customary view of accountability fails to recognize that people can gain more from a proactive posture than from a reactive one.

Take, for example, a situation that has intrigued us for some time. We have constantly been amazed at the manner in which local government officials determine when and where to install stop signs and traffic signals. We recall a particularly dangerous intersection with terrible visibility and horrendous traffic speeds. Traffic officials had been exceptionally slow to install traffic signals at this intersection. Rather than tracking complaints about the safety of the intersection, officials only tracked the number of accidents. After mishaps reach a certain number, officials install a stop sign. If a few fatalities occur, they erect a traffic signal. Now that many accidents and some fatalities have occurred at that bad intersection, it has graduated from a four-way stop sign to a traffic signal. How sad that it took pain, suffering, damage, and even lives to achieve the proper result. That's why we so dislike a reactive view of accountability and insist on a more proactive one instead. After the fact, it's too late to adjust behavior and avoid the negative consequences that can follow.

Pop psychology, whether intentional or not, has often encouraged people in our society to blame all their woes and problems on a single or few experiences in their lives, thus promoting a lack of accountability for current and future behaviors, attitudes, and feelings. It is not unusual for people to explain their nightmares, eating disorders, compulsive cleanliness, anxieties, drive for self-improvement, physical ailments, financial problems, and impatience on some singular and pivotal problem or experience that occurred earlier in their lives. Blaming everything on their past wounds, they explain their vulnerability to fad diets, their awkwardness in relating to their children, or their feelings of alienation and loneliness, as if no other modern adult suffers these problems. The fact is, whether you are a true victim or a pseudovictim, you will never overcome a hurtful past until you develop a present- and future-oriented view of your own accountability for getting more out of life. To achieve such a shift in how you view things, we suggest that you start with our more powerful, more proactive definition of accountability.

JOINT ACCOUNTABILITY

The Oz Principle's definition of accountability emphasizes the fact that accountability works best when people share ownership for circumstances and results. The old definition of accountability leads people to assign individual responsibility without acknowledging the shared accountability that so often characterizes organizational behavior and modern life. Not surprisingly, whenever the blame game singles out an individual as the one responsible for poor results, everyone else heaves a sigh of relief now that they're off the hook. Assigning singular responsibility may comfort the majority, but the fact remains, organizational results come from collective, not individual, activity. Hence, when an organization fails to perform well, it represents, ultimately, a collective or shared failure. A complete understanding of accountability in organizations must include the principle of joint accountability.

For example, imagine a baseball team where each defensive player assumes responsibility for covering an area of the field. No hard-and-fast rules prescribe the exact point where one player's area ends and another's begins. Given such overlapping areas of responsibility, getting good results—i.e., covering the whole field—becomes a team effort wherein individual accountability shifts according to circumstances, and coaches train players to go for the ball, whenever they can reach it, even when more than one player can do so. For example, you have probably observed the occasion when a batter pops up a ball into shallow left-center field. Immediately, the shortstop, the left fielder, and the center fielder converge at the same time with none of them completely sure who should catch the ball. Sometimes, the ball gets dropped because the players run into one another or, thinking it could be anyone's ball, they all wait for the other guy to make the catch, not certain who will take responsibility for it this time. In many ways, the organizational game is a team sport where everyone shoulders his or her individual responsibility, where everyone contributes to the final score, and where joint accountability governs play.

One company president characterized what joint accountability meant to him this way: "Everyone working together so that we don't drop the ball; but when it does get dropped, everyone dives for the ball to pick it up." "Unfortunately," he continued, "too many of our people see the ball land on the ground between players, but react by saying, 'That was your ball.'" In most organizations it would be easy to recount a litany of projects in which someone had missed a critical deadline, incurred an unexpected expense, quit in the middle of a job or failed to pay attention to a crucial detail. In such cases, no one jumps in to pick up the dropped ball. Everyone just sits smugly on the sideline, saying, "Well, Bob [or Sue] really messed things up this time." This same company president described how his people used to think about quality. "We would ask who's accountable for quality?" In response, he said, "one hand would go up and everyone else would be pointing at them." Then, he described how their thinking changed after understanding joint accountability. "Today, when we ask who owns quality, all hands go up."

One client enlisted our help in launching an Information Technology implementation of a system-wide integration of all information that would require a significant reengineering of business processes. Since the client's executives worried about making the implementation work, they drew upon specialists from all over the company, with every major organizational function represented on the team. Getting this varied group of people to work together, particularly when people would need to make trade-offs to meet the highest priority, seemed a foreboding task! The fact that they had never seen an IT implementation come in on budget and on time only intensified their concerns. In the past, they would end up changing the due date four or five times and then run over budget. During the September kickoff, we helped the team create an environment of positive accountability for all of the behaviors and mind-sets needed to accomplish the mission by September 5, exactly one year later. In effect, the executives created a Culture of Accountability emphasizing "What else can I do to achieve the result?" rather than the traditional, "I'll just do *my* job." Amazingly, the implementation team worked into the night on the Saturday before the due date to finish sixteen hours early and come in under budget! This was the first time in the company's history that IT achieved anything like this. The implementation now serves as the model for our client for all major IT implementations.

In the diagrams on the next page we illustrate how creating joint accountability for results can impact performance in organizations. When people look at their accountability to the organization they usually view it strictly in terms of their own individual responsibility. As a result, things tend to fall through the cracks because they fall outside the boundaries people have drawn around independent aspects of their job. Often, organizations try to fix this problem by redefining roles, hiring more people (thus filling in the cracks by adding more

Individual Responsibility

Joint Accountability

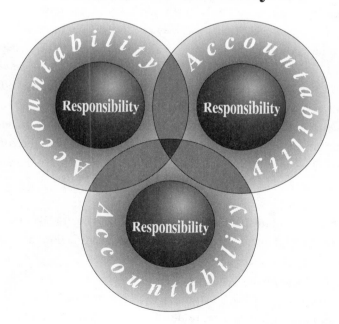

circles), or restructuring the organization. However, when people view their accountability for results as something larger than their responsibility for doing
their own job, they find themselves feeling accountable for things beyond what
a literal interpretation of their job description might suggest, e.g., profits, customer complaints, sharing information, project deadlines, effective communications, sales, and the success of the overall company. When people assume this
attitude of joint accountability for all aspects of a project, the cracks or boundaries disappear, and people see their ongoing responsibility as making sure the
ball is not dropped.

Jack Welch, former CEO of General Electric, remained vigilant in his quest
for more joint accountability or "boundarylessness," as he called it: "If this
company is to achieve its goals, we've all got to become boundaryless. Boundaries are crazy. The union is just another boundary, and you have to reach
across the same way you want to reach across the boundaries separating you
from your customers and your suppliers and your colleagues."

For many people, the idea of joint accountability is elusive because they
have been programmed to think only in terms of the *one* responsible, rather
than the *group* responsible. Yet, you may ask, can people in an organization
really assume accountability for the same things, the same results? Doesn't that
translate to *no one* being responsible? Not at all. In their book, *Revolutionizing
Product Development,* Kim Clark, dean of the Harvard Business School, and
coauthor Steven Wheelwright, describe the significant strategic and competitive advantages that result when team members understand this concept of
joint accountability. After forming product development core teams, consisting
of dedicated personnel from various functional departments in the organization, they observe:

> Each core team member wears a functional hat which makes him or
> her the focal point and manager responsible for a function that deliv-
> ers its unique contribution to the overall project.
>
> But each core team member also wears a team hat. In addition to
> representing his or her function, each core team member accepts re-
> sponsibility for overall team results. In this role, the core team shares
> responsibility with the heavyweight project manager for the develop-
> ment procedures followed by the team, and for the overall results that
> those procedures deliver. The core team is accountable for the success

of the project, and can blame no one but itself if it fails to manage the project, execute the tasks, and deliver the performance agreed upon at the outset.

What is unique in the core team members' responsibilities is not so much their accountability for tasks in their own function, but the fact that they are responsible for how those tasks are subdivided, organized, and accomplished.

Yes, it is vital that each individual in an organization be accountable, but, in addition, they must also share joint accountability with others.

Consider the following story. A manufacturer of dishwashers and other home appliances ran two parallel assembly lines, separated by a row of inventory-handling offices and storage units. Each line functioned autonomously for the most part, and each developed its own unique operating culture. Under the leadership of the line supervisor, the workers on assembly line one became adept at quickly identifying a faulty subassembly from any one of the twenty workstations on the line. When someone identified a bad subassembly, the supervisor immediately confronted the operator responsible for the problem and, with everyone watching, embarrassed that person into correcting the problem and improving future performance. Naturally, everyone else on the line, protected by an illusion of safety, would blame the erring operator for slowing them down. Over time, however, people began hiding their mistakes, hoping to remain sheltered from blame, and would not acknowledge an error even when confronted by the supervisor. As a result, production output had been declining and defective subassemblies and scrap had been increasing for several months.

Next door on assembly line two, the workers had developed a markedly different kind of operating culture. When an operator made a mistake at a workstation, other workers would immediately offer assistance in solving the problem quickly and without a lot of discussion. Functioning as part of a team, each worker felt jointly accountable for the end result of assembling quality products on time. Free from the illusion of safety created by explanations and victim stories, the workers appreciated and helped one another, quickly identifying mistakes but never accusing one individual of hurting the group effort. As a result, production on line two remained high, with defective subassemblies and scrap near zero.

The workers on assembly line one spent a lot of time *Below The Line,* denying their errors, blaming each other for mistakes, and generally walking, talking, and thinking like victims. In contrast, the workers on assembly line two enjoyed their work, liked working with each other, felt fulfilled, and got great results. Organizational behaviorists could speak eloquently about the many differences between these two work cultures, citing innumerable variables that explain the differences in results, but we see one fundamental difference between the two: One practiced joint accountability, the other did not.

In his best-selling book, *The Seven Habits of Highly Effective People,* Stephen R. Covey observes:

> On the maturity continuum, dependence is the paradigm of you—you take care of me; you come through for me; you didn't come through; I blame you for the results.
>
> Independence is the paradigm of I—I can do it; I am responsible; I am self-reliant; I can choose.
>
> Interdependence is the paradigm of we—we can do it; we can cooperate; we can combine our talents and abilities and create something greater together.

We think that while dependent people need others to get what they want, and independent people attempt to get what they want through their own effort, interdependent people combine the best of both worlds.

The most powerful working environments apply the principles of interdependence and joint accountability, where people don't fear accountability but teach and coach each other in order to win whatever game they're playing. While each individual accepts accountability for his or her own performance and results, each also knows that it takes teamwork and a sense of shared responsibility to achieve overall objectives. For people working in such environments, accountability propels everyone forward. Yes, you still must account for your own mistakes, but you know such an accounting will drive toward a better future. In such an environment, people spend less time and fewer resources creating excuses and more time and resources uncovering problems, taking risks, and initiating positive action to solve problems. Learning replaces punishment, success replaces failure, and victimization gives way to accountability.

When problems like product recalls, missed sales targets, or cost overruns arise in organizations where joint accountability hasn't taken root, you'd better look out—because you are in for a large dose of apathy and finger pointing. Too often unaffected departments sit on the sidelines and rest quietly, relieved that the problem lies outside their realm of accountability, grateful that they are not the one on the critical path. In contrast, people functioning in an environment of joint accountability realize that problems extend beyond functional lines and often require solutions that necessitate wide-scale involvement.

Recall when the astronauts on Apollo 13 uttered the immortal words, "Houston, we have a problem." Can you picture people on the ground standing around and waiting for someone to do something? No way. Instead, those words prompted quick action. People scrambled, offered assistance, and anticipated related contingencies that could develop. There was only one problem, *everyone's* problem, and we had to solve it: How do we bring our men safely home?

But how does joint accountability really work, and how do you manage it? How do you avoid getting dragged *Below The Line* when someone with whom you share accountability gets stuck in the victim cycle? Joint accountability can be hard to find because it can be so difficult to create. Can you create an environment where people collectively own achieving the result, but do so without surrendering individual accountability? At what point does one's quest to help solve the problem actually get in the way of engaging others in doing the same? Can my own individual accountability obfuscate another's? When do we cross the line into confusion where everyone feels accountable for everything? Tough questions. And they require tough answers.

HELPING PEOPLE "RING THE BELL"

All answers to these questions come from a total focus on results within the organization. When everyone is accountable for achieving organizational results, and not just doing her job, the right things tend to happen. When people make a direct connection between their job and the organization's desired results, they breathe purpose and vision into their lives and become highly motivated. It all hinges on getting people to work on the right things and to know why they're doing what they're doing at every level in the organization. Otherwise, they can get lost in the process of doing the job and lose their focus on results.

One client, the leader of an international sales group, met this problem head on. Within his developing sales organization, people naturally focused on process, on how they did their jobs. Those in the field who were traveling heavily, away from home and family for weeks at a time, began to feel burdened by the process and that distracted them from concentrating on the results that mattered most. How could the leader turn that around? How could he get everyone in the department constantly thinking about what mattered most: making the sale? In short, how could he keep them from getting lost in process? Pondering this question, he hit upon a simple idea. One morning he installed a large bell on the wall outside his office in full view of the department. Whenever someone closed a sale, he would clang the bell repeatedly. It made quite a racket!

As you might imagine, the bell caught people's attention, not only in the department but throughout the company as well. Before long everyone began to talk in terms of doing things that would ring the bell. They knew the bell would not ring for procedures and policies, for processes and posturings, but for concrete results.

Clanging bells can come in all shapes and sizes, from bonuses and rewards to words of glowing praise. What can you do to get people to focus on the things that ring the bell in your organization? This is, perhaps, the greatest challenge of leadership, made all the more difficult by today's fast-paced, technology-driven environment. It's just so easy for all the noise to drown out the bell's clear ring.

To keep our own organization focused on results in the face of noisy activity, we speak of ringing the bell often. When new projects begin, a discussion ensues about *what*, at the end of the day, rings the bell. Our people translate this phrase to mean: "We know there are a lot of things we need to do to make this happen. We also know that some of these things may be extremely difficult and may seriously test our team, but in the end, we've accomplished nothing until we get this one most important result." Again, accountability begins, without exception, with clearly defining the results you want and need to achieve.

Throughout the chapters in Part One of this book, we have tried to show how people in organizations can succumb to the temptation to seek protection *Below The Line*. When they do so, they become experts at concocting explanations and victim stories. While that may provide an illusion of safety, that illusion is easily shattered by reality.

THE BENEFITS OF APPLYING ACCOUNTABILITY
THE OZ PRINCIPLE® WAY

Viewing accountability *The Oz Principle* way doesn't come without its costs. You must abandon the who-done-it game and the illusion of safety that arises when you pin blame on someone else. You must also become more involved both in coaching others and in checking yourself, always bearing in mind the need for *both* individual and joint accountability.

In our experience, however, the benefits far outweigh the costs. You save the costs of endless explanations from people hiding *Below The Line.* You save the costs of missed results that stem from insufficient action. You save the costs of all the dropped balls someone must, sooner or later, pick up. And you save the costs of wasted time spent micromanaging everything and everybody in sight.

To illustrate the benefits of applying accountability *The Oz Principle* way, consider Dennis Antinori, the vice president of sales for what used to be IVAC, a large medical products company, who anxiously awaited an upcoming national sales meeting at which the company would launch several new products. Two months before the meeting, Dennis received word that the new products would be a full twelve months late. Astonished by the news, he struggled with three enormous challenges: (1) how to keep himself *Above The Line,* refrain from blaming the new product development people for his predicament, and work to hit his numbers without the help of new products, (2) how to help his sales management team stay *Above The Line,* and (3) how to assist his sales managers in keeping their sales reps committed to achieving their sales targets despite the lack of new products.

Having learned to operate *Above The Line* and view accountability in a new light, Dennis met with his eighteen sales managers to take a new look at their circumstances. After letting people spend some time *Below The Line* in the victim cycle, concocting reasons for why they felt let down by the rest of the company, Dennis consciously moved the discussion *Above The Line.* Viewed from *Above The Line,* the huge obstacles to achieving sales targets still looked formidable, but not insurmountable. Dennis asked: "Given the obstacles we face, and they are huge ones, what else can we do to rise above these circumstances and achieve the results we want and the company needs?" At first the question baffled the sales managers. "How," they asked, "do you solve a new products problem without new products?" "That's not our *real* problem," Dennis suggested, "the *real* problem is a sales problem, not a new products problem. We must accept the reality that we will receive no new products this year and that the company still needs us to hit our numbers. Assigning blame to the new product development folks won't remove our responsibility to deliver on budgeted sales." After much lengthy discussion, the team climbed *Above The Line* and began asking: "What else can we do to achieve this year's sales targets, despite no new products?"

In the months following this meeting Dennis Antinori and his sales management team found many new and creative ways to boost sales and meet the targets set at the beginning of the year. By year's end they turned in an outstanding performance, one of the best in the history of the company: a healthy 15 percent increase in sales over the previous year.

One year after the accountability session, Dennis and his sales management team got together a few weeks prior to the national sales meeting. During the discussions Dennis asked his team: "What most contributed to our sales success last year?" As he recounts: "Everyone felt that we took an *Above The Line* approach to the situation, wasted no time blaming new product development, and really challenged ourselves to find and implement solutions, positively rather than negatively. When the bull charged, we took it by the horns and wrestled it to the ground. We got focused, rather than frustrated, and we made it happen, despite the odds stacked against us."

LOOKING FOR PEOPLE WHO ARE REAPING, OR FAILING TO REAP, THE BENEFITS OF ACCOUNTABILITY

As we read the newspaper and watch or listen to the news on any given day, we see *The Oz Principle* repeatedly applied and ignored. In fact, we decided to test this theory by randomly choosing a day and then searching the paper to see *The Oz Principle* at work (or not). We picked income tax filing day, April 15, in *The Washington Post*, the *Los Angeles Times*, *The* (London) *Times*, *The Boston Globe*, *The Wall Street Journal*, and *The New York Times*.

In the *Los Angeles Times*, we found a story about L-tryptophan and Betsy

DiRosa. As you read the following excerpt, you might take a minute to think about who was accountable and who could have been more accountable in this story:

"Two years after taking the over-the-counter sleeping aid L-tryptophan, schoolteacher Betsy DiRosa began suffering skin blotches, joint and muscle cramps, tingling in her arms and legs, even damage to her heart and lungs. The symptoms remain with DiRosa and with thousands of other victims of L-tryptophan, which was lifted from shelves across the country and is now the focal point of about 1500 lawsuits brought by victims of the debilitating disease EMS, for which L-tryptophan is blamed. This week, DiRosa, 42, became the first plaintiff in the nation to win a lawsuit against Showa Denko K.K., the Japanese manufacturer of the pill, but DiRosa and her attorney reacted with disappointment Wednesday, saying they had hoped for more than the jury's award of slightly more than $1 million." The article goes on to say, "She was 'upset' about the jury's verdict, saying she continued taking L-tryptophan after watching a news report that said a handful of people in New Mexico had developed mild symptoms as a result of using the pills." DiRosa exclaimed, "There was no mention of recalls, and I never saw another report. L-tryptophan was still on the shelves, with no warning sign anywhere in sight. I don't feel the least bit responsible for causing all of the horrible things that have happened to me. Was it really my fault?" DiRosa had been seeking $144 million but received less than even the $1.5 million offered in a proposed settlement by Showa Denko K.K. The jury found DiRosa partially at fault because she continued taking the pill after news accounts warning of its dangers. After the case concluded, Showa Denko's attorney John Nyhan said, "The result should tell the plaintiffs and the plaintiffs' lawyers that jurors do not believe the company should be punished for its conduct." But then, according to DiRosa's attorney Patrick McCormick, "Fault has been established. We clearly showed that Showa Denko K.K. manufactured a defective product, one that never obtained FDA approval, and which has had a devastating impact."

As with most victim stories, there are clearly two sides to this case: Both DiRosa and Showa Denko could have done more to avoid the tragedy. Showa Denko could have performed more testing and gained FDA approval before marketing its product. DiRosa could have stopped taking the pill as soon as she learned there might be a problem with the product. The jury rightly faulted Showa Denko for producing a bad product; but, honestly, the money DiRosa received seems inadequate compensation for the difficulties she has faced and will continue to face throughout her life because of L-tryptophan. However, the jury based its decision on the principle of "what else might DiRosa have done." Think of the situation in light of the Tylenol-tampering scare a few years ago. How many people, when they first heard of the tampering problems, stopped buying and using the product? How many people waited for the recall before they stopped using Tylenol? In our opinion, accountable consumers immediately discarded their Tylenol capsules and waited until Johnson & Johnson assured them that it had removed the risk of product tampering before they resumed using the product. DiRosa's story highlights an important aspect of *The Oz Principle:* Even when we are truly victimized, as Betsy DiRosa was, we may still show some accountability for the outcomes that we experience. To be sure, you can be a 100 percent victim, but it probably happens a lot less often than you might think or want to believe.

In *The Boston Globe* we found the insightful story of two sixth grade conflict managers, Cheryl Mauthe and Carrie McManus: "When Grade 6 students Cheryl Mauthe and Carrie McManus put on their pink baseball hats and head out to patrol the playground at Betty Gibson school, they go looking for trouble. The two girls are conflict managers, part of a program at the Brandon elementary school where students mediate non-physical disputes among their fellow schoolmates during recess. 'It's a good feeling knowing that you're putting effort into making our playgrounds a safer place,' Cheryl says. 'We're helping people instead of them just getting into fights,' adds Carrie. The conflict managers, who have been patrolling the school's playground since March 8, are not supposed to try to solve problems themselves, take sides or break up fights. Instead, they're taught to ask the children involved how the problem can be solved, how to avoid future fights and attempt to get an agreement from everyone involved." What marvelous *Above The Line* behavior! How might schools today improve if kids on all our playgrounds helped their schoolmates talk rather than fight, encouraged those with conflicts to find their own solutions and identified conflict as something that does not need to mar school life?

Each of these examples and many others appeared in the news on one day. As you read or watch the news today, look for examples of people reaping or failing to reap the benefits of accountability. It won't take long for you to see the need for *The Oz Principle* in virtually every aspect of human behavior.

PREPARING TO CLIMB THE *STEPS TO ACCOUNTABILITY*®

Throughout this chapter we have redefined accountability and shown how *The Oz Principle* definition can help you more fully appreciate the difference between *Below The Line* and *Above The Line* behavior. To summarize this chapter, and the importance of purposefully moving *Above The Line*, we'd like to share the following story.

In the early 1990s, Guidant Cardiac Rhythm Management (then known as CPI) made an unyielding commitment to improve new product development. At the time Guidant CRM had not produced a major new product in years, and the attitude in the industry was that the company couldn't develop its way out of a paper bag. At that time, then president Jay Graf described the company "as an organization going ninety miles per hour on an icy road headed toward a cliff because no one is willing to take responsibility for the situation, and, worse, no one really understands how bad things are." Despite all the clear signs of the company's precarious competitive situation, many people in the organization focused on "coping with growth" as its biggest problem, unwilling to recognize or acknowledge the impending product development challenges that could easily knock them *Below The Line*. Jay could foresee the competition's eventual rise to unquestioned market leadership just two years down the line, and he feared that their continuous introduction of high-quality new products into the market would create a game of leapfrog that would keep CRM in a defensive posture and render its products also-rans as soon as they hit the market.

As Guidant CRM began to *See It,* management noted that as engineers were designing a device, someone would always request an additional feature. The engineers would definitely deliver on the additional feature and then someone else would request another feature. It was clear to management that CRM would never deliver a new product if they continued to succumb to what they referred to as *creeping elegance.*

As this fundamental problem was recognized company wide, they began to address it with concerted effort. They implemented frequent project review meetings that provided more timely coaching and guidance for product development teams. They put into effect a new system of succession planning that distinguished between top players who accepted accountability for results and those who failed to do so. Ultimately, they involved the entire company in a process of organizational transition that focused the company on changing the corporate culture from one characterized by "finger-pointing, confusion, and complacency" to one noted for "accountability and ownership." Over the next few years, Guidant took accountability for delivering new products to the marketplace. People throughout the organization ceased to react solely in terms of their product development strategy. They aligned around a concept for a new product, and then they delivered. Over the next few years Guidant CRM became what management referred to as a new product development machine, delivering fourteen new products in just fourteen months.

It is interesting to note, according to Barb Reindl, vice president of HR at Guidant CRM, that while "new product development has become a significant and dependable strength of our company, today's markets have changed from the early nineties. No longer is it sufficient to just have great technology."

As Guidant worked to produce the world's smallest and most sophisticated defibrillator in the late 1990s, many people "had been placed on mandatory overtime for about a year because of the impact this device was certain to have on the company's performance. Management at Guidant was shocked when their innovative and highly celebrated product did no more than bump the business a little in market share."

Jay Millerhagen, director of heart failure marketing, explained that because of the company's singleness of vision, Guidant would release a great new product and then stand around and say, "We don't get it. Why doesn't it take us to number one in market share?"

"It was a real wake-up call," said Dale Hougham, director of quality assurance. "Our approach—that the best technology will keep us on top—had been shattered. It was going to take more than that." Reality had hit Guidant right between the eyes for the second time in a decade.

Once again this management team took accountability to shift the way they viewed their business. They began to think about their business from the patient and customer perspective instead of from an internal R & D only viewpoint. They put patients and customers first. They emphasized their role as a company in Guidant. They energized their people around this new view and created great emotional appeal throughout their organization.

Additionally, Guidant focused on the results of a key study as a way to energize both customers and employees. The company had pioneered the practice of sponsoring clinical trials in defibrillator therapy. While the results from one major trial helped identify patients who needed defibrillators, only 20 percent of them were actually receiving a device.

Janet Babka, director of quality information and technology, observed, "The results of a more recent study showed even more people needing device therapy. If they did nothing, the number of high-risk people receiving a device was going to decline further." Acknowledging the reality of the current tragedy, Guidant rallied to action. "Instead of focusing only on how their devices were different from competitors', they started focusing their message on the larger issue—that people were needlessly dying without therapy. They worked to change this reality and consequently, to change the very dynamics of the industry."

Guidant CRM began steering toward "a new understanding of competitiveness, which went beyond great products to include great sales, service, technical support, training, and every other aspect of their business. They began to focus on doing twenty things well, rather than just two or three."

Finally, Guidant CRM focused on improving its message and its distribution system. They took accountability for how they were viewed in the marketplace. The experts would attest to the fact that Guidant CRM's products were superior, but everyone agreed that Guidant CRM had failed to declare that same message. Guidant CRM ultimately acknowledged that great technology doesn't sell itself. Today, every strategic imperative ends with the phrase, "and get credit for all of it."

As for its distribution system, Guidant CRM's U.S. sales force has expanded more than five-fold: from 215 reps in 1997 to 1134 reps in 2003.

CLIMBING THE *STEPS TO ACCOUNTABILITY*®

It takes time, effort, commitment, and sometimes even emotional trauma, to get onto the *Steps To Accountability* and stay there, but we have never found an individual or organization, who, after experiencing life *Above The Line,* wanted to return to the blame game. You may slip. In fact, you will slip. However, you'll know you're slipping and you'll want to catch yourself before you sink too far.

In Chapter Two, we provided some telltale signs of getting stuck in the victim cycle so you could recognize *Below The Line* attitudes and behavior. We'd like to conclude this chapter with some telltale signs of climbing the *Steps To Accountability* that can help you remain *Above The Line.* In the next four chapters, we will address the various *Steps To Accountability.*

You can improve your own ability to remain *Above The Line* by watching for the following clues that indicate accountable attitudes and behavior:

• You invite candid feedback from everyone about your own performance.

• You never want anyone, including yourself, to hide the truth from you.

• You readily acknowledge reality, including all its problems and challenges.

• You don't waste time or energy on things you cannot control or influence.

• You always commit yourself 100 percent to what you are doing, and if your commitment begins to wane, you strive to rekindle it.

• You *own* your circumstances and your results, even when they seem less than desirable.

• You recognize when you are dropping *Below The Line* and act quickly to avoid the traps of the victim cycle.

• You delight in the daily opportunity to make things happen.

• You constantly ask yourself the question, "What else can I do to rise above my circumstances and get the results I want?"

When you think and act in these ways you're functioning *Above The Line.* Rising above your circumstances to get the results you seek is the soul of *The Oz Principle,* just as it was the empowering theme in L. Frank Baum's land of Oz.

Part 2

The Power of Individual Accountability: Moving Yourself *Above The Line*®

The universally applicable **Steps To Accountability**®, **See It**®, **Own It**®, **Solve It**®, *and* **Do It**®, *weave the tapestry of every business success scenario, without exception. In Part Two, we examine each of the* **Steps To Accountability**, *one at a time, to help you understand, internalize, and apply each step. You'll learn how to muster the courage to see and acknowledge reality; find the heart to own your circumstances, no matter how difficult that may prove to be; obtain the wisdom to solve any problem or overcome any obstacle that stands in your way; and exercise the means to make things happen, allowing you to get the results you want.*

Chapter 4

THE LION: MUSTERING THE COURAGE TO *SEE IT*®

"Do you think Oz could give me courage?" asked the Cowardly Lion.

"Just as easily as he could give me brains," said the Scarecrow.

"Or give me a heart," said the Tin Woodsman.

"Or send me back to Kansas," said Dorothy.

"Then, if you don't mind, I'll go with you," said the Lion, "for my life is simply unbearable without a bit of courage."

—*The Wizard of Oz,*
L. Frank Baum

It always takes courage to acknowledge the reality of a difficult situation, and even the most heralded institutions can fail to do so. Schering-Plough recently recalled almost sixty million of its inhalers because some of them did not contain the necessary active ingredients for alleviating asthma attacks. Critics like Dr. Sidney Wolfe, director of Public Citizen's Health Research Group, have called it bad management and sloppy manufacturing. Long known for its disciplined manufacturing, Schering-Plough began surprising analysts, shareholders, and eventually customers in recent years with a growing number of product recalls, FDA fines, and sanctions. Apparently, management poured money into marketing and sales for blockbuster products such as Claritin while delaying plant upgrades and over-relying on the past strength of manufacturing systems. Fortunately, Schering-Plough's executives are demonstrating the sort of courage we'd like to see from all corporations. CEO Richard Kogan told shareholders, "I am taking full responsibility for resolving these matters in a timely manner and securing the FDA's confidence." He launched a manufacturing improvement program, formed a worldwide quality operations unit to address quality issues, implemented technology upgrades, added hundreds of quality control people and scientists to make the changes last, and established a review board composed of former FDA officials to oversee FDA compliance. Congratulations to Schering-Plough, CEO Kogan, and the entire executive team. It takes courage to see reality, admit mistakes, and recognize the need for improvement, the first step to rising *Above The Line.*

It isn't easy to see reality, and you can't do it overnight, but you will get there much more quickly if you proceed one sure step at a time. As you begin taking the first step *Above The Line,* bear in mind the words of Jack Welch, former CEO of General Electric, who defines management as "looking reality straight in the eye and then acting upon it with as much speed as you can."

TAKING THE FIRST STEP *ABOVE THE LINE*®

Even the most accountable people get stuck in the victim cycle from time to time. And sometimes, people who usually practice accountability can get stuck on a particular challenge. Regardless of whether you're stuck *Below The Line* all the time or only on a particularly pesky problem, you must still take the first step out of the victim cycle by recognizing that you are stuck in a circle of denial. That recognition requires the courage to acknowledge the reality of your situation, no matter how unpleasant or unfair that reality may seem. Without such acknowledgment, you can never expect to respond to it effectively. According to Andrew S. Grove, chairman of Intel, every company faces a critical point when it must change dramatically to rise to the next level of performance. If the company fails to see and seize that moment, it will start to decline. The key is courage.

It's astonishing to see such giants as Enron, WorldCom, and Arthur Andersen, at one time the unchallenged leaders in their respective world markets, suddenly fall. In a short period of time, hundreds of thousands of people became victims of the actions of a relative few. However, in the mire created by such circumstances, many courageous people are taking bold actions to see the reality of their situations and to stave off further calamity. Take, for instance, one intimate interview with Jim Copeland, CEO of Deloitte & Touche. In this interview, *Fortune* magazine reporters captured the essence of this CEO's choice to face reality. "As the news that employees in Arthur Andersen's Houston office had destroyed thousands of Enron-related documents scrolled across a TV news ticker one afternoon in early January, Copeland's stomach turned. He knew instinctively that the focus of all the public outrage, the government investigations, and the breathless media coverage would shift to Andersen and, by extension, to the rest of the accounting profession." Copeland, knowing his firm would not escape scrutiny and criticism, mustered the courage to face the situation head on. One of the toughest realities he had to face was the need to separate consulting services, a very lucrative part of the firm, from accounting and auditing services. Deloitte & Touche had long tied consulting and accounting services together because of the natural synergies and benefits to clients, and the firm was committed to maintaining that strategy until one morning when Manoj Singh, head of the firm's consulting services business in the United States, showed up in Copeland's office. *Fortune* reported the pivotal moment: "Singh had just learned that a big audit client was backing out of a contract to use Deloitte Consulting for a multimillion-dollar restructuring and cost-reduction study. The client was concerned about the perception of a conflict. Copeland nodded sadly and picked up the phone. He dialed Douglas McCracken, the head of Deloitte Consulting worldwide, and William Parrett, the managing partner for Deloitte's American accounting, tax, and related services. That afternoon the four men—Copeland, McCracken, Singh, and Parrett—

locked themselves in a conference room for five hours. They emerged, Copeland recalls, with tears in their eyes. They began working the phones, hosting marathon conference calls with partners around the world. Their message was simple: The one-firm model was dead. Deloitte & Touche would reluctantly separate from Deloitte Consulting." With that message the whole company took one firm step *Above The Line.*

WHY PEOPLE FAIL TO *SEE IT*®

People most frequently fail to see reality because they choose to ignore or accept changes in the external environment. For example, *The Wall Street Journal* reported that ". . . Connie Plourde and the other sales representatives at American Telephone & Telegraph Co.'s Sacramento, California, office lost their desks. They were given laptop computers, cellular telephones and portable printers and told to create 'virtual offices' at home or at their customers' offices. It wasn't an easy change for the extroverted, 19-year AT&T veteran, who delighted in the camaraderie of the workplace. 'Until the real-estate people came in and started moving our cubicles out, we just continued to come in,' she recalls. 'It was a comfort zone, I guess.'" Ignoring or refusing to deal with such a change can quickly thrust you *Below The Line.* Dun & Bradstreet's Michael Bell, one of a new breed of corporate real-estate managers, was surprised to encounter such strong resistance to AT&T's telecommuting initiative. Why couldn't people see that "the office isn't a place to come, sit down and stare at a computer screen or talk on the phone all day? If you want to do that, you can do it at home." Even corporate decision makers, who climbed the corporate ladder at a time when clout was measured by office size and location, found it hard to embrace what Mr. Bell has dubbed the un-real-estating of corporate America. Resistance to such a trend could, however, undermine the competitiveness of a company that has found itself in a dogfight for market share. Larry Ebert, director of real estate at Ernst & Young, says there will be a lot of cultural resistance to such office changes. If those changes are inevitable, then those who resist them will inevitably fail.

In another case of people failing to see reality and accept their own responsibility for that reality, consider the current family dysfunction game. While most people agree that the home environment affects a person's habits, it has become fashionable, even epidemic, for adult children to blame all their woes on dysfunctional childhood homes. Who do you blame for compulsive shopping disorders, sex addictions, poor eating habits, alcoholism, spouse and child abuse, work ruts, personality disorders, uncontrollable urges to please others? Everyone but yourself, it seems. "It's not my fault, it's my family's fault." Talk show hosts from Oprah Winfrey to Jerry Springer daily exploit America's penchant for playing the dysfunction game by parading celebrities as well as ordinary people across the nation's television screens, perpetuating the notion that none of us need shoulder full responsibility for our problems. The raging popularity of such shows emphasizes just how much the nation's television audiences enjoy hearing other people recount their victim stories. In turn, many TV watchers use such victim stories to justify their own *Below The Line* behavior, making the blame game a new national pastime. After all, according to popular lecturer and author John Bradshaw, 96 percent of the population comes from dysfunctional families.

While we agree that family problems can plague people far beyond their childhoods, we take issue with Bradshaw's claim, not just because we question the accuracy of the percentage, but because reliance on that percentage lets 96 percent of the population off the hook for their current behavior. If you comfort yourself with the knowledge that 96 percent of your fellow Americans can blame their dysfunctional families for their problems, you're probably stuck in the victim cycle. Oh, you may justly feel that early experiences have contributed to your problems, but chalking everything up to those problems prevents you from taking charge of your life and doing something about your problems. In this sense, the current dysfunctional fad strikes us as just one more indicator of people's inability and unwillingness to acknowledge their own accountability.

Indeed, the whole dysfunctional movement would strike us as funny, if it didn't pose such a dangerous threat to our country's well being. Consider, for instance, these excuses for overdrafts at the now-defunct House Bank for the U.S. House of Representatives, as reported in *The Wall Street Journal* during 1992:

1. Representative Mary Rose Oakar, a Democrat from Ohio who sat on the House Administration Committee that oversaw the House Bank and racked up 217 overdrafts, said, "When I came to Congress, they didn't tell us there was another way to get your check."
2. Representative Robert Mrazek, a Democrat from New York with 972 overdrafts, said, "I have never bounced a check."

3. Representative Tim Penny, a Democrat from Minnesota, blamed his overdrafts on his office manager.

4. Representative Edolphus Towns, another Democrat from New York, attributed many of his 403 overdrafts to embezzlement by a former employee.

5. Former Representative Newt Gingrich, a Republican from Georgia and House Republican Whip, dismissed his overdrafts as "no big deal."

Well, we think it is a big deal because elected officials should serve as role models for more responsible behavior, both before and after the fact. Not doing so represents a singular lack of courage. For people languishing in the victim cycle and unable to come to grips with the reality of their situations, it takes a lot of courage to:

1. Recognize when they fall *Below The Line;*
2. Realize that remaining *Below The Line* not only ignores the real problem but leads to increasingly poor results; and
3. Acknowledge and accept reality as the first step toward taking accountability.

Acknowledging *Below The Line* behavior and facing up to the reality of your situation does take courage. Failure to muster that courage results in an unwillingness to pay the price for greater accountability and results. In most troublesome situations, people do know, in the back of their minds, that acknowledging reality means they'll have to change something that many of us fear, and even resist. That change generally begins with choosing to see a situation in a different way, and viewing a situation differently often means admitting that you did something wrong, that you yourself could have done more and didn't. Deciding you can't do anything to remedy the situation, you may as well move on. Why solve a problem when you can run away from it? For those who have been truly victimized, at the hands of a criminal, for example, it may mean deciding that you can't allow that particular event to hold you back throughout your life. After all, success on the heels of real victimization is the best revenge you can exact on the situation.

Doing something differently about your situation often requires doing things you dislike doing, such as taking a risk you've been avoiding or confronting an issue or person you've been ducking. At Hartmarx Corporation, the Chicago-based maker of men's suits, the board of directors failed to confront the inability of the company's chief executive officer, Harvey Weinberg, to halt a string of losses that eventually totaled $320 million. Only then did the board force Weinberg to resign. According to *The Wall Street Journal*, the board didn't act sooner because it "didn't want to be seen as pulling the plug too early." Unfortunately, the wait-and-see attitude significantly contributed to the company's stock value plummeting from $600 million to $200 million.

Embracing such realities can prove difficult because doing so involves shedding the protective cocoon of a victim story. It seems so much safer to remain *Below The Line*. But, in reality, the cocoon offers only an illusion of safety. Eventually the time will come to pay the piper for your inaction. When you give yourself permission to do nothing about your situation, when you don't act, don't learn, don't acknowledge your responsibility, don't admit having done wrong, don't face the facts, don't give up the sympathy that a victim story attracts, and don't look for what else you can do to achieve results, or improve your life, your behavior gets you nowhere. To get somewhere better and to solve your problems, you must abandon the illusion of safety *Below The Line* and take the risks involved in rising *Above The Line*.

When you encounter a difficult situation, ask yourself whether you want to remain mired in the difficulty or attempt some sort of breakthrough to extract yourself from it. Even the most habitual victim would rather be leading a better life. But achieving a breakthrough usually requires a break with past actions and attitudes. That means that any person feeling victimized must replace his or her victim story with a willingness to see things as they really are and not as they appear from the tenuous safety of a *Below The Line* attitude.

THE CONSEQUENCES OF NOT *SEEING IT*

When Christopher J. Steffen resigned as chief financial officer at Eastman Kodak after less than three months on the job, his exit exposed the growing vulnerability of boards of directors who must assess the reality of their companies' needs in a timely fashion. According to *The Wall Street Journal*, "Management experts say boards of directors everywhere are under greater pressure nowadays to fill top jobs quickly. Directors sometimes fail to gauge whether a new executive—especially below the chief executive officer's level—will mesh with existing senior management." According to the article, in Eastman Kodak's case, Steffen's resignation "knocked $1.7 billion off market value of the company's stock." Not seeing reality, especially at the board level, can deliver devastating, and sometimes lightning-swift, consequences.

We recently worked with a client who, because of the sensitive nature of the story and our desire to protect the privacy of the individuals involved, must remain disguised. It's a true story, however, and it exposes the inexorable consequences of not seeing reality. Tim Langley, president and CEO of CET, a $400 million insurance company, had recently hired Jed Simon as his new vice president of underwriting to resolve a sales volume shortfall in the near term and to build a world-class underwriting organization in the long term. Langley believed he had hired the perfect man, and after the first year together, Langley awarded Simon a rave review for his work and even implied that his protégé would someday succeed him as CEO of the company.

Soon after joining CET, Simon had introduced an organizational effectiveness program that created greater openness and productivity throughout the company's underwriting operations and quickly ended the sales shortfall. In addition, Simon drafted a new policy manual, hired new staff, and beefed up the organization's capabilities to meet anticipated future demand. Since his actions enabled the company to surpass all its annual goals, Langley took to calling Simon "the best underwriting vice president in the business."

Then, as the year ended and the new year began, Langley shifted CET's emphasis from increased sales to better customer service. Simon's reputation plummeted almost overnight. In stark contrast to last year's review, his next one nailed him to the wall. From Langley's perspective, Simon had been ignoring vital feedback from the sales force about CET's dismal customer service. According to the sales force, poor service quality made it impossible for them to sustain and increase sales.

When we dug into the situation, we discovered that Simon responded to this feedback from deep within the victim cycle. Here's how he described his feelings to us: "How can I get a review like this? I have never received such a horrible review. What do these salespeople know anyway? They can't even make accurate sales forecasts for one quarter. The sandbaggers! They want a sure thing in terms of their sales quotas, and they never stretch for higher goals. They haven't even looked at the monthly graphs that clearly show customer complaints down and sales up. Furthermore, we have rolled out so many new products prematurely that we have ended up doing the job of the development people along with our own. You know, I really think Langley's got an ego problem and feels threatened by me. Last year he told me and many others that he thought I was the best underwriting vice president in the industry. He even told me I would succeed him someday. Now he's telling me I'm doing a rotten job. I don't think he knows what he wants. He changes his priorities every time I turn around. He's the one who's got a problem, not me."

While there may have been some truth to Simon's perceptions, he was clearly wallowing *Below The Line* by refusing to acknowledge the reality of his circumstances. Through a series of rationalizations, he convinced himself that the alleged service quality problem shouldn't fall in his lap. Worse, he considers his current course of action productive, appropriate, and destined to yield superior results, when, in fact, it won't.

Before Jed Simon could *See It* he needed to (1) acknowledge his own *Below The Line* behavior, (2) recognize the reality (and not necessarily the accuracy) of his boss's perception that he has failed in the area of service quality, and (3) realize that as long as he stays *Below The Line* he will remain ineffective. Simon's inability and/or unwillingness to acknowledge reality has created a growing chasm between himself and his boss, and no matter how unjust it may seem to him, when it comes to a showdown, he'll lose, Langley will win.

Simon isn't the only leader to fail to see reality and subsequently face the consequences. Think back to IBM's memorable decline over the last decade. As recorded in *Time* magazine: "For years, IBM stubbornly attempted to ignore the trend away from big mainframes. Instead of adapting, it tried to protect its base. . . . But with sales slowing and price pressure mounting, IBM has finally faced up to the trend. Akers signaled IBM's intention to shift away from its mainframe business, which is down 10 percent this year." This situation did not occur overnight, and a number of IBM's competitors had already paid the price for not mustering the courage to see it coming. Wang Laboratories filed for bankruptcy. Unisys, created by the merger of Burroughs and Sperry, suffered $2.5 billion in losses, and Digital Equipment almost sank under similarly huge losses, which resulted in the ouster of Digital's founder and president Kenneth Olsen. Clearly, the handwriting was on the wall: The old non-mainframe strategies no longer worked. IBM, however, ignored the signals, even when upstart Apple Computer surpassed IBM as the leading PC maker and tacked up a stellar performance, partly due to a "tiny frame" computer, the laptop Power-

Book. Aggressive price cutting in the industry sparked great demand, which Apple and IBM compatible Compaq rushed to fill. IBM also failed to anticipate the workstation revolution and sat by as Sun Microsystems and Hewlett Packard took the lead in that market. As the *Time* article concluded, "Although it developed superb technology years ago, the company sat on it out of fear that it would cannibalize IBM's bread and butter mainframe business." Failing to see the reality of its situation, IBM lost both the value of its bread and butter business and the chance to position itself advantageously for the future.

When did the downfall occur? In an earlier story, *Fortune* magazine pinpointed the time precisely: "To understand fully just what a disaster IBM has been, and just how blind its own management was to the depth of its problems, step back to a moment in late 1986. IBM was more than a year past a boom period and struggling. Revenue growth was miserable, earnings growth was nonexistent, and IBM's stock, then $125 a share, had lost nearly $24 billion in market value from a peak of $99 billion just seven months earlier." In an interview with *Fortune,* Chairman John F. Akers nonetheless exhibited gritty confidence: "Four or five years from now," he asserted, "people will look back and see that the company's performance has been superlative." Almost five years later, reality proved Akers dead wrong. IBM stock continued to fall, losing another 18 billion in market value. Revenue grew at less than half the industry average for the period, and IBM's worldwide market share fell from 30 to 21 percent, a whopping $3 billion in sales for each percentage point. When asked by *Fortune* what went wrong and why his prediction of superlative performance didn't pan out, Akers replied, "I don't think anything went wrong." *Fortune* reporters responded, "Then why, one might reasonably ask, did he tell his managers in May [1991] that IBM was 'in crisis,' a characterization made in private and quickly leaked to the press? And, if IBM stock has lost $42 billion in value since 1986, just how far would it have fallen if something really had gone wrong?" Akers later claimed he only meant to emphasize that Big Blue's industry is so volatile that no company can anticipate all the unexpected changes that sweep through it. To his credit, however, he admitted that IBM could not blame any outside force for its stupendous loss of market share.

In 1994, IBM's woes grew even worse than in 1991 and 1992, and the company's new chief executive officer, Louis Gerstner, must have felt much like the Wizard of Oz, from whom everyone expected an improbable miracle. When IBM's new leader came aboard, he immediately began to help the company see the reality of its situation and to act on it. Now, almost ten years later, almost everyone acknowledges the problem. In his first meeting at IBM as described in his book *Who Says Elephants Can't Dance,* Louis V. Gerstner, Jr., writes, "It is not helpful to feel sorry for ourselves. I'm sure our employees don't need any rah-rah speeches. We need leadership and a sense of direction and momentum, not just doom around here. I want can-do people looking for short-term victories and long-term excitement. I told them there was no time to focus on who created our problems. I had no interest in that. We have little time to spend on problem definition. We must focus our efforts on solutions and actions."

Not wasting any time, he then proposed the following five ninety-day priorities:

1. Stop hemorrhaging cash. We were precariously close to running out of money.

2. Make sure we would be profitable in 1994 to send a message to the world—and to the IBM workforce—that we had stabilized the company.

3. Develop and implement a key customer strategy for 1993 and 1994, one that would convince customers that we were back serving their interests, not just pushing "iron" (mainframes) down their throats to ease our short-term financial pressures.

4. Finish right-sizing by the beginning of the third quarter.

5. Develop an intermediate-term business strategy.

The very basis of IBM's historic turnaround was established in this first meeting lasting all of forty-five minutes. It isn't always easy to see reality, but you must see it if you expect people to move *Above The Line* and take ownership for their results.

With that in mind, let's now look at how you can assess and develop your own ability to acknowledge reality and thereby avoid the unpleasant and inevitable consequences of failing to *See It.*

SEE IT® SELF-ASSESSMENT

Picture in your mind's eye something we see all too often: the sales vice president of a midsized computer manufacturer telling his colleague, the marketing vice president, that the company's sales are weak because its products don't meet customer needs, but the marketing vice president dismissing the argument. In such a situation, the sales vice president perceives that the marketing vice president never listens to his group's input while the marketing vice president thinks that the sales vice president never appreciates the sales group's input. Both feel victimized by the other, and both remain stuck *Below The Line,* unwilling to acknowledge reality. Unless these two executives can *see* reality, they will squander their time and energy blaming each other, fostering confusion, promoting organizational discord, and creating an environment in which their people wait and see if their leaders will work things out. So how do these vice presidents begin recognizing their *Below The Line* attitudes and behavior?

The first step requires careful and honest self-assessment. To facilitate your own self-assessment, we have developed the *See It* Self-Assessment, which will give you a general idea of your ability to recognize a *Below The Line* posture. Take a few minutes to evaluate your ability to *See It* in the context of your work, home, team, club, community, church, or association, answering each question as honestly as you can.

SEE IT®
Self-Assessment

		Never	Seldom	Sometimes	Often	Always
ONE	You quickly recognize when you get stuck in the victim cycle.	7	5	3	1	0
TWO	You accept coaching from others who point out ways in which you helped contribute to the problem you currently face.	7	5	3	1	0
THREE	You willingly acknowledge that you make mistakes that impair your ability to get results.	7	5	3	1	0
FOUR	You openly listen when people offer you perspectives of the problem that are different from yours.	7	5	3	1	0
FIVE	You look first at what you are personally doing, or not doing, that is getting in the way of progress as opposed to solely looking at how others are preventing your progress.	7	5	3	1	0
SIX	You strive to broaden your scope of understanding about the problem you face by seeking greater understanding from a wide array of resources.	7	5	3	1	0
SEVEN	You readily acknowledge existing problems and clearly understand the consequences of not resolving them.	7	5	3	1	0
EIGHT	You test your view of reality with other people when faced with a perplexing problem.	7	5	3	1	0
NINE	You consciously and actively work to get *Above The Line* by objectively acknowledging reality.	7	5	3	1	0
TEN	When explaining your lack of progress, you quickly acknowledge how you contributed to a lack of results.	7	5	3	1	0

After you have completed the *See It* Self-Assessment, total up your score. The following table provides some guidelines for evaluating your ability to recognize when you're stuck *Below The Line.*

Once you have assessed yourself, don't get discouraged if you discover that you need help seeing it. You can get a lot of help if you ask others familiar with your situation to give you perfectly candid feedback.

SEE IT®
Self-Assessment Scoring

TOTAL SCORE	EVALUATION GUIDELINES
50+ points	Indicates a serious inability or unwillingness to *See It*. You need outside help. Call 911, immediately!
30 to 50 points	Suggests that you often find it difficult to *See It*. Learn to seek feedback (see next section). Ask someone sitting near you to slap you in the face, right now!
10 to 30 points	Reveals a fair ability to *See It*. Keep working on it. If you have created a victim story, write it on a piece of paper, bury it in the back yard, and move on!
0 to 9 points	Verifies a strong ability to *See It*. Ask a good friend or colleague to give you a pat on the back!

HOW FEEDBACK IMPROVES YOUR ABILITY TO *SEE IT*®

You can gain great insight from frequent, regular, and ongoing feedback from other people. Although it can cause a great deal of pain and embarrassment at times, honest input helps create the accurate picture of reality that lies at the core of accountability. Since no one individual can mandate a perfectly accurate description of reality, you must draw from many other people's perceptions to imbue your reality with the deepest possible understanding of its many hues and shades. In our experience, accountable people constantly seek feedback from a wide range of associates, be they friends, family, business partners, consultants, or other advisers. Remember, other people's perceptions of reality, whether you agree with them or not, always add important nuances to your own perception. The more perspectives you obtain, the more easily you can recognize when you're stuck *Below The Line*, move *Above The Line,* and then encourage others to do likewise.

To better grasp the importance of seeking and giving feedback, picture in your mind a common situation we encountered with one of our clients: Betty Bingham, a corporate staff human resources vice president of a large corporation, who has been temporarily reassigned to clean up a division's human resources policies and practices. The people in the division naturally view her as an intruder, and she assumes, after a few weeks, that all the bad press she's getting automatically comes with such bad-guy assignments. Several months later, when she thinks it's time to return to her corporate staff assignment, she learns that headquarters doesn't want her back. Worse, she receives no salary increase. Devastated by this turn of events, Betty feels victimized and confused because she had received no direct feedback about her performance from headquarters or from the division president to whom she has been temporarily reporting. Instead of feeling sorry for herself, however, she begins seeking direct feedback from the people she's been working with over the last nine months. As she seeks and receives this input, she discovers that her clean-up methods have caused deep resentments and frustrations. For example, one vice president confided in her that he thought she did not respect others' points of view, that she did not acknowledge the previous accomplishments of the organization or her staff, and that she tended to take credit due others.

This sort of feedback helped Betty gain an awareness of how she had caused much of the bad press herself, which made it difficult for her to get the results she needed now. Armed with honest feedback, she set out to turn around the negative perceptions and win back the confidence of people in both the division and at headquarters. To her delight, more and more people began to confide in her, and she soon built a reputation as a credible and useful executive. Before she got the feedback, she felt victimized, powerless, and unable to

Feedback Creates Accountability

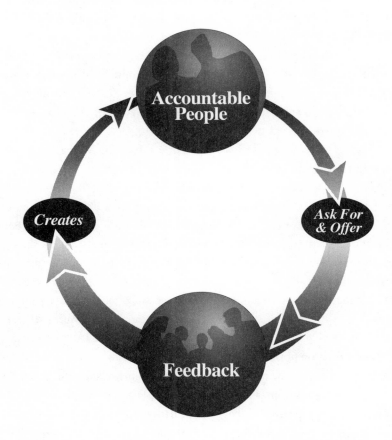

change things; she was truly unaware and unbelieving with respect to how others viewed her. Had she remained trapped in that resentment, she would undoubtedly have sought employment elsewhere. After the feedback, however, she could *See It* more clearly and consequently felt more empowered to do something about her predicament. In short, she had moved herself *Above The Line*.

If you find yourself continually surprised by your performance appraisals, we suggest you do what Betty did and seek *more* feedback about your performance, not just from your superiors, but from others whom you respect and trust. It's easy to go home and rant against your superiors over what you perceive as unjust treatment; it's hard to ask your family to help you understand why you've gotten the review you did. But you must do it right. Over the years we have observed both right and wrong ways to seek feedback. If you don't do it right, you may only hear what people think you want to hear. To gain the most honest feedback, try these tips:

1. Ask for feedback in the right environment (a comfortable, quiet place free from interruptions and distractions).
2. Tell the person from whom you're seeking feedback that you want completely honest input about a particular situation or concern. Emphasize your sincerity, and explain your motivation.
3. Remember, the feedback you're requesting represents an important point of view, so don't get defensive, even if you strongly disagree with something the person says.
4. Listen carefully and ask for elaboration, but be sure not to invalidate feedback off-handedly with which you disagree.
5. Make sure you express your appreciation for your advisor's time and help.

Once you have more fully examined your own *Above* and *Below The Line* behavior, consider the substantial benefits that automatically flow to someone who has mustered the courage to face reality.

THE BENEFITS OF *SEEING IT*®

As we indicated at the beginning of this chapter, even if you consider yourself a highly accountable person, you can still get stuck in the victim cycle when facing a particular challenge, as we ourselves did not long ago with an important client. To protect our client's privacy, we'll refer to the organization as DALCAP.

We always strive for superior customer service with our clients, but something in our consulting engagement with DALCAP over a six-month period caused certain key executives there to perceive us as *Below The Line* in terms of customer service. Had we somehow failed to practice what we preach? While we saw them as our most demanding client, we had also felt that we had risen to the occasion time and time again. While we knew that our client harbored certain concerns, we pretended not to know they resented what they saw as inaccessibility. Each time a DALCAP executive cited an example of our inaccessibility, we were stunned. How could she say that after all the extraordinary things we had accomplished for the firm? We rationalized it all as false expectations on their part, by convincing ourselves that no matter what we did, we could never make this client happy. Eventually, however, after a lot of discussion, we realized that in order to maintain a successful relationship with DALCAP, we had to acknowledge that we were falling short of their expectations. We knew that we must get *Above The Line* and demonstrate the *See It* attitude we emphasize so much in our consulting work. As a first step, we wrote the following memo to DALCAP's executive staff:

To: DALCAP Executive Staff Members
From: Partners In Leadership, LLC
Subject: Customer Orientation

We reviewed our recent proposal to DALCAP with Barbara Kowal this morning and were pleased to hear that we will probably go forward with the project. We appreciate your confidence in our ability to continue to assist DALCAP.

Barbara very graciously shared with us some constructive feedback about our work during one of your recent executive staff meetings. Some people honestly feel *Partners In Leadership* has not been as accessible as it should be. This deeply concerns us because it seems to indicate that some at DALCAP question our commitment to customer service.

We want you to know that we will do everything we can to prove our commitment. Your feedback will help us to grow, and that will help us help you. We promise this: *Partners In Leadership will* be accessible.

We understand that perceptions do not change overnight, but we have already begun to work on establishing this new perception. Specifically:

1. Throughout our engagement, we will call Barbara Kowal weekly to review progress and to determine whether we should meet with any of you or any of the trained facilitators.
2. While our travel and our work facilitating off-site sessions may prevent us from getting back to you right away, we will personally respond to

your voice mail messages no later than the evening of the day on which you call.

3. If you need to reach us for an immediate response please call our office number (909) 694–5596. Emphasize that you have an urgent message and need to reach us right away. We will make sure our people remain alert for all such calls and that they relay them to us immediately. We will get back to you within four hours.

If at any time you doubt our accessibility, tell us so at once. We need your continued feedback to foster our own accountability for results.

We look forward to our ongoing relationship and the growth of both our organizations.

Sincerely,
Partners In Leadership

While this response may not appear extraordinary, it did communicate to our client that we heard their feedback, acknowledged their concern, and would respond to their needs. Less than one month after receiving the memo, the president of DALCAP signed a new long-term agreement with us, larger than our two previous ones with the company.

It would have been much easier for us to continue denying or rationalizing DALCAP's perception of our inaccessibility, but doing so would have robbed us of the substantial benefits we gain from such a valuable client. By acknowledging the reality, we ran the risk of appearing "wrong," but until we decided to do something about our client's perception, we would never have climbed *Above The Line,* and changed their perceptions.

PREPARING FOR THE NEXT STEP *ABOVE THE LINE*®

Oz's Lion symbolizes the first dimension of accountability, mustering the courage to see reality. However, Dorothy would need to understand all four dimensions of accountability before she would fully understand that only she could rise above her circumstances and return to Kansas. Not surprisingly, along her yellow brick road journey she learned to love and cherish her companions for each of their unique qualities. In the end she was able to combine what she had learned from and with her companions to escape feelings of powerlessness and rise *Above The Line* to get the results she wanted. In the next chapter, you will see how the Tin Woodsman symbolizes the heart to *Own It,* and in the process you'll learn how to do that yourself. Keep in mind that to get the results you want at the end of your own journey, you'll need what all the Oz companions gained on theirs.

Chapter 5

THE TIN WOODSMAN: FINDING THE HEART TO *OWN IT*®

"I might have stood there always if you had not come along," he said; "so you have certainly saved my life. How did you happen to be here?"

"We are on our way to the Emerald City, to see the great Oz," she answered, "and we stopped at your cottage to pass the night."

"Why do you wish to see Oz?" he asked.

"I want him to send me back to Kansas; and the Scarecrow wants him to put a few brains into his head," she replied.

The Tin Woodsman appeared to think deeply for a moment. Then he said: "Do you suppose Oz could give me a heart?"

"Why, I guess so," Dorothy answered.

—*The Wizard of Oz,*
L. Frank Baum

Everything seemed out of control. As hard as he tried, Dave Schlotterbeck, CEO of ALARIS Medical Systems, just could not get the organization to perform. ALARIS Medical Systems, a company with $500 million in revenues and 2900 employees worldwide, had resulted from the merger of two medical device companies, IVAC and IMED. While this combination should have produced strength and great potential, a huge debt load and under-performance stalled all efforts at realizing that potential.

Of particular concern was the disposable products division. Product quality had leveled off at 88 percent, i.e., only 88 percent of all products met the company's quality threshold for shipment. Successful deliveries, those completed within twenty-four hours after receipt of the order, had leveled off at 80 percent. They had a backlog of nine thousand instruments, with five thousand spare parts on order. Overall, ALARIS, as a whole, had missed both top and bottom line performance numbers for three years running. Nothing Dave did made any difference. As he described his frustration to us he said, "These were problems that I was personally giving a lot of attention to, in fact higher levels of attention than I had given to anything in the company, but regardless of the approach I took personally, I really saw no improvement." Using *The Oz Principle* to help every group in the company focus on ownership and accountability, everyone began to mobilize—especially the disposable products division.

Over a two-year period, product quality dramatically increased to 97 percent and twenty-four-hour delivery success climbed to 99.8 percent. Every department began turning in similarly improved results. With the organization hitting and, in many cases, exceeding their monthly numbers for the first time since the merger, Wall Street rewarded this impressive turnaround with an equally impressive increase in stock price, a whopping 900 percent. Capturing this success, *Money Magazine* listed ALARIS as the top performing stock of 2003 for the last twelve months in the whole country.

The results were spectacular, and all this was done while simultaneously cutting inventories in half. Dave Schlotterbeck's assessment of the change in the level of ownership, accountability, and performance was sweet and simple: "People in the organization owned their circumstances, established their own targets, and made the improvements; and that's without me paying any attention to it. This is simply the result of their being more accountable, going at this in a very teamwork oriented fashion, and giving each other a lot of feedback on what we needed to change."

The breakthrough at ALARIS was the result of focused effort at every level of the organization. People recognized the problem and how they could personally change it. They began to articulate the issues, problems, frustrations, and disappointments, all because they had developed a clear and consistent sense of ownership. No matter what your current circumstances, once you come to See It, you must take the next step to Own It. Only by accepting full ownership of all the past and present behavior that keeps you mired in your current circumstances can you hope to improve your future situation.

TAKING THE SECOND STEP *ABOVE THE LINE*®

We'll never forget a speaking engagement at a client's national sales conference in Hawaii where we witnessed a curious example of what happens when people do not feel a sense of ownership. As we toured the island during the scheduled recreational breaks in the conference, we saw people happily driving cars over the rough lava beds. The vehicles were taking a real beating. "Ten-to-one those are the sales reps," we joked; "there's no way those people own those cars." Later, during our session, we launched the discussion of Owning It by humorously suggesting that self-guided tours through Hawaiian lava beds by rental car might exemplify what we mean by a no-ownership attitude. The embarrassed laughter loosened things up and helped us drive home a crucial point: "Ownership of your circumstances isn't circumstantial."

All too often people view unhappy circumstances as accidents of chance; yet when they find themselves in more pleasant circumstances, they automatically take credit for a job well done. Ownership should not depend on the quality of your circumstance. If you selectively assume accountability for some circumstances, yet conveniently reject it for others, you cannot stay on the *Steps To Accountability*. Such occasional accountability not only prevents people from fully owning their contribution to all of their circumstances, it also keeps them stuck, mired in the victim cycle, as the following disguised-to-protect-the-guilty story aptly illustrates.

Brian Porter and Andy Dowling were driving to work together one morning, when the radio announcer reported the mugging of a twenty-five-year-old man who now lay in a coma at the local hospital.

"Do you ever think that could happen to you?" asked Andy.

Brian thought for a moment, then said, "It did happen to me."

"You're kidding!"

"Well, not the way you might think, but I was definitely mugged."

"Tell me about it."

As Brian told it, during his final year in the MBA program at Northwestern University, he had been interviewing with prospective employers and had almost decided to accept what appeared to be an imminent offer from Citicorp in its international division. Given the fact that it was early May, and many of Brian's classmates had already accepted offers, Brian was feeling a little anxious.

To his surprise, Brian received a telephone call from the owners of a $15-million-a-year southern California–based pool supply distributor where he had worked the previous summer. Sam and Dave, the two founding partners of Sunshine Pool Products, had grown up in southern California and were close friends with Brian's older brother, a physician practicing in Anaheim. Now, on the telephone, the two men urged Brian to fly to Orange County to "talk over a great opportunity." Although Brian told them he intended to accept an offer from Citicorp should it materialize, the partners insisted Brian come anyway. "Bring your wife, Christie, all expenses paid, just keep an open mind," they urged. Flattered by this show of interest, Brian decided it wouldn't hurt to listen.

A few days later, Brian and Christie were met at the LAX Terminal by the two partners, who drove the group to a beautiful house in Palos Verdes. If the Mercedes-Benz 500SL hadn't been enough to impress Brian and Christie, the house certainly was: a rambling Spanish-style ranch home nestled among lush gardens and overlooking the Pacific Ocean. To top it off, the two partners' wives welcomed their guests to a festive table set with antique china and stunning silver.

After a wonderful dinner, Brian joined Sam and Dave for a walk along the moonlit ocean cliff, during which he listened to a powerful sales pitch for why he should join Sunshine Pool Products as vice president of marketing and sales. The starting salary and the luxurious benefits, including immediate stock options and any car of his choice, made his head swim. Equally alluring was the fact that, fresh out of grad school, Brian would oversee thirty people. Sam concluded the pitch by putting his arm around Brian's shoulder and saying, "Brian, we have a vision of the three of us building a great company together that will make us all wealthy. You have the skills we need to pull it off. It's the opportunity of a lifetime."

The next day Brian and Christie flew back to Chicago wondering how they could turn down such an offer. Brian especially relished the looks on his classmates' faces when they heard about the salary. Suddenly, Citicorp seemed like a pale prospect by comparison. Later that same day, Brian called Sam to accept the job.

On July 1, Brian went to work as the Sunshine Pool Products vice president of marketing and sales. After his first three months he felt things were rolling along beautifully. His summer with the firm had prepared him so well for the job that he eased smoothly into his new responsibilities. With his people beating their sales targets, he knew he had made the right career choice. He and Christie were even planning to make an offer on a new home, so they could move out of his brother's house, where they had been staying since moving to southern California.

Then, on October 8, lightning struck. When he came to work that day, Brian heard a rumor that the company had been sold. Shocked, Brian confronted Sam and Dave, but they simply said, "That's business, kid. You never know what's gonna happen next!" They went on to assure Brian that his job was secure, hinting that they just might be able to offer him another "opportunity of a lifetime" in the near future.

Brian felt betrayed. What had happened to the vision of the three of them building a great organization? His anger soon gave way to resignation, however, and he decided to hang on and make the situation work.

Over the next few months, Brian watched forlornly as sales took a nosedive. Unaccountably, some of Brian's best salespeople were just not performing. After several weeks of sagging orders, he confronted the two people who seemed to have fallen off the most. As the three sat in Brian's office, Don, the more open of the two salesmen, admitted, "Brian, we have to be honest, the new president of the combined companies doesn't have much confidence in you. He approached us both a couple of months ago and told us we could receive a higher commission rate if we turned our sales directly over to him, rather than through you. What could we do?" Halfheartedly thanking Don for his honesty, Brian immediately called Morgan, the new president, who worked in an office a few miles away, and demanded an appointment. "Sure," said Morgan. "Tomorrow, 10 A.M."

When Brian walked into the president's office the next day, he didn't mince words. "Morgan, is it true that you're offering more commission to some of my salespeople if they turn over their sales directly to you?"

Morgan's face did not betray any surprise. He chuckled. "Yeah, it's true. Look, Brian, I like you, but you're just out of graduate school, and I really can't afford an inexperienced guy running the marketing and sales side of this business. I've got to keep hold of the reins myself to take this company where I want it to go. But, hey, there's a place for you here. I'm glad you dropped by, I've been wanting to talk about your future."

Brian shot back, "I already know about my future. I quit. Just pay me the $8,500 in commissions you owe me."

Morgan's expression finally cracked with a frown. "Hold on, Brian. Most of that money represents commissions on personal sales, and as far as I'm concerned, those sales are house accounts. No vice president of marketing and sales should get commissions for such sales. We only owe you $2,500."

Without uttering another word Brian spun on his heel and left the office. Reaching his car, he yanked open the door, climbed in, and left a smoking strip of rubber as he shot out of the lot. During his one-hour commute home, he replayed in his mind the illusion of good fortune he once held. Imagining himself the victim of a terrible ruse, Brian found a lot of gut-wrenching questions racing through his mind: What am I going to tell Christie? What will my friends from Northwestern think? Worse, what will my brother think? Brian arrived at his brother's house in a black mood. Anger, confusion, and embarrassment boiled up as he felt more and more victimized by Sam, Dave, and Morgan. Fuming, he pounded the steering wheel, muttering, "I'll never trust anyone again."

Three years later, the episode still infuriated him. "So," he sighed, as he finished recounting the story to Andy Dowling, "anybody can get mugged, and I mean really beaten up by people who are supposed to be looking out for your welfare. I don't know how that guy in the hospital feels about his attacker, but I bet it would be even worse if it had been a friend doing the job on him."

Finally, Andy spoke up. "Don't take this wrong, Brian, but the way you told your story, it sounds like you had nothing to do with the outcome."

Brian frowned. "I didn't!"

"But, Brian, wasn't there something you could have done to prevent what happened to you?"

"Yeah, I could have gone to work at Citicorp in the first place. Hey, what is this? I thought you'd be on my side."

"I am. That's why I think we should talk through what happened to you."

Andy then tried to help Brian consider what he might have done differently. The two continued their discussion for a week as they commuted to and from work. Uncomfortable at first, Brian actually began looking forward to the talks because they afforded him an opportunity to examine feelings he had not shared with anyone but his wife.

Gradually, Brian came to see that he had only been looking at the facts from the victim's point of view, while, in fact, another viewpoint actually existed. Such a realization represents a crucial step for anyone who wants to move beyond feeling victimized. While a situation may seem starkly black and white from a victim's angle, within the context of accountability it may take on more shades of gray.

For instance, from the standpoint of accountability, Brian could see how he had let himself get sucked in by the promise of a quick road to wealth and prestige. The luxurious cars and houses owned by the two partners lay just around the corner, or so Brian imagined. He had been seduced by the image of himself as a vice president right out of graduate school, with an income higher than almost everyone in his graduating class. From the victim's point of view, Brian had been sandbagged, but from an accountability point of view, perhaps Brian himself had been too greedy, shortsighted, immature, and vain. Together Brian and Andy reviewed the following questions to help Brian adopt a more accountable attitude:

1. What facts, which you knew to exist, did you choose not to acknowledge?

2. If you were to face this situation again, what would you do differently?

3. What were the warning signs along the way?

4. What could you have learned from your previous similar experiences that might have helped you avoid or minimize the negative outcome?

5. Can you see how your behavior and actions prevented you from getting the results you wanted?

With Andy's help, Brian tried, sometimes painfully, to answer those questions. Not surprisingly, he began to probe some aspects of himself that he had selectively screened out of his consciousness.

One of the facts Brian chose not to acknowledge or remember was a conversation that had taken place the summer before with his boss, Sunshine Pool Products' then vice president of marketing and sales, Bill Wold, prior to Bill's resignation. When Brian had asked Bill why he was working for Sunshine and what he expected to happen down the road, Bill had spoken confidentially of the pact he had made with Sam and Dave to make great things happen in the future. When Brian heard Sam suggest a similar pact almost a year later, he had ignored or suppressed that earlier conversation. This time the two partners really meant it because, after all, they were talking to Brian Porter, whiz kid extraordinaire.

Brian had missed other hints as well. During his second month as vice president of marketing and sales, he got a speeding ticket driving his new Corvette, and when he showed the highway patrolman the car's registration, he discovered that it had been leased on a temporary, monthly basis. That clue might have tipped off Brian that his bosses had made something less than a long-term commitment to his career.

When Brian received his first paycheck it turned out to be somewhat less than the agreed-upon salary. Dave assured Brian that the difference would quickly come in the form of commissions on personal sales, so Brian chose to overlook the discrepancy. After all, he should lead the way in sales, setting an example for his team.

Why hadn't Brian demanded a written confirmation of his salary and benefits? Friends should trust friends, he had decided. When doing that, Brian set aside the memory of a partnership he had formed while in college with a buddy that had soured when the buddy absconded with $3,000 in profits, saying, "Sue me. We don't have anything in writing." Unfortunately, Brian elected not to apply that lesson to Sam and Dave.

Brian came to realize that as soon as he had learned that Sam and Dave had sold Sunshine Pool Products he should have sat down, right then, with Morgan to clarify everyone's expectations and commitments. However, because Brian didn't know Morgan well enough to feel comfortable with him, he decided to let the situation slide, hoping that things would iron themselves out naturally over time.

Should Brian therefore accept accountability for what eventually happened to him? In many ways, yes. Even though others did take advantage of and mislead him, he learned through objective self-examination that he himself must shoulder some responsibility. After Brian opened up with Andy and pondered Andy's feedback, he finally came to appreciate both points of view: that of the victim and that of the accountable individual. Finally, Brian was ready to own his circumstances and create a better future. In our experience, however, too few people take this step toward greater accountability.

OWNERSHIP IN THE FACE OF CHANGE

Too many people in today's society have lost the heart to own their circumstances, and that loss of heart has begun eroding the very foundation of organizational performance and competitiveness. A *Time* magazine article on the contemporary workplace details one particularly alarming aspect of that erosion:

> This is the new metaphysics of work. Companies are portable, workers are throwaway. The rise of the knowledge economy means a change, in less than 20 years, from an overbuilt system of large, slow-moving economic units to an array of small, widely dispersed economic centers, some as small as the individual boss. In the new economy, geography dissolves, the highways are electronic. Even Wall Street no longer has a reason to be on Wall Street. Companies become concepts and, in their dematerialization, become strangely consciousless, and jobs are almost as susceptible as electrons to vanishing into thin air. The American economy has turned into a bewilderment of good news–horrible news, depending on your point of view. After two years of record profits, Bank of America recently announced that thousands of employees would become part-timers, with few benefits. Beneath some of the statistics of economic recovery lies stress and pain.

A companion article entitled "Disposable Workers" identifies America's growing reliance on temporary staffers as a trend that's shattering the tradition of employee loyalty and commitment: "The corporation that is now the largest private employer in America does not have any smokestacks or conveyor belts or trucks. There is no clanging of metal on metal, no rivets or plastic or steel. In one sense, it does not make anything. But then again, it is in the business of making almost everything. Manpower, Inc., with 560,000 workers, is the world's largest temporary employment agency. Every morning, its people scatter into the offices and factories of America, seeking a day's work for a day's pay."

As behemoth *Fortune* 500 companies strive to "rightsize" themselves by shrinking their payrolls, Manpower, based in Milwaukee, Wisconsin, fills the vacuum, supplying the bodies and brains those companies still need to accomplish their goals. The United States has entered a new era, the freelance economy, where the ranks of part-timers, temps, and independent contractors are expanding while the traditional full-time work force is shrinking. According to the *Time* article, "Their ranks are growing so quickly that they are expected to outnumber permanent full-time workers by the end of this decade." While this trend may benefit the bottom line, it can take its toll not only in terms of alienated relationships among coworkers, but also in terms of pride in product quality and customer satisfaction. Will temps care as much as full-time workers about the long-term consequences of their jobs? Will they be as willing to go beyond their job descriptions in order to get the result? Or, will they use their job descriptions as justification for why they failed to get results? Will they feel victimized by an organization that wants to "rent" their services, but requires them to "own" their jobs? For their own sake, we hope they don't, because no matter how much your work may change over your lifetime, you will never achieve the success and satisfaction you deserve if you reject accountability in favor of victimhood.

The *Time* article continues with Robert Schaen, former controller of Ameritech and now publisher of children's books, observing, "The days of the mammoth corporations are coming to an end. People are going to have to create their own lives, their own careers and their own successes. Some people may go kicking and screaming into the new world, but there is only one message there: You're now in business for yourself." In the freelance economy, owning your circumstances, whether for a week temping in an unfamiliar organization, a few years in a career-enhancing position, or for a lifetime in your own business, will become more and more critical for every worker throughout the world.

In a report on *Fortune* magazine's "Most Admired Corporations," reporters highlighted employee involvement, which includes ownership and accountability, as one common thread among the most admired firms: "Most admired companies treat their employees exceptionally well, which is a factor in, and a result of, their success." Robert Haas, CEO of Levi Strauss Associates, thinks employee engagement and satisfaction are fundamental to running a strong business. He says, "You have to create an environment where everyone feels like a representative of the company. Unless you have people who know what you stand for, and want to make every transaction the best, you're going to stub your toe." As an example of the sense of ownership felt by Levi Strauss employees, *Fortune* described what happened at a manufacturing plant where factory workers identified a serious problem and began working with a local businessperson to recycle some of the millions of pounds of denim scraps Levi took to the landfill every year. The workers approached Levi headquarters with the idea and won approval for the plan. As a result, all Levi Strauss interoffice stationery is blue because it contains recycled denim. The manufacturing plant has cut paper costs 18 percent while taking a little pressure off the local landfill. Now that's ownership!

WHY SO MANY PEOPLE FAIL TO *OWN IT*®

People most often fail to own their circumstances because they cannot bring themselves to accept the accountable side of their story. The old cliché "there are two sides to every story" is generally true. The victim side stresses only one side of the story, the one that suggests you played no role in creating the circumstances. In a difficult situation, it's easy to feel had or let down and to let yourself off the hook. But when you focus on that single perspective, you screen out the other side of the story, the one where certain facts suggest you contributed to creating the circumstances you now face. In our experience, victim stories tend to screen out all evidence of accountability.

To establish ownership, you must find the heart to see both sides of the story, linking what you have done or failed to do with your current circumstances. Such a shift in perspective requires that you replace your victim story with an accountable one. However, seeing and owning the accountable side of a story does not mean suppressing or ignoring the victim facts; rather it means seeing the whole story, including the part that may not bode well for your ego.

The people who consistently achieve results, people like former Chrysler chairman Lee Iacocca, quickly acknowledge their mistakes and own the resulting circumstances so they can avoid getting bogged down in the victim cycle and set to work improving things. Here's what Iacocca told *Fortune* magazine about one of his mistakes: "I've made a lot of them. Let's say moving the Omni/Horizon cars to one plant and then to another before discontinuing them, at a cost of $100 million, was a mistake. Why argue? We made a $100 million mistake." That sort of willingness to own the whole reality and admit mistakes allowed Lee Iacocca to save Chrysler from bankruptcy and make it a viable automobile manufacturer.

On a personal level, consider the story of Home Mortgage Service scams reported in *The Wall Street Journal:* "If you get a letter advising you that servicing your mortgage has been taken over by a new company, check it out before you send a check. It may be a scam. That's what homeowners in Texas learned recently after receiving a letter announcing that an outfit calling itself Mortgage Bankers of America had 'acquired ownership of your previous mortgage company.' The letter asked that future payments and other correspondence be sent to a post office box in Houston. Although the letter says Mortgage Bankers is the fifth largest mortgage banking company in the United States, law enforcement authorities say it doesn't exist." While Robert Pratte, a St. Paul, Minnesota, attorney who represents mortgage lenders, says the company's solicitation shouldn't fool people, it does every day. People living *Above The Line* would take the time to investigate the situation; those living *Below The Line* will lose their shirts. The former own their circumstances, while the latter become willing victims.

At the University of Southern California Business School, Richard B. Chase, professor of business administration, taught a class on the management of service operations where he offered students a money-back guarantee of $250 if they weren't satisfied with his performance by the end of the course. That offer represented a big risk in an academic environment not known for its emphasis on accountability. Chase wanted to impress upon his students, as they studied the superior service practices of companies such as Federal Express and Domino's Pizza, that customers expect the service they pay for. While some of Chase's colleagues worried about the implications of his experiment, we admire it as a clever way of communicating accountability. Professor Chase owns his circumstances, and even though he could have ended up paying as much as $13,000 if all his students demanded their money back, he was willing to take the risk. However, just to make sure he didn't take an inordinate amount of the responsibility for what his students learned, he required that they request rebates before they obtained their final grades.

Some health care businesses are also trying to make sure they please their customers. In a *Wall Street Journal* story entitled, "Pleasing Hospital Patients Can Pay Off," the reporters found a few hospitals owning their circumstances and enhancing profits as a result: "As the health-care industry moves into an era of accountability and cost-cutting, the desire to relate patient feedback directly to the bottom line is likely to grow, say hospitals and management service companies." Take St. Barnabas Medical Center in Livingston, New Jersey, for example: "All patients are asked to evaluate quality of food, cleanliness and staff courtesy, using a questionnaire that provides a measuring stick for a novel contract that links profit to patient satisfaction. Hospitals that farm out certain hospital services—including St. Barnabas, Faulkner Hospital in Boston, and Park Ridge Hospital in Rochester, N.Y.,—are in the forefront of what may be a key operating strategy for the future: Share the risk. Contracts that contain incentives have been around for years, and so have patient surveys. But 'partnering' has linked the two formally, and raised the ante higher for vendors, who are sometimes expected to invest in state-of-the-art equipment for use in the hospital they have contracted with. A performance-linked contract 'is a vendor's gamble,' concedes Ronald Del Mauro, President and Chief Executive Officer of St. Barnabas. But he adds: 'If we're successful, they're successful.'" For St. Barnabas, owning their circumstances, and getting their affiliates and suppliers to do likewise, results not only in happier patients but also in healthier profits.

Unfortunately, millions of people keep themselves from achieving the results and happiness they so desperately pursue because they just can't bring themselves to see both sides of the story and own their circumstances. According to an Associated Press series of articles entitled "Are We Happier?" by Leslie Dreyfous, "The number of books on the topic [happiness] has quadrupled in recent years and the therapy industry has more than tripled in size. Excruciatingly frank talk shows dominate afternoon TV, and entire catalogues are devoted to marketing meditational tapes and inspirational videos. People pay hundreds of dollars and travel thousands of miles to retreats like Esalen (the granddaddy of human potential centers in Big Sur, California). Still, baby boomers are four times likelier to say they're not satisfied with their lives than are people of their parents' generation, according to an Associated Press poll. Experts estimate the incidence of psychological depression is ten times what it was pre–World War II." In our increasingly complex and changing world, it seems more and more people think they exert less and less control over their happiness.

Just like Dorothy and her friends in *The Wizard of Oz,* a lot of people take the trek to the Emerald City, where they hope that a personal audience with the wizard will solve all their problems. All too often, such people blame their lack of happiness on perplexing circumstances that seem totally beyond their control. Rather than own their circumstances by seeing the whole story, they choose to view themselves as incapable of modifying their situations through their own actions, resigning themselves to being acted upon by influences and forces rather than the other way around.

It seems ironic that, in this information age, millions of people feel such a lack of control over their lives. Obviously, the communications revolution has done little to overcome, and may even have contributed to, a feeling of detachment and disconnectedness with circumstances and other people. As a result, our world has come perilously close to becoming a society of victims, in which its citizens, no matter the nation, feel paralyzed rather than empowered by what they observe and learn every day. In such a climate, it's not terribly surprising that so many people resist ownership of the consequences of their own behavior.

A society of observers is not a society of participants. If you sit on the sidelines watching "the game of your life" play out before your eyes, you relinquish your ability to affect the final score just as much as a spectator watching a football or baseball game from the bleachers. To remedy this darkening malaise, people must abandon the bleacher seats and jump onto the playing field. You can take an important step in that direction by embracing the whole story and accepting ownership for your circumstances, no matter what the condition or history of those circumstances. Failure to do so invites dire consequences.

THE CONSEQUENCES OF NOT *OWNING IT*

After the *Columbia* space shuttle tragedy, space-exploration supporters became even more critical of the government and NASA for putting too much emphasis on cost cutting at the expense of safety. According to *The Wall Street Journal,* "Nine months ago, the former chairman of NASA's Aerospace Safety Advisory Panel testified before Congress that the agency's budget constraints would eventually affect space-shuttle safety. To rebut those complaints—or at least deflect them from lawmakers—the House Appropriations Committee yesterday released tables with historical NASA budget information showing that the agency's funding has closely mirrored its requests to Congress." Not surprisingly, no one wants to own the full circumstances surrounding the worst shuttle disaster since the *Challenger* explosion over twenty years ago. NASA complains about the lack of funding, the Administration complains about spending overruns, and Congress claims they only did what they were asked to do. It will take years for NASA to recover from the *Columbia* tragedy and even more years for government executives and lawmakers to face the reality that safe, productive space exploration may cost more than they are willing to pay. In the wake of the disaster, three high-ranking decision makers have been put in new assignments. Of this, a Cleveland paper, *The Plain Dealer*, editorializes: ". . . what is happening in the shuttle program is about far more than putting engineers' heads on pikes. . . . No one should lose sight of the 'cultural problems' NASA's best-informed critics continue to lament. The problems that were fatal to *Columbia* and its crew of seven had a great deal more to do with administrative systems, policies and traditions than with any three particular decision makers." Truly owning the circumstances that you face requires you to make a link between what has happened and all the factors contributing to the problem, however much that linkage may implicate you. Then, and only then, can you effectively move to the next step. Ownership is the ability to connect current circumstances with what I have done and the ability to tie future circumstances with what I am going to do. If you can't make these connections, you'll never *Own It* and you won't ever *Solve It*. We all know the old adage, "If you are not part of the solution, you are part of the problem." Well, ownership implies that "If you are *not* part of the problem, you are *not* a part of the solution." Tragically, you will always suffer the consequences of not owning the full extent of your circumstances, both present and future. *Owning It* requires a candid effort to acknowledge what everyone would rather sweep under the carpet, *before* it's too late.

In contrast, Bradco, the largest privately owned drywall and plaster company in California, found the heart to own its circumstances when the initial actual costs on a major project started coming in much higher than estimated. If the cost-to-budget discrepancy were allowed to continue, the company would face an enormous loss by the end of the project. Promptly, one of the estimators on the project started spending his evenings, on his own time, scouring the project plans and budgets to figure out what had gone wrong. No one in the company had assigned him this responsibility and no one had blamed him for the problem, but nevertheless he chose to own the company's problem and spend countless personal hours reviewing stacks of paper and blueprints to get to the bottom of things.

To his chagrin, he not only isolated the problem, but also discovered he himself had caused it. During the estimating phase of the project, he had overlooked a single wall in the detailed plan from which he had developed his estimate. In a domino effect, that same wall was omitted from all eighteen floors of the building. When the estimator informed company executives of his mistake, he knew he was putting his career on the line, but instead of receiving a pink slip he won praise from higher-ups, who thanked him for his investigation and his willingness to bring the problem to light without regard for his own reputation.

Because the accountable estimator located the problem early, Bradco could adjust to allow for completion of the project on time and within budget. In the months following the incident, the estimator's story was told and retold throughout the company as an example of what it means to *Own It* at Bradco.

Before you create an *Own It* culture where people buy in, sign up, and invest themselves in achieving results, you must first learn to assess and develop your own ability to own your circumstances.

THE *OWN IT*® SELF-ASSESSMENT

As we have said, owning your circumstances depends on seeing both the victim and accountable sides of a story. You should therefore begin your assessment by identifying a current situation in which you feel victimized, taken advantage of, or otherwise find yourself languishing *Below The Line.* If you can't think of a current situation, consider a past one, choosing a story from your work, home, personal, community, social, or church life. Once you have selected your story, complete Part 1 of the *Own It* Self-Assessment form that follows by listing facts that describe why you feel or felt victimized or taken advantage of. Try to list the victim facts of your story in a way that will persuade someone else that you really weren't at fault.

OWN IT® SELF-ASSESSMENT
PART 1 - VICTIM FACTS ABOUT A
CURRENT OR PAST CIRCUMSTANCE

1.
2.
3.
4.
5.
6.
7.
8.
9.
10.

As we discussed earlier in this chapter, most people quite naturally focus on the facts that make them feel victimized or taken advantage of while screening out the accountable facts that support their own role in creating their circumstances. Therefore, in Part 2 of the *Own It* Self-Assessment, you want to move beyond such filtering, focusing instead on the accountable facts of your story: that is, the other version of your story where you delineate your own actions or inactions, which contributed to your circumstances. The following five key questions will help guide your assessment.

OWN IT SELF-ASSESSMENT
PART 2 - ACCOUNTABLE FACTS ABOUT A
CURRENT OR PAST CIRCUMSTANCE

1. _____ Score: [____]

2. _____ Score: [____]

3. _____ Score: [____]

4. _____ Score: [____]

5. _____ Score: [____]

6. _____ Score: [____]

7. _____ Score: [____]

8. _____ Score: [____]

9. _____ Score: [____]

10. _____ Score: [____]

1. Can you cite the most convincing point of the "other side of the story" that "they" are telling?
2. If you wished to warn someone in similar circumstances not to make the same mistakes, what would you tell them?
3. What facts did you choose to ignore?
4. What facts should you add to the story that you have left out?
5. What would you do differently if you faced this situation again?

With the aid of these five questions, complete Part 2 of the *Own It* Self-Assessment by listing at least four accountable facts. Once you've done that, we'll show you how to score your responses.

After you have listed an accountable fact, score your willingness to *Own It* by asking yourself how accountable you feel for that fact on a scale of 1 to 10. A score of 1 means you do not feel at all accountable for a particular fact, whereas, a score of 10 signifies that you feel fully accountable for that fact. Then add up your total combined score and divide that score by the number of facts that you listed. Finally, evaluate your cumulative score by using the table that follows.

While a low score suggests that you are failing to assume ownership for your situation, it may also indicate that you truly are a victim of your current

OWN IT®
Self-Assessment Scoring

TOTAL SCORE	EVALUATION GUIDELINES
8 to 10 points	Indicates that you see your accountability and own circumstances.
5 to 7 points	Suggests that you only partially own your circumstances or vacillate between owning and not owning them.
1 to 4 points	Reveals that you have probably gotten stuck *Below The Line*, and are unable or unwilling to see your accountability and own your circumstances.

circumstances. Even so, you do not want to remain in the victim cycle. A person who owns his or her circumstances never allows the actions of someone or something else to keep them stuck *Below The Line.* Instead, the accountable person accepts whatever ways in which his or her own behavior contributed to the situation and sets about overcoming those circumstances, no matter how difficult.

At the same time, every day people tell compelling, legitimate stories about how they were truly victimized without any opportunity to have changed the outcome. Whether their stories detail violent crimes, natural disasters, or a slow economy with layoffs and prolonged unemployment, these people usually have fallen victim to circumstances beyond their control. However, we believe that even true victims cannot move toward happier times until they can be accountable for where they go from here.

In one case, we heard about a husband and wife in Florida whose home was destroyed by a hurricane. Devastated by the loss of all their personal belongings, the couple retreated to their vacation home on the island of Kauai to recuperate and to wait out the rebuilding of their Florida home. Shortly after their arrival, another hurricane struck the Hawaiian Islands, demolishing their vacation home. Clearly, these two people had gotten battered by these natural disasters, suffering deep grief and frustration as a result, but even so they resolved that these calamities would not destroy their lives. Instead, they acknowledged the fact they had built their homes in areas vulnerable to such disasters, and they committed themselves to relocating and rebuilding with optimism and faith. After all, they had survived two disasters, and they had come through with their health and human abilities still intact. What a good lesson for us all. Owning our circumstances gives us the strength to overcome the powerlessness that comes from being a victim and allows us to move forward and achieve more satisfying results in life.

THE BENEFITS OF FINDING THE HEART TO *OWN IT*®

In Japan you can see the *Own It* attitude at work in the public transportation system. *The Wall Street Journal* reported:

> In the Tokyo area, millions of rail commuters can count on reaching their destination at pretty much the same minute every day—and that says as much about the Japanese as it does about their trains. "It's the

people that delay the trains," says Shoji Yanagawa, a spokesman for Tokyo's Eidan subway company. "But then again it's people that keep the trains running on time." Tokyo's train system is so finely tuned that it has eliminated almost all sources of extended delay, to the point where a major cause of lateness is the "jumper," or suicide. Tokyo elementary schools teach children the basics of train riding. In the stations, riders are bombarded with messages in schoolmarmish voices: "It's dangerous, so please don't run onto the trains." (People who rush often get stuck in the closing doors, which delays departure.) To keep straphangers from cramming into doorways, the railways lash them with a bit of shame. "We put extra workers on the platforms, and mostly they stand there and look at the passengers," says Mr. Yanagawa. "That usually works." Rigorous, maybe, but the commuters thronging the platform at Otemachi Station are eager adherents.

That could work only in Japan, you might say, but the principle of ownership cuts across all cultures and companies: when everyone buys into the problem or situation and treats it as their *own,* results always improve.

In another example, Josh Tanner traveled the fast track with his former blue-chip company and had won accolades from the organization for his analytical prowess and political savvy. In four short years, he had learned how to get things done so well in a large, bureaucratic organizational structure that most everyone applauded Josh as a high-potential employee, capable of making it to the top. Josh's reputation not only spread throughout the company, but also captured the attention of headhunters always on the lookout for talented people.

It didn't take long for an executive recruiter to grab Josh's interest, with an intriguing opportunity to work for a small start-up company with enormous potential. Within a few weeks, Josh left the security of his large-company job for a smaller, albeit riskier one, where he knew he could shine even more brightly than before. He relished working in a more entrepreneurial, fast-paced environment where he could really put his analytical and political skills to the test. In fact, he saw himself almost single-handedly turning the start-up into a blue-chip company as the years flew by.

Not long after Josh joined the new firm, however, he was hit with a landslide of feedback that threw him for a loop. Given his political savvy, Josh knew how to listen, but he just couldn't believe the feedback he was hearing. People at the new company weren't impressed with Josh's analytical bent and bureaucratic orientation. For several weeks, Josh denied the feedback, thinking to himself, "I've already accomplished so much in my career; I was a star in a blue-chip company; people here should feel lucky to get someone with my experience; I gave up a lot to come here." Eventually, Josh learned that he would not receive the promised promotion to vice president of marketing, and worse, if his performance did not improve, he would not be with the organization much longer. This turn of events dealt a shocking blow to Josh, who simply could not believe this was happening to him. "This is worse than a bad dream," he moaned, "it's my worst nightmare!" Soon he began to mourn the loss of his fast-track career with his former company and lament the fact he had reached a dead end in his current situation.

At this point, the company's management asked us to work with Josh. Immediately after contacting him, we began coaching him to move *Above The Line.* It wasn't easy, but Josh was at least willing to acknowledge the reality that he was no longer the star in his old company, but someone who needed to improve. Still, he continued feeling victimized by the new job and other people. He told us, very convincingly, one side of the story, moving through the victim cycle with ease and familiarity as he identified each level and anxiously explained how "they" had knocked him *Below The Line.* Finally, he explained what we recognized as a wait-and-see attitude: He was hoping that time would disprove his new associates' initial assessment of him.

As we worked with Josh, it became clear that his greatest challenge lay in forging the link between his own behavior and the perceptions of his new associates. While he understood the perceptions, his unwillingness to accept their accuracy was rendering him unable to *Own It.* At this point, we asked Josh to retell his story, this time focusing on the accountable facts of his circumstances instead of just the victim facts. Slowly, he began describing how people might have misinterpreted some of the things he had done after joining the company, but after each such admission he would say something like, "but only an idiot would draw that kind of conclusion." As he continued to identify how his actions could have contributed to the perceptions of others, he gradually found it easier to recognize the things he did or did not do to contribute to his present predicament. As he did so, his anger began to abate. We explained to Josh that owning his circumstances did not mean accepting the perceptions of his new associates as total truth, but rather acknowledging a connection between his behavior and their perceptions.

Finally, when we asked him the question, "What extra steps could you have taken?" Josh stopped to reflect on how he could have started off by asking people what kind of job they thought he was doing. Recognizing the differences between his new and old environments and acknowledging that he had ignored the new culture's bias against excessive analysis and bureaucratic process, Josh finally admitted that he could have taken more care explaining to others the motives and principles behind his actions.

As Josh's sense of accountability increased, so did his feelings of liberation: "I should have worked more closely with the people and the culture of the new company to obtain their ideas and involvement in the programs I was trying to implement. I could have been more open to their suggestions, and I should have involved myself more with their plans, purposes, and priorities. Wow, did I make a mistake by withdrawing into myself when the negative feedback started coming in!" Not until that moment did Josh fully address the other side of the story and own all the facts, particularly those that linked his behavior with his circumstances. He was not saying that he should shoulder 100 percent responsibility for everything that had happened, nor was he saying that the people in the new company had given him a 100 percent fair assessment, but he was finally admitting that he himself had done, or failed to do, certain things that contributed to his circumstances. "Man," he said during our final coaching session, "getting stuck *Below The Line* feels like being trapped in a room with no windows or doors. Now that the doors are open, and I see the whole story, I can start changing my circumstances. Things can only get better!"

Josh came to own his circumstances when he made the connection between his behavior and the perceptions of his new associates. When he saw the reality that his past behavior had contributed to his present circumstances, he realized that his behavior from now on could create an entirely different and better future. This realization gave him the heart he needed to begin working to shift the perceptions of those with whom he worked, and, before long, he lost all the distaste he had developed for his new associates. After a little more than three months of *Above The Line* behavior, Josh had so completely shifted the perceptions of his subordinates, peers, and boss that he won that promotion to vice president of marketing.

The benefits of owning your circumstances more than compensate for the

heart-wrenching effort involved. When you find the heart to own your circumstances, you automatically gain the commitment to overcome and change those
circumstances for the better.

THE NEXT PHASE OF ACCOUNTABILITY

As this chapter shows, the Tin Woodsman from the land of Oz symbolizes the
second dimension of accountability, finding the heart to own your circumstances, and it further fuels Dorothy's realization that results come from within
ourselves. In the next chapter, the Scarecrow will show you how to acquire the
wisdom to *Solve It*. And he will teach you how to put your *See It* and *Own It*
abilities to work in conjunction with a new *Solve It* attitude that can help you
remove the obstacles on your path to results.

Chapter 6

THE SCARECROW: OBTAINING THE WISDOM TO *SOLVE IT*®

"Who are you?" asked the Scarecrow when he had stretched himself and yawned, "and where are you going?"

"My name is Dorothy," said the girl, "and I am going to the Emerald City, to ask the great Oz to send me back to Kansas."

"Where is the Emerald City?" he inquired; "and who is Oz?"

"Why, don't you know?" she returned, in surprise.

"No, indeed; I don't know anything. You see, I am stuffed, so I have no brains at all," he answered, sadly.

"Oh," said Dorothy; "I'm awfully sorry for you."

"Do you think," he asked, "if I go to the Emerald City with you, that Oz would give me some brains?"

"I cannot tell," she returned; "but you may come with me, if you like. If Oz will not give you any brains, you will be no worse off than you are now."

—*The Wizard of Oz,*
L. Frank Baum

A few years ago, Toyota began to put its collective brainpower to work solving a problem its competitors hadn't yet seen or owned. The world's second largest automaker had been expanding capacity and building new plants despite an environment of serious global overcapacity, sluggish sales, and plant closings around the world. Using its head, while others were losing theirs, the $100 billion company began rethinking everything. A *Fortune* magazine article told the story: "Toyota is big, famously conservative, and hugely successful. Why mess with a good thing? In fact, the company that the Massachusetts Institute of Technology report 'The Machine That Changed the World' called the most efficient automaker anywhere, is rethinking almost everything it does. Turning Japan's unnerving stubborn economic slump into an opportunity, Toyota is reorganizing its operations, putting still more high technology into its factories, and reworking its legendary 'lean production' system. Even if some of the measures fail, Toyota is likely to emerge an even more vigorous global competitor." Not overreacting to declining profits for a second year, the company continues hammering out solutions for the future. While some European and American automakers are closing plants, Toyota keeps opening new ones, increasing the company's total capacity to one million vehicles per year. The company would rather rely on cost cutting to improve efficiency. As a prime example of a *Solve-It* company, Toyota is setting the pace for competitors. According to *Fortune*, "Just when the rest of the world started to catch on to Toyota's lean production system, Toyota is adapting it to accommodate new workers and advanced technology." A perpetual problem solver, Toyota thrives on challenges, always searching for ways to do things better and swiftly adapting to change. Donald N. Smith, a manufacturing expert at the University of Michigan's engineering school and a longtime Toyota watcher, warns Toyota's competitors to assume that Toyota will constantly improve in the future. To think otherwise could court disaster. We agree. Toyota's undying and unwavering *Solve It* attitude will undoubtedly ensure its standout performance among global corporations for years to come.

We must issue this warning, however: *Solve It* means solving real problems, not tackling illusionary ones or just changing for change's sake. In another *Fortune* magazine article, reporters recount the saga of Ann Taylor Stores: "Through the 1980s, Ann Taylor was the place for women to shop for stylish, well-made career clothes at better than department store prices." That strategy seemed sound until the 1990s "when Joseph Brooks, former head of Lord & Taylor and

Merrill Lynch bought the company from Campeau Corp. for $430 million." As Chief Executive Officer, Brooks began changing things for change's sake, substituting synthetics for silk, linen, and wool blends and squeezing suppliers. One supplier, Irving Benson, President of Cygne Design, bemoaned the situation to *Fortune*'s reporters: "You get nothing for nothing. When Brooks told me he wanted to pay less to make a jacket, cuts had to come from either the fabric or how the garment was made." At the same time, Brooks expanded the operation from 139 to 200 stores. When customers did not materialize, the board forced Brooks to resign. The cost? Ann Taylor lost $15.8 million on sales of $438 million. To redirect the company's problem-solving efforts, the board picked Frame Kasaks, who had run Ann Taylor in the 1980s before she left to take over Talbots and then the Limited's Abercrombie and Fitch division. Frame Kasaks improved the company's private-label fashions, increased sales monitoring, hired experts in specialty retailing, and developed lines of casual and weekend clothes. Within a few years, Ann Taylor had regained its former glory and profitability. It doesn't take a genius to solve the sort of problems Kasaks inherited; it just takes persistent functioning *Above The Line,* discovering real problems, and designing appropriate solutions.

Every organization wrestles from time to time with pesky problems that stand in the way of significant performance gains. The credit card division of one of the largest banks in the world utilized our services and implemented *The Oz Principle Accountability Training* workshop in an effort to create greater accountability and ownership at every level of the organization, particularly at the front line. They focused in particular on the call center where turnover had been exceptionally high and results in terms of "handle time" needed improvement. The call center handles a very high volume of calls from current and potential customers. This high volume of calls equates time to money: Every second of additional handle time equates to a million-dollar drop in profit at the end of the year. With this thought planted firmly in mind, the leadership group in the call center determined that they would create accountability for reducing the average handle time by 50 percent, no small task since they had been struggling unsuccessfully to reduce handle time for years.

Surprisingly, getting everyone to buy into this lofty objective wasn't as tough as management had anticipated. However, when it actually came down to figuring out how to bring about change, the going got a lot tougher. Still, as every member of the management team signed up and began looking for ways to improve performance, before long, they had changed the way they hired people; and they had implemented new software solutions. They also began measuring and reporting performance on a daily basis. Additionally they implemented a balanced scorecard and focused their training to impact high priority skills and behavior. The *Solve It* mentality flourished. Ideas poured in from everywhere as everyone from top management all the way to the front line took accountability for reducing the time needed to handle a call. The result: an increase of $143 million a year to the company's bottom line.

Unfortunately, many people attempt to solve problems without seeing or owning reality, which makes the whole problem-solving effort nonsensical and misguided, as in the case of the U.S. Air Force's fight against ozone depletion. *The Wall Street Journal's* sarcastic article entitled "Survivors Will Glow in Happiness, Knowing the World Is a Safer Place," provides an apt example: "Fear not: The U.S. government will protect the ozone layer in the event of a nuclear holocaust. To do its bit to save the planet, the U.S. Air Force plans to retrofit its nuclear missiles with cooling systems that don't use chlorofluorocarbons. Those CFCs are blamed for depleting the atmosphere's ozone layer, which protects people from skin cancer, glaucoma and other diseases by screening out harmful rays from the sun. Never mind that each intercontinental ballistic missile packs three to 10 bombs that can wipe out entire cities, making skin cancer and glaucoma moot concerns." Good PR, perhaps, but silly problem solving.

Simply acknowledging reality and accepting your role in creating your circumstances will achieve little if you fail to tackle real problems and remove true obstacles on your road to results. To do so, you must exercise wisdom.

ATTAINING THE THIRD STEP *ABOVE THE LINE*®

Getting to the *Solve It* step quickly can often make all the difference in the world. *Solving It* can begin even before you fully take the step. Consider the *CNN/Money* report on the so-called underemployed people, or Duppies, "tough times have spawned a new class of 'depressed urban professionals.'" These folks were involved largely in the tech industry where they went from high paying jobs to low wages, swelling the ranks of the millions of underemployed people who long to do more, but just can't find the work. Sadly, they have not only lost wages, they have lost the stimulation provided by more challenging and interesting jobs. As the article reports, "according to government statistics, 4.8 million individuals are underemployed. That's on top of the 4.2 million non-working who don't bother." People who have been unemployed for some time rightfully take whatever work they can get, even if it means flipping burgers. Along with a smaller paycheck, they often talk of feelings of depression and discouragement, particularly as the time goes on and the ideal job doesn't materialize. While usually temporary, these periods of underemployment can become prolonged, and in either case they force a fairly abrupt and major change in lifestyle.

So what does *Solving It* look like to the victim of a tough industry, an economic downturn, or a massive layoff that doesn't care who gets in the way? First, it begins with preparation, particularly if you work in a sector prone to swings in employment. Becoming "professionally nimble" and preparing yourself for the three-career life where an occasional job change is more the norm than the exception. It means keeping up on your technical skills with continuing education, networking with people outside of your industry, and making sure you've set aside a nest egg that will help smooth such a transition. The wisdom to *Solve It* includes anticipating what could occur and preparing for the worst. When it does come, moving quickly to the *Solve It* step can make a huge difference. Janet Crystal, 51, says the loss of her job as a new-products planner for companies like Lucent hasn't brought "much of a shift" in her lifestyle for several reasons. First, she was lucky enough to cash out stocks before the market crashed. Second, the Boston-area resident has lived through layoffs before and was good about saving. Finally, Crystal says she learned long ago the satisfaction of living simply: She savors her garden, good books, and friendships.

The *Solve It* attitude and behavior stem from continually asking the question: "What else can I do?" By constantly and rigorously asking this question, you avoid slipping back down into the victim cycle whenever certain events occur that would otherwise seem to block the road to results. Since solutions to thorny problems often do not readily reveal themselves, you must diligently search for them, but beware of wasting time *Below The Line* because that will only dull your senses and discourage your imagination from discovering creative solutions. Remember, getting *Above The Line* is a process, not a singular event, and the road to results is strewn with hindrances and obstacles that can easily thrust even the most accountable person back *Below The Line*—particularly if he or she stops asking the central question: What else can I do to rise above my circumstances and achieve the results I want?

In a *Harvard Business Review* article entitled "Empowerment or Else," author and company owner Robert Frey describes how he got his organization *Above The Line* to *Solve It*. He recounts how bad the situation got after he and a partner purchased a small Cincinnati company. Founded in 1902, Cin-Made was a troubled company. It manufactured composite cans (sturdy paper containers with metal ends) and mailing tubes. Shortly after Frey's purchase, things began to spiral downward. Poorly negotiated labor contracts that have driven wages to an unsustainable level, a stagnant product line that had not changed in twenty years, and old plant equipment all conspired to drive profits from a meager 2 percent of sales to zero. Unless something happened quickly, the company would soon go under.

It quickly became clear to Frey, the new president of Cin-Made, that renewed profitability depended on guiding the company out of the victim cycle, prompting people who had grown lethargic to act quickly and wisely to solve the firm's problems. As Ocelia Williams, then a sheet-metal worker, later recalled, "When I first came to Cin-Made, the place was like a circus. There was a ten-minute break every hour, and people walked off the line at anytime to go to the ladies' room or get a candy bar." People just did not *See It* or *Own It*. They didn't understand their role in the company's situation or the need to revolutionize the way they did things.

Frey and his partner immediately set out to make the necessary changes to move the organization *Above The Line* and solve the problems the company faced. After some difficult negotiations and concessions with the union, people finally began acknowledging the company's dire circumstances. They especially appreciated that executives like Frey were beginning, for the first time, to share previously guarded information on the company's performance.

Although Frey was making steady progress moving the organization *Above The Line,* he still struggled to get employees to *Own It* and *Solve It*. Only they, after all, could lift the company out of the quagmire. As Frey recalls, "I wanted the workers to worry. Did any one of them ever spend a moment on a weekend wondering how the company was doing, asking themselves if they'd made the right decisions the week before? Maybe I was unrealistic, but I wanted that level of involvement." He continued, "After a bad start, I had begun to see that the workers knew more about the company and its operation than I or the new managers I'd hired. They were better qualified to plan production for the next day, the coming week, the month ahead. They had more immediate knowledge of materials, workload, and production problems. They were ideally placed to control costs and cut waste. But how could I give them some reason to care?"

As the organization gradually moved *Above The Line*, people began to change the way they viewed their roles, especially in terms of responsibility and accountability. It wasn't easy, as Frey himself admits: "Change of any kind is a struggle with fear, anger, and uncertainty, a war against old habits, hide-bound thinking, and entrenched interests. No company can change any faster than it can change the hearts and minds of its people . . ." To help capture their hearts and minds, to get them spontaneously to act in the *Solve It* mode, Frey implemented an innovative profit-sharing plan, establishing a pattern of cause and effect that would link what people did with what people got.

After realizing that his managers habitually resorted to a command-and-control, "tell them what to do" approach to the job, he found that the workers had grown complacent with it, too. "My managers believed that managers should manage and that hourly workers should do what they were told. The trouble was, most of the workers were perfectly happy with that arrangement. They wanted generous wages and benefits, of course, but they did not want to take responsibility for anything more than doing their own jobs the way they had always done them." Such behavior, he knew, kept people from doing anything more than just complaining about the company's problems. After all, why try to fix something you don't own? He also knew that such a culture of complaint would eventually destroy Cin-Made.

Frey continues, "It was bad enough forcing them to use new equipment, but I was also forcing them to change job descriptions, to change work habits, to think differently about themselves and the company. What my employees were telling me, both in deeds and in words, was, 'We don't want to change, and we're much too old to change. Anyway, we don't come to work to think.'" Ocelia Williams recalls how the union president actually argued that it was "nonunion" for employees to take on so much responsibility. "That bothered me," says Williams. "I kept asking myself if I was truly union. But I couldn't see how we were going to protect ourselves and keep our jobs if the company went under. And I couldn't see how the company could work unless we all took our share of the responsibility. A lot of people thought those ideas were off-the-wall." Frey further observes, "But which of us is ever eager to take on new responsibilities?"

Recalling how his people reacted, he says, "They never dreamed how much re-sponsibility I wanted to lay on their shoulders, but they disliked what little they had seen so far."

Coaching people into the *Solve It* mode took patience. Frey states, "I made people meet with me, then instead of telling them what to do, I asked them. They resisted. 'How can we cut the waste on this run?' I'd say, or, 'How are we going to allocate the overtime on this order?' 'That's not my job,' they'd say. 'Why not?' I'd say. 'Well, it just isn't,' they'd say. 'How in the world can we have participative management if you won't participate?' 'I don't know,' they'd say. 'Because that's not my job either. That's your job.' And I'd lose my temper. In the beginning, I really did lose my temper every time I heard the words, 'It's not my job!' "

With persistent effort to overcome that lethargy and convince people that *Solving It* is not an extra activity, but part of the job, Frey finally started to see results. He recalls, "gradually hourly workers in general began to take on some of the work of problem solving and cost control. I pushed and prodded and re-quired people to help solve problems related to their own jobs. Sometimes I felt like a fool, albeit a very pleased fool, when they came up with simple solutions to problems that had persistently stumped me and my managers."

Having moved the organization *Above The Line* and taken the *Solve It* step, Cin-Made now finds itself well on the way to prosperity. It enjoys a highly dif-ferentiated product line that Frey observes, "is doing well in a demanding mar-ket and making a lot of money." On-time customer delivery has risen to 98 percent, absenteeism has practically vanished, full-time employees now moni-tor temporary workers in an effort to reduce waste, productivity has improved 30 percent, grievances have declined, strict adherence to job descriptions is a thing of the past, and people are making more money than other workers in comparable industries.

As the Cin-Made story illustrates, *Solving It* requires an ongoing commit-ment to ask the question, "What else can I do?" Moving *Above The Line* and adopting the *Solve It* attitude can do more than almost anything else to help fledgling or struggling companies become robust and thriving enterprises.

Nestle Purina illustrates the point nicely. The company had planned to in-troduce an easy-to-open Alpo dog food can by April 2003, but highly success-ful preliminary market tests convinced the marketing department to accelerate the new products launch. Using concepts and principles from our *Oz Principle*

Accountability Training—such as continually asking, "What else can we do to get the results we want?"—the Alpo EZ-Open Can team got to work. Coordinating the activities at three plant locations—Weirton, West Virginia, Allentown, Pennsylvania, and Crete, Nebraska,—the EZ-Open team assembled people across several functions to accomplish the impossible: cutting market introduction by more than a year. For their extraordinary efforts, the Alpo EZ-Open Can team received the company's prestigious Pillars of Excellence Award. Marketing manager Kristin Pontius expressed her elation with the results in a recognition letter that went out to everyone involved. "I wanted to write a quick note of congratulations to the Alpo EZ-Open Can team. On Tuesday of this week, this team was awarded the prestigious Nestle Purina Petcare Company (NPPC) Pillars of Excellence Award by CEO Pat McGinnis. This award is very well deserved. You worked at an incredible rate with great dedication to accomplish your goal. EZ-Open cans began shipping one year and one week prior to original plans. Not only did you meet your goal; you exceeded it as EZO cans shipped even three weeks earlier than expected. You did all of this while facing multiple obstacles, including needing to design special lids, having to hand orient cans until equipment arrived, and needing to fill an overwhelming volume push while maintaining quality and integrating everything into the NPPC supply system. All goals were met, and many beaten, through the hard work of a team that wouldn't fail to overcome all obstacles." The Allentown, Crete, and Weirton factory teams did it in a way that set a powerful example for the rest of the company. Their answer to "what else can I do?" The seemingly impossible!

Remember Mike Eagle? As President of IVAC corporation, a midsized medical instruments company, he also helped his senior team and people throughout the company take the *Solve It* step and stay *Above The Line*. The company developed a new Model 570 set of instruments, composed of seventy different pieces of equipment, and promised Sparrow Hospital in Lansing, Michigan, one of IVAC's first customers for the new product, delivery before Christmas. One day, late in the year, Mike learned that the delivery could not take place as promised because the new Model 570 instruments required last-minute changes in their printed circuit boards. Determined to keep IVAC's commitment and to solve this problem, he asked what else IVAC people could do to hit the target date. After intense discussion, a possible solution emerged. Could a concerted effort from an ad hoc project team close the gap? Some said, "Maybe." Mike said, "Yes!" Immediately he assembled the new team with representatives from product development, instrument operations, engineering, quality assurance, and shipping, urging them to invest every brain cell in effecting the circuit board changes within a week.

Just one week later, the Model 570 instruments were ready for shipping. But then a new obstacle arose: Due to heavy holiday orders, all commercial shipping services were already overbooked. Once again, Mike asked, "What else can we do?" And the answer came, "There is nothing else we can do short of renting a Learjet to get this product there on time." Mike didn't miss a beat. "So we rent a Learjet!"

Astonished at Mike's get-it-done attitude, the team enthusiastically went to work. The shipping department raced to rent a Lear jet and reconfigure its interior to accommodate the Model 570. Then, at the last minute, it turned out that the company had miscalculated the size of the order. Even with the reconfigured jet interior, all the boxes simply would not fit. Unwilling to accept defeat so close to the goal line, freight packers opened each box and repacked all seventy different instruments. Finally, at 3:00 P.M. on December 17, the Learjet left the San Diego airport for Lansing, Michigan.

In anticipation of any further problems and intent upon doing whatever else it took to get the result, a product manager from IVAC accompanied the flight. A few hours later, the jet arrived in Wichita, Kansas, for refueling. While taxiing down the runway to take off again, the pilot detected a broken altimeter. Able to fly but a short distance at low altitude, the pilot took the aircraft two hundred miles to Lincoln, Nebraska, where the product manager got on the telephone with the company's Traffic Coordination Department to track down the faulty altimeter part, a task quite out of the ordinary for this department. After five hours of intense communications with airlines and manufacturers, the part was secured, flown to the airport, and installed in the jet. At 3:30 A.M. on December 18, the shipment left Lincoln for Lansing, where it arrived at 5:45 A.M. Meanwhile, IVAC's in-service and training personnel, who were scheduled to instruct the people at Sparrow Hospital in the use of the new Model 570 instruments, had gotten stuck in a snowstorm in Chicago and had traveled all night by car to arrive at the hospital on time the next morning.

At 7:30 A.M. the following day IVAC unveiled the Model 570 instruments at Sparrow Hospital on time, as expected, and commenced with its service and training operations.

Unlike the people at IVAC, Cin-Made, and Nestle Purina, many in other organizations do not ask the question "What else can we do to rise above our circumstances and achieve the results we desire?" That, as much as anything else, explains why so many of their problems go unsolved.

WHY PEOPLE FAIL TO *SOLVE IT*®

As people begin solving problems they almost always encounter obstacles, both expected and unexpected, that can cause them to sink *Below The Line* into the victim cycle. To avoid this, people must fully commit themselves to stay *Above The Line* during problem solving, particularly when an unanticipated crisis attacks.

One of our clients has demonstrated an uncanny ability to cope with and beat the often powerful temptation to fall *Below The Line*. Again, to protect the privacy of this organization and the individuals involved, we have disguised the circumstances and details of the story, but we assure you it's otherwise true.

Joe McGann, the store operations vice president for a midsized department store chain, had experienced a trying year in which retail sales declined alarmingly. Without any new merchandising or marketing programs over the last three years, Joe and his eighty-four store managers felt as if they were fighting a battle without any bullets. However, as some people in the company began to recognize and own the circumstances, new life and hope spread throughout the organization, and along with it a new merchandising campaign that breathed fresh optimism and a can-do attitude into the store managers. Even the sales clerks applauded. However, even as sales increased and morale climbed higher, the company still needed to do a lot more just to catch up with their more successful competitors. Yes, the department store chain was making progress, and, thankfully, people were attempting to stay *Above The Line* with a strong problem-solving attitude, but it wasn't easy, particularly for the store managers, who fought in the trenches for retail sales each and every day.

Late one night, in a hotel at the Dallas–Fort Worth International Airport, Joe met for a brief meeting with his five regional managers, each one of whom supervised fifteen to eighteen stores. All six of them were flying somewhere else and had arranged a quick stopover for this unusual meeting. As they gathered in a small conference room, each person wanted to appear accountable, willing to own their circumstances, and committed to operating *Above The Line,* but all of them were strained by the high expectations of senior management for continued improvements in performance. Their strain was intensified by the diminishing effect of the latest merchandising program and the delay of promised incentive compensation plans.

Before the meeting officially started, one of the regional managers asked somewhat hesitantly, "Before we begin, can we drop *Below The Line* for just a few minutes? We need to talk about what's going on." Everyone laughed but then unleashed a lot of pent-up anxieties, airing their thoughts about what was going wrong in the company, who deserved the blame, and why the situation was terribly unfair. After about fifteen minutes, Joe waved his hand, "Okay, now that we've gotten that off our chests, let's get back *Above The Line* so we can determine what else we can do to achieve the results we want." Having aired their frustrations, the regional managers could finally engage in a productive discussion of what they could do to solve the problems and remove the obstacles that confronted them. While they all knew that remaining *Below The Line* would get them nowhere, they had consciously dropped into the victim cycle for a brief moment to vent their frustrations and recite their discouragement with their current circumstances. Without their increased awareness of the fruitlessness of remaining *Below The Line,* Joe and his team may have unwittingly prevented themselves from rising *Above The Line* to solve their problems. Without such awareness, it's awfully easy to succumb to the urge to stay *Below The Line.* The trick is to go there only briefly and be committed to get out of there quickly.

When people give up asking the *Solve It* question, as Joe McGann and his team felt tempted to do, they drop back *Below The Line* into the victim cycle where they will never find the creative solutions they need to fashion a better future. In a *Fortune* magazine article by Brian Dumaine, "Leaving the Rat Race Early," the author cites a Roper survey in which a mere 18 percent of those polled (1,296 people) felt that their "careers were personally and financially rewarding." According to the *Fortune* article, the dissatisfaction with full-time work is growing as more and more Americans find themselves overworked and overstressed. The article makes an intriguing and revealing point but fails to make another more important one: that 82 percent of those surveyed are stuck *Below The Line,* victimized by their circumstances, and could, in fact, make their jobs more personally and financially rewarding if they would only accept accountability for that result. The article makes the point that you can gain greater personal and financial satisfaction by retiring early, but it never explores the possibility of making the workplace itself more personally and financially rewarding. Instead, the article reflects the general attitude that people in organizations lack control over their circumstances. As pawns and victims, they feel helpless to do anything but settle for what they can get. Believe us when we say that anyone at any level of an organization who acknowledges reality and owns the circumstances surrounding their dissatisfaction with their job can, indeed, develop the wisdom to *Solve It* and remove the obstacles presently impeding them from obtaining the job satisfaction they desire.

Anyone who chooses, as the article urges, the early retirement path will run into plenty of obstacles there, too. It claims that "dropping out, i.e. early retirement, requires foresight and discipline but isn't as difficult as you might have feared." Perhaps so, but that doesn't mean you'll stroll down a primrose path. You'll still need the wisdom to *Solve It*. Whether you stay employed full time or drop out, you can always sink *Below The Line*. To its credit, the *Fortune* article does spell out what someone must look out for if he or she drops out of the rat race early: "Sounds great, but how on earth can you leave your job with no pension or social security and hope to survive? Financial planners recommend a three-pronged approach. First, expect to cut back on your lifestyle. You might have to buy a smaller house in a less expensive part of the country, tell your kids they can't count on Ivy League tuition, and buy used cars rather than new ones. Second, you'll probably have to work a few months a year or hours a week, either for your old employer or for a new one (including yourself). Third, you'll have to save enough money to supplement your newly reduced income." In other words, even when you retire early, you must go on asking yourself what else you will need to do to attain your goals. Retiring early changes the landscape, not the journey. You must still learn to rise *Above The Line* as you encounter the challenges that will come with new landscape. If it sounds like the process of moving *Above The Line* to solve your problems requires some personal risk, that's good, because it does. But residing *Below The Line* poses an even greater risk, the risk of never obtaining the results you most earnestly seek.

Regardless of whether you're trying to keep, revolutionize, or retire from your current job, you'll never do it successfully unless you overcome the temptation to fall *Below The Line*. Indeed, you must focus your efforts on removing the obstacles standing between you and the outcomes you desire. As always, unhappy consequences await those who fail to do so.

THE CONSEQUENCES OF NOT *SOLVING IT*®

According to a *Wall Street Journal* article, college textbook publishers stand to lose their entire market unless they assume a *Solve It* attitude:

> A technology revolution is sweeping higher education. Entering freshmen at schools such as Drew University receive laptops. Professors assign Web sites rather than books. Professor Norman Lowrey was among the first to teach musical composition using software that enabled students to compose music on their computers and then play it back. Students at Cornell's veterinary school worked on computer simulations that allowed them to examine animals, complete with audible heartbeats, before experimenting with treatments. "They get really upset if they kill Fluffy the dog," says Kathy Edmondson, an administrator, "even though it's just on computer." But most college textbook publishers aren't ready for this high-tech conversion. Despite such advances as CD-ROM, interactive computer software, and other so-called multimedia developments, the publishers in the $2.6 billion market for college books could miss a potential gold mine in new product sales. They have a fortune sunk in the making and marketing of standard textbooks that are increasingly behind the times and technology.

While most publishers see this rapidly emerging reality, and some even *Own It*, few have started converting their problems into opportunities. An exception is Robert Lynch, director of McGraw-Hill's Primis service, a database operation that allows professors to customize textbooks, who says, "If we do things right and develop the full potential of high-tech educational publishing, this could be a $50 billion business instead of a $2.6 billion business." If college students will some day buy more computer disks than books and more books that their professors tailor for their needs from databases, foresighted textbook publishers can reap huge benefits from that revolution, but only if they *See It, Own It,* and *Solve It.*

As our next case demonstrates, it's not uncommon for people to negotiate the first two steps then stumble on the third. At CreativeWare, a computer software company disguised to protect the privacy of one of our clients, four directors in the programming and development area had come to their wits' end dealing with their boss, the vice president who oversaw their department. Bob simply would not fully accept responsibility for meeting both tight deadlines and high quality standards. Brilliant in other regards, he would blithely promise to meet impossible target dates and then release a rushed and compromised product.

On the other hand, the four directors, each responsible for a different segment of the programming and development operation, saw the reality of the situation clearly and even owned their circumstances, but they could not *Solve It*. Stuck on the *Own It* step, they kept complaining that "we're trying, but nothing's working." Creative solutions eluded them.

With the four directors manifesting all the familiar signs of the victim cycle, the department continued to languish under the mismanagement of the vice president. Each time they moved *Above The Line* to *Solve It*, they would fall back *Below The Line*, frustrated and discouraged. Because of the vice president's approach, they felt helpless to change the circumstances and powerless to alter the things they really needed to change. Without new products, CreativeWare's credibility in the marketplace declined as dealers, distributors, and retailers began to disbelieve the company's promises to deliver products on time and bug-free, even when the company did meet the goal, a heavy price for a failure to *Solve It*.

In a similar example, General Electric's and Emerson Electric's *Below The Line* behavior brought tragedy and heartache to hundreds of families. In an ABC *PrimeTime Live* broadcast, Chris Wallace reported how a malfunction in General Electric's coffeemakers, manufactured with Emerson Electric fuses, caused the appliance to burst into flames, destroying hundreds of homes. Both manufacturers knew about the problem but ignored it. According to Wallace: "Over the past 12 years, hundreds of people have had problems with GE coffeemakers. Defective machines have burned down houses, caused serious injuries, and even killed people. But GE for years denied responsibility, contesting claims against its coffeemakers with all the resources a big corporation can muster." General Electric documents from ten years prior to the *PrimeTime Live* report show that the company expected an estimated 168 claims that year and rated the prospect of "no injuries" associated with the claims at only 42 percent, evidence that the company recognized the reality. One year later, GE recalled two hundred thousand coffeemakers, proof that the company even owned the problem.

However, the company's efforts to improve the appliance didn't stop fires from breaking out. As Wallace reported, "GE considered adding a second backup fuse, but didn't do it." A couple of years later, GE sold its coffeemaker division to Black & Decker, which, to its credit, solved the problem by adding a second fuse. During this same period of time, GE sued Emerson Electric for its faulty fuses and won. One GE official testified that the company had been "disgusted with the reliability" of the Emerson fuses for several years. Nevertheless, prior to selling the division, GE did little to solve the problem either.

Even if an organization enjoys the collective talent, wisdom, experience, and integrity of companies like GE, they must remain vigilantly alert or risk losing it all on one trip *Below The Line.*

THE *SOLVE IT®* SKILLS AND SELF-ASSESSMENT

Over the years we have helped friends and clients translate their understanding and ownership into problem-solving action with a list of key *Solve It* skills. These skills provide a solid foundation for an assessment of your own ability to move from *See It* and *Own It* to *Solve It.*

SOLVE IT® SKILLS

1. Stay Engaged. Often, when a pesky problem persists, people naturally feel inclined to give up and stop trying—to wait and see if things will get better on their own. As you implement the *Solve It* step, avoid this trap by staying engaged in the process of finding solutions. Don't focus on what can't be done and, as a result, stop looking for and thinking about creative alternatives.

2. Persist. You must constantly ask the *Solve It* question: What else can I do? The repeated asking of this question makes it possible for you to formulate new and creative solutions that make progress possible. As one leader said, "That which we persist in doing becomes easier for us to do; not that the nature of the thing itself is changed, but that our power to *do* is increased."

3. Think Differently. Albert Einstein once said, "The significant problems we face cannot be solved at the same level of thinking we were at when we cre-

ated them." In other words, the same thinking that got you into the problem won't get you out of it. Always solicit and strive to understand perspectives other than your own.

4. Create New Linkages. Many solutions require innovative approaches that tap into new ways of both thinking about and doing things. Often, such approaches involve forging new relationships that involve others you may not have previously considered to offer keys to the solution. Such relationships may include your competitors, your suppliers and vendors, or someone in another department in the company. Always consider creating new linkages.

5. Take the Initiative. The *Solve It* step requires that you assume full accountability for discovering solutions that will ultimately deliver desired results. Such solutions generally come only when you take the initiative to explore, search, and question even after you think you have done everything you can. Understanding that others often do not share the same level of ownership or desire to achieve your goal, you must take the initiative to get the result. Which would you rather be: someone who makes things happen, someone who watches things happen, someone who wonders what happened, or someone who never knew anything happened?

6. Stay Conscious. Perhaps this sounds unusual, but we assure you, it is a crucial point. Staying conscious means overcoming the auto-pilot mode and paying attention to everything that may relate to potential solutions, particularly those things that we take for granted or that we have come to accept as "the way we do things around here." Always challenge current assumptions and beliefs in an effort to break through to a new level of thinking that may take you out of your comfort zone.

To assess whether, and to what extent, you practice these six skills, complete the following *Solve It* Self-Assessment. Evaluate each of the skills by determining whether your attitudes and behavior always, never, or sometimes reflect them.

Circle the description after each skill that best characterizes your attitudes and behavior:

		Often	Sometimes	Never
ONE	Do you stay engaged in solving a problem when things get difficult?	3	2	1
TWO	Do you persistently ask the *Solve It* question: "What else can I do to achieve the desired results?"	3	2	1
THREE	Do you take the initiative to explore, search, and question when solutions elude you?	3	2	1
FOUR	Do you stay conscious by challenging your current assumptions and beliefs about how you do things?	3	2	1
FIVE	Do you create new linkages in order to arrive at innovative solutions?	3	2	1
SIX	Do you try to discover new ways of thinking about problems?	3	2	1

SOLVE IT®
Self-Assessment

Now, take a few minutes to weigh the implications of your assessments. An honest appraisal of each of the *Solve It* indicators will reveal areas where you can work to increase the wisdom to *Solve It*.

By taking the *Solve It* step to greater accountability you will enhance your wisdom to solve problems and remove the obstacles you will encounter as you progress in your journey *Above The Line*. The benefits will delight you.

THE BENEFITS OF DEVELOPING THE WISDOM TO *SOLVE IT*®

The folks at one North American oil company reaped all the benefits of taking the *Solve It* step. They wanted to improve safety, reduce accidents, and drive the OSHA recordable rating to 0 (no accidents), a lofty and ambitious target. With

SOLVE IT Self-Assessment Scoring	
TOTAL SCORE	EVALUATION GUIDELINES
Often 18 to 13 points	Indicates that you see your accountability, own your circumstances, and diligently pursue a problem-solving course of action. Congratulations!
Sometimes 12 to 7 points	Shows that you feel ambivalent about problem solving. Such wavering courage, heart, and wisdom will only take you on a roller-coaster ride, *Above* and *Below The Line*. Work on it!
Never 6 to 1 points	Reveals a need for much greater effort. Reread this chapter!

a current OSHA recordable level of 8, the plant faced a long trip to 0. Getting everyone *Above The Line* wasn't easy because accidents, by their very definition, are "not my fault." But if no one accepted responsibility, how could the plant possibly change anything that would lower the accident rate? As the organization began practicing *The Oz Principle,* however, things began to happen. The recordable level began to drop. In every meeting people asked, "What else can we do to improve safety and eliminate accidents?" As discussions evolved, no one spent much time *Below The Line* as everyone searched high and low for creative solutions. The end result—a safety rating less than 1, a miniscule 0.7! Along with this huge improvement in safety came other benefits, such as cost savings from a reduction of wasted time, energy, effort, and resources discovered along the way. While the organization has not yet achieved a zero rating, it has markedly improved overall performance.

Earlier in this chapter the four directors in CreativeWare's programming and development department recognized their reality and even owned it but felt powerless to *Solve It.* After a lot of soul searching and debate, they finally decided to overcome their feelings of powerlessness and take the *Solve It* step by asking the question, "What else can we do to rise above our circumstances and get the results we want?" To answer this question they decided to air their concerns at a company retreat during a series of group discussions. As you might imagine, *The Oz Principle* helped them focus the retreat exclusively on new product-development projections. Just three weeks prior to the meeting, CreativeWare had presented an annual profit plan to the parent company describing how three new product introductions would account for 25 percent of their projected profit. Now, however, the projected product introductions sketched in that profit plan were running six months to one year behind schedule. An audible moan could be heard across the room as that information sank in.

After two days of intense scrutiny of such apparently unrealistic projections, CreativeWare's president acknowledged the reality that the company would not be able to introduce any new products in the coming six to twelve months. He then encouraged all his senior managers to acknowledge that same reality. They then began to own and solve the problem, immediately implementing a series of actions throughout the organization that would emphasize a collective effort to *Solve It.* Over the next eighteen months, CreativeWare successfully introduced three new products and reversed the rising credibility concerns among the company's dealers, distributors, and retailers.

Despite pressure to perform in the short term, the president of CreativeWare and, ultimately, his people, patiently worked through the *See It* and *Own It* steps before attempting to solve the problem. Impatience would have resulted in just the sort of scheduling mishaps and quality defects the company wished to eliminate.

Once everyone had fully seen and owned the problem, then people could start asking the *Solve It* question, which they did persistently until solutions began to take shape. Their persistence led to the new and creative solutions that would never have materialized otherwise.

Feelings of powerlessness had prevented the four directors from getting out of a rut from which the problem appeared insoluble. While the vice president never did come to grips with that issue, and, as a result, lost his job, the four directors did finally accept the fact that the power to get the results the company desired really did lie within themselves. While the four directors kept their jobs, none of them moved up to the vice president's position. Yes, they had each learned a valuable lesson, but they needed more seasoning in terms of accountability before they would be ready for such a promotion.

Each journey *Above The Line* begins, and is fueled by, a single question: "What else can we do to achieve the result?" The journey never ends until the problem gets solved. CreativeWare may not have perfected its delivery of new products, but it had achieved measurable progress in that direction; the journey continues.

As the CreativeWare case suggests, getting *Above The Line* to *Solve It* can make all the difference in the world, no matter what you're trying to do or achieve. Languishing *Below The Line*, you can expect only lackluster performance.

THE FINAL STAGE OF ACCOUNTABILITY

The Scarecrow symbolizes the wisdom to solve problems, a capability, as it turned out, he possessed all along. By this time in the story, Dorothy herself was coming closer to realizing that the results she was seeking would also come from within, but she would need to discover one more dimension of accountability before she could click her heels and return to Kansas. Having learned a great deal from her Oz companions, she finally reached the threshold of fully understanding the power of living *Above The Line*. In the next and final chapter in Part Two, you will discover how Dorothy pulls all four *Steps To Accountability* together to *Do It*.

Chapter 7

DOROTHY: EXERCISING THE MEANS TO *DO IT*®

Oz, left to himself, smiled to think of his success in giving the Scarecrow and the Tin Woodsman and the Lion exactly what they thought they wanted. "How can I help being a humbug," he said, "when all these people make me do things that everybody knows can't be done? It was easy to make the Scarecrow and the Lion and the Woodsman happy, because they imagined I could do anything. But it will take more than imagination to carry Dorothy back to Kansas, and I'm sure I don't know how it can be done."

—*The Wizard of Oz,*
L. Frank Baum

Former Wal-Mart CEO and current chairman of the executive committee David Glass emerged as the world's most admired CEO in *Fortune* magazine's annual survey. *Fortune's* article, "David Glass Won't Crack Under Fire," explains why this *Do It* executive deserves the praise of his peers: "Sam Walton had to try several times before he could persuade Glass to join the company as executive vice president of finance 16 years ago from the Consumer Markets chain in his home state of Missouri. Walton was forever stirring the management pot. In 1984 he pulled a high-level job swap, naming Glass, then the CFO, president and chief operating officer and requiring vice chairman Jack Shewmaker to give up the stores for the financial chores. The switch created a very public succession race in which Glass became the front-runner." Now, as CEO of the $55 billion retailing powerhouse, Glass lives in the stores more than in his office headquarters because that's where the action is. Wal-Mart's success hinges, he recognizes, on knowing what's happening in store aisles, in competitors' showrooms, and in each employee's daily work. Notebook in hand, Glass asks a million questions for every answer he gives. His constant questioning and searching for better ways to do things personifies the *See It, Own It, Solve It,* and *Do It* executive, who consistently strives to work *Above The Line*. Employees never fear a visit from Glass because they know he shares their hopes and concerns. And Wal-Mart executives respect him as well, knowing that Glass's down-to-earth style does not mean he'll tolerate mediocrity. As a senior executive told *Fortune,* "There's no question that his expectation is 110 percent. I mean, he never has to tell you. You know what it is before you ever talk to him." Not surprisingly, a lot of companies and executives want to learn from Glass. As the *Fortune* article points out, "Although Wal-Mart's rah-rah style is sometimes criticized by sophisticated types, a steady stream of corporate heavyweights finds its way to Bentonville to see what the noise is all about. GE boss Jack Welch was a welcome visitor. When former Procter & Gamble CEO John Smale took over as chairman of General Motors, one of his first exercises was to cart CEO Jack Smith and other GM executives to a Wal-Mart management meeting, presumably to learn how to make a decision without using a calendar. Executives from IBM, Eastman Kodak, Southwest Airlines, Sara Lee, P&G, and Anheuser Busch have all made the trek." Despite Wal-Mart's impressive growth and success, David Glass believes the best lies ahead. In other words, you don't just *Do It* and then rest on your laurels, you keep on doing it 24/7.

A recent *BusinessWeek* article on Wal-Mart and David Glass tells more of the story: "Just three years ago, it looked as though Wal-Mart Stores Inc. had finally hit the wall. Profit growth was slowing, and investors were fleeing. But David D. Glass, Wal-Mart's CEO since 1988, has managed to infuse the retailing giant with much-needed new energy and direction. His biggest success: a foray into the grocery business, with giant 'supercenters' that sell general merchandise and food. And now Glass, 63, is experimenting with smaller food markets, too. That's helped revive Wal-Mart on both Main Street and Wall Street." Glass's secret? His undying commitment to making things happen and building the chain into a global brand. "Wal-Mart's earnings—and stock—are soaring. And after years of costly investment, even international is now adding to the bottom line." And his replacement, president and CEO H. Lee Scott, Jr., comes from the Walton-Glass mold.

When you combine the first three steps of accountability with the fourth and final step, *Do It*, then and only then will you experience the full power of living *Above The Line* and getting the results you want. Sam Walton's famous Sundown Rule still guides Wal-Mart people to do it today, rather than waiting until tomorrow: "In this busy place, where our jobs depend on one another, it's our standard to get things done today—before the sun goes down. Whether it's a request from a store across the country or a call from down the hall, every request gets same-day service."

REACHING THE FOURTH AND FINAL STEP OF ACCOUNTABILITY

Ultimately, personal accountability means accepting full responsibility to achieve results and *Do It*. If you don't *Do It*, you'll never reap the most valuable benefit of full accountability: overcoming your circumstances and achieving the results you want. Despite the many benefits that accrue from applying the other three steps, results only come when you put all four steps together and passionately, proactively, and persistently *Do It*!

Illustrating what it means to *Do It*, FedEx posted the following stories on their Web site under the heading of their key philosophy: "Absolutely, Positively Whatever It Takes." Buster Knull, a FedEx driver, arrived at Alcoa Company to pick up a wheel shipment that had to go out that evening. The wheel stems, an essential part of the wheel, had arrived late and still needed to be installed.

Rather than waiting and watching, Buster jumped into the fray and helped install the stems and lubricate the wheels so that the shipment could be moved on time. Then consider the case of Steven Schott. "During one shift, Steven completed his FedEx deliveries by repeatedly refilling the radiator of his overheating van. He returned to the station and loaded packages into another van, but that vehicle also broke down. Determined, Steven asked a customer if he could borrow the bicycle she rode to work. He then attached a FedEx crate to his backpack and placed the packages inside. In 90-degree heat, Steven pedaled 10 miles up and down steep hills to complete all of his deliveries, he ran 3.6 miles to deliver packages 'on the clock,' then walked an additional 2.2 miles to pick up another shipment during his break. Steven finished his route on foot." As we see with both Buster and Steven, the only way to win the race for results is to *Do It.*

The *Do It* step bestows accountability, not just for activities, circumstances, or feelings but for future accomplishment. When you combine the notion of accountability with the objective of accomplishing better results, you create an empowering and guiding beacon for both personal and organizational activity. This form of accountability comes after you have progressed through all four steps *Above The Line.* By stopping at any step short of *Do It,* you may, for a time, keep yourself out of the victim cycle and the blame game, but you will never fully achieve a permanent position *Above The Line.* Any effort that falls short of making it happen and getting it done simply indicates a lack of full acceptance of accountability.

Doing It requires that you work continually to stay *Above The Line,* avoiding the occurrences inherent in daily circumstances and problems that can tempt you back *Below The Line.* As we constantly stress in this book, accountability is a process, and you can fall into the victim cycle just as easily from the fourth step as from any of the others. Staying *Above The Line* requires diligence, perseverance, and vigilance. It also requires a willingness to accept risk and to take the giant step that's often necessary to get what you want out of your life or your organization. Fear of the risk of failing can so debilitate many people that they build walls between *Solve It* and *Do It.* However, only by accepting the risk can you penetrate the walls and break down all the barriers to success.

In the final analysis, *Do It* means embracing your full responsibility for results and remaining answerable for your progress toward those results, regardless of how or why you managed to get into your current situation. Consider the example of an American Van Lines driver who established his accountability and stayed *Above The Line,* even when the going got tough. It all started at the Teradata Corporation, a company founded in a garage in Los Angeles and now a division of NCR. Teradata strove to fill a niche in the computer database market unserved by larger companies such as IBM. After the first two years of hard effort, they finally sold the first Teradata computer to a *Fortune* 500 company headquartered on the East Coast. That accomplishment prompted quite a celebration among Teradata's fifty-two employees, who had worked together as a veritable family for two long years. Now, after all that effort, the company had turned the corner and was about to ship its first product.

On the Saturday morning scheduled for shipment of the computer, all the employees and their families gathered at the Teradata facility, a renovated warehouse that had replaced the garage in which the company had begun its operations, to give it a rousing send-off. Streamers and signs hung from the rafters and the eaves of the warehouse roof. Everyone sported T-shirts with the words *The Big One* screened on the front and back. Even the American Van Lines driver who had contracted to deliver the shipment got caught up in the festivities as he climbed into the cab of his eighteen-wheeler.

As the contract driver pulled out of the parking lot with The Big One in tow, the Teradata families formed a parade route to cheer his departure. Moved by the moment, the driver waved back, shouting that he would not let them down. Indeed, the driver felt he had joined the Teradata team, even if only for this one haul, and he felt a strong sense of ownership and pride over the role he was playing in Teradata's first major achievement.

Almost eight hours into his trip, the American Van Lines driver pulled into his first weigh station only to discover that his load was five hundred pounds over the legal limit. He knew the overweight problem would require additional paper processing and approvals that could create a full day's delay and prevent Teradata from meeting the promised delivery date. At this point, you can imagine how easy it would have been for this driver to fall *Below The Line,* blaming the company for the overweight problem. After all, it wasn't his fault. You can also imagine how easy it would have been for the driver to check into a motel to await further instructions. However, the driver stayed *Above The Line* by choosing to own the situation. Only he could save the delivery date. Recognizing the reality of his situation and owning the circumstances, he quickly moved to *Solve It.* In minutes he turned the truck around and drove to the nearest truck stop where he dismantled the truck's front bumper, removed its extra water containers and spare chairs, and then hid all the apparatus in a nearby ditch under some brush. He recalled thinking of the risk of losing the hidden items; after all, he would be held accountable by the company that owned the rig, but such thoughts quickly evaporated. He accepted the risk knowing it was the only way to get the shipment delivered on schedule. When he returned to the weigh station, the truck checked in fifty pounds under weight. With a sigh of relief and a great deal of pride and satisfaction in his accomplishment, he drove on to the East Coast where he delivered The Big One on time. He had done it!

After hearing about the driver's experience, the people at Teradata celebrated his *See It, Own It, Solve It, Do It* attitude by, among other things, incorporating his story into the company's new employee orientation program as a parable to reinforce the power of working *Above The Line*.

In another example of how seeing, owning, solving, and doing combine to make extraordinary things happen, consider how one of our clients, who has utilized *The Oz Principle* and our training for over a decade, epitomizes the connection between daily effort and company results.

Remember Guidant, a $3.5 billion medical products manufacturing company? Their CRM division consistently makes business unit objectives clear to individuals. How do they do it? At one recent employee meeting, they asked one simple question of every employee: "What are you prepared to do?" According to Guidant, "That way everybody is thinking about what they can contribute to the overall goal." Has it made a difference? Absolutely. Each new CRM employee attends required accountability and cultural training in which they learn to *See It, Own It, Solve It, Do It,* and to constantly ask the question "What else can I do to get the result?" As Guidant works toward its goal of becoming more customer focused, for example, employees have become much more aware and committed to that goal by continuing to ask what they can do as individuals to satisfy customers. And the results have been impressive. In one recent situation, a patient ready to receive a Guidant defibrillator implant was at risk because of potential interference with another implanted device for stimulating nerves to relieve back pain. The doctor did not know whether the two devices would interact positively or negatively and, when he couldn't contact the nerve device manufacturer, he called Guidant. The tech services employee at Guidant who took the call immediately faxed several articles regarding the Guidant device and its interaction with other devices to the Guidant field representative who, in turn, read them to the doctor over the phone. The doctor finally felt comfortable performing the critical implant. After the surgery, the Guidant field rep E-mailed the tech services employee: "Without your help the patient wouldn't have received the much-needed defibrillator therapy. You saved the day!" Dale, then manager of Guidant's twenty-four-hour on-call tech services group, says this happens every day at Guidant. "I can't tell you how often sales reps or physicians compliment us for always having highly trained people available to answer questions." Guidant wins kudos in the industry for providing technical support, thanks to one simple question: "What are you prepared to do?" Of course, it's easier to ask that question than to answer it.

WHY PEOPLE FAIL TO *DO IT*®

Most people who fail to *Do It* find it difficult to resist the gravitational pull from *Below The Line,* which can so easily pull you back into the victim cycle, wasting valuable time, energy, and resources; ignoring and denying; making excuses; developing explanations; pointing fingers; getting confused; and waiting to see if some wizard will make things better. In our experience, this happens most often because of a natural resistance to the perceived risks associated with becoming fully responsible for results. A fear of failure can create a terrible burden that makes taking the final step to accountability virtually impossible. It seems so much easier to hide in a false sense of security, citing excuses for avoiding the dangers associated with risk. Nothing will keep you in the victim cycle more surely than an unwillingness to take the risks so often associated with action.

We see it all the time. Just as the line between the *Steps To Accountability* and the victim cycle separates effective organizations from ineffective ones, the line between *Solve It* and *Do It* separates good companies from great ones. Great organizations welcome the risks associated with action, regardless of the inherent danger in those risks.

To get people personally involved and accountable for results, many companies have initiated new ways to empower workers to take risks. Such organizations have learned what it means to create a sense of urgency about doing it, regardless of the existing structure or past traditions. A story in *USA Today* shows what happens when a group of people do get personally involved: "Chevrolet had a problem. Its Camaro muscle car—an important lure for young buyers and a big part of Chevy's performance image—had become a clunky rattletrap a few years ago. *Consumer Reports* magazine condemned it. Even sympathetic auto enthusiast magazines couldn't ignore loose gearshift levers, leaky windows, and chattering dashboards. Pontiac—Chevy's sibling division at General Motors—was suffering too. Its Firebird shared hardware with, and was built alongside, the better selling Camaro. GM's generic designation for these cars is F car. 'Sales were off. Quality ratings were way down,' said F car engineering manager Richard DeVogelaere. 'Water leaks, squeaks and rattles, poor driveability, electrical problems—probably no secret to any Camaro or Firebird owner. We just hadn't paid as much attention as we should have.'"

However, GM did not let large company bureaucracy stand in the way of improvement, allowing DeVogelaere and a small, underfinanced team to tackle the problem. As a result, the team managed to improve quality and cut defects so much that warranty claims fell by half in just two years. DeVogelaere described how his team did it: "The budget was very, very small, but it was all blessed upfront, so we didn't have to justify anything. They gave me the money and said, 'Get it done.' That really made it work. It didn't take several signatures. If you say it, it gets done. That was refreshing. You hear about driving the responsibility down to the levels where people really know. Well, this is a case of it." On the other hand, some companies fail to engender this kind of accountability in their people because they can't resist the impulse to tell people what to do, all the way down the line.

The era of debt financing that took the United States by storm and helped bankrupt many companies, eventually plunging the country and the world into a nagging recession, seemed to tempt everyone but Morgan Stanley. As reported in *Time* magazine: "During the heyday of takeover lending and junk bond financing, the patrician investment firm Morgan Stanley was often the butt of ridicule. While more aggressive firms plunged into risky new techniques, Morgan, despite a leading role in corporate takeovers, seemed stuck in its stodgy habit of underwriting stock for blue-chip companies and selling investment-grade bonds. The new breed was playing high-stakes Monopoly, the joke went, while the stuffed shirts at Morgan were playing Trivial Pursuit." To its credit, Morgan Stanley chose to risk losing investors with its conservative policy, but in the long run, and with hindsight, that policy proved correct. Accepting full responsibility for the consequences of its actions, Morgan saw the shortsightedness of the junk bond craze and owned its circumstances despite ridicule and criticism. It solved its problems by diversifying into various other fields rather than jumping on the junk bond bandwagon, and it acted decisively when it adhered to its well-established values of trust and integrity. In the end, what Morgan Stanley did was to become one of the most profitable investment banking firms on Wall Street.

COUNTING THE CONSEQUENCES OF NOT *DOING IT*®

If you fail to *Do It,* you not only fail to improve your circumstances or obtain the results you want, but you also set yourself up for a continuing cycle of disappointment. The story of Strategic Associates proves the point.

As do many small service organizations, Strategic Associates (not its real name), a management consulting firm, ran into difficulty sustaining its overhead and continuing its growth. The firm had learned to pinpoint the "cliff of no sales" that usually lay two to four months beyond current engagements. Since all the key people in the firm both sold and delivered the company's services, they naturally watched for the dangerous cliff and turned their attention from delivering service to sales whenever they saw themselves swerving too close to the edge.

While SA's organizational culture had become adept at avoiding the cliff, the situation began to change a few years ago when the cliff became steeper and more threatening. In fact, unknown to the rank-and-file employees of the firm, the president himself mortgaged his home to meet payroll demands for two months. As word of the predicament leaked, however, people began to wonder about just how bad the situation had become and worried that the company might start laying people off if things didn't get better.

In this atmosphere of dread, the entire firm dropped *Below The Line* as everyone began blaming other people, internal programs, and outside events for lack of performance and for the ever-increasing cliff problem. Although SA's management conducted objective personal interviews with all employees to assess their performance, most people felt they were receiving unfair blame for the company's problems, which lay beyond their control. After a lot of emotional venting at a weekly staff meeting, management and employees agreed that the time had come to stop the blame game and turn the situation around.

Subsequently, management invested a lot of time interviewing all the employees to better understand the real nature of the problem. Then, at a historic company-wide meeting, they laid everything they had discovered on the table, holding nothing back, unveiling charts and graphs that summarized all the pertinent facts of the situation. Open discussion and dialogue ensued, with the express aim of solving the overriding issue of sales. It wasn't hard to *See It* because the problem had become so pervasive. As the meeting progressed tumultuously, no one held anything back because, after all, what could honesty cost them? Clearly, unless the current situation changed within the next two months, SA would start laying off people. The meeting sounded a loud wake-up call as every employee came to appreciate both the gravity of the situation and the fact that they personally were doing little to help solve the problem.

Senior management had certainly made its share of mistakes, but employees too had avoided the sales issue because they didn't feel responsible for it. Even those who had tried to sell in the past had failed to get good results, while others had not even tried to sell because they received no incentive for it. While some blamed management for poor training or the lack of attractive commissions, they also started seeing the limitations of their own comfort levels and unwillingness to challenge themselves and assume responsibility for SA's problem. Everyone had allowed the burden of sales to rest upon the shoulders of the executive group, especially the president. After all, since those key executives had always made the necessary sales to sustain the firm's growth, why should anyone else worry about it? Now, of course, with the very life of the organization at stake, the realization dawned that everyone must worry about it.

Management too obtained from the meeting a growing realization that they had not acknowledged some important realities. In the past, the top salespeople had received a lot of recognition for saving the day, and until now, they had shied away from sharing the glory and the wealth. Luckily, they had always steered SA away from the cliff, but at this juncture luck alone wouldn't carry the day. As the senior staff listened to their people, they realized that all SA's sales success stories starred the president and the chairman. In fact, the chairman always treated the selling of intangible consulting services with a certain mystique reserved for only the elite among consultants. Whenever SA dug up promising leads for new business, the firm invariably put its very best salespeople, the chairman and the president, to work on them, a habit that had further fostered the perception that sales remained the domain of people at the top.

As a result of the meeting, the chairman and president also learned that while they knew how to sell, they did not feel confident that they could train others to do so. That feeling stemmed in part from their own need to bask in their accomplishments. After all, successful selling cemented their positions as stars in the company.

As the chairman and president owned the facts surrounding SA's dilemma, they realized that all their employees needed to gain confidence so that they could help *Solve It*. If people could define themselves as part of the problem and own their own circumstances, they could help everyone else see themselves not only as part of the problem but as part of the solution. Given the gravity of the situation, each person needed to demonstrate 110 percent ownership of the situation, no matter how small their contribution to the problem. Otherwise SA could not possibly turn things around permanently.

As the president and chairman shared this insight during the meeting, more and more people began talking about how they could and would do whatever it took to accomplish the firm's objectives. Emotion ran high. Enthusiasm gained speed. Confidence soared. In a very real sense, these feelings boosted the organization's power to get results tenfold as everyone developed a strong sense of ownership.

As the president led the group into the *Solve It* phase, he asked, "What else can we do to achieve the results we want?" The ensuing discussion revealed a pent-up enthusiasm for solving the firm's ever-recurring sales problem, not only for the immediate term but for the long term as well. The group began crafting a sales plan that listed the immediate involvement of every person in the firm, outlining what each might do to keep SA from falling over the cliff. For the first time in SA's history, each and every employee began thinking of what they could personally do to increase sales leads and improve the overall sales performance of the company. Some even considered friends and acquaintances they could tap for sales leads.

Even more important than this short-term effort, they hammered out a long-term plan to involve the entire consulting staff in keeping the firm well away from the cliff. This plan centered on developing the sales skills of all the consultants. Eventually, everyone bought into the long-term solution: categorizing all incoming business into three different groups based on income potential. Any lead for a company with annual sales under $250 million fell into the C category, which any consultant could count without the aid of a member of the executive team. This would immediately expand the sales team by allowing more people to call on prospective clients without risking the loss of more lucrative accounts. Over time, all consultants would gain selling experience that would prepare them for selling to bigger prospects.

The B category included companies with over $250 million but under $1 billion in annual sales. These prospective clients would be contacted by any consultant and a member of the executive team other than the chairman or president. The A companies, exceeding $1 billion in annual sales, would receive the direct attention of the chairman or the president, along with one of the consultants, who might lead the ultimate engagement.

To implement this program, the senior consultants outlined a training and certification process for each category, and by the end of the meeting the entire group felt both enthusiastic and empowered to meet the challenge ahead. Most people felt they now stood in a position to benefit both themselves and the company with the new sales approach, and the president himself felt that the new program would remove all limits and boundaries to the firm's successful future. Not only would the solution expand the sales force immediately, it would further develop all SA's people, creating a machine capable of producing sales and keeping SA permanently away from the cliff.

After the meeting, SA's people were finally ready to *Do It*. It never happened, though. Just as people turned their attention to the need for immediate sales during the weeks after the memorable meeting, the president snared the firm's largest contract ever, causing everyone to heave a sigh of relief that SA had solved its immediate crisis.

Almost overnight the long-term concern of permanently avoiding the cliff and sustaining perpetual growth became a dim memory as all the consultants went back to doing what they had always done: implementing the work sold by top executives. The picture looked rosy because this one huge sale, combined with SA's annual sales to date, enabled the firm to achieve its best revenue year ever. As a result, the chairman and the president perpetuated the myth that only they could slay the big dragons, and they let the training and certification program fall by the wayside. While from time to time an employee lamented the return to business as usual, none of the new sales development plans ever materialized. With neither management nor the consultants willing to take the risks associated with the new approach, SA soon fell back *Below The Line,* waiting for the next cliff to appear, hoping that it wouldn't be so steep the next time.

Of course, a year later, the cliff did reappear and SA found itself right back where it started. Once again, the chairman and president shouldered the responsibility. Unfortunately, by not taking the step from *Solve It* to *Do It,* the firm could not stay *Above The Line* and get the results it really needed. Imagine what might have happened had SA followed through on its original plan.

DO IT® SELF-ASSESSMENT

Your own ability to *Do It* will arise from your willingness to hold yourself fully responsible for your circumstances and totally accountable for your progress toward results. The following questionnaire will help you determine whether you are willing to take the risks associated with doing it. If you find yourself unwilling or hesitant to *Do It,* review Chapters Four through Seven, to renew your understanding of the *Steps To Accountability.* Now, take a few minutes to weigh your behavior and attitudes when it comes to doing it.

Once you have completed the *Do It* Self-Assessment, total up your scores, then consult the following table for some guidelines on evaluating your ability to stay *Above The Line* and *Do It.*

We often use this questionnaire with clients because it helps people generate feedback from others. While you may gain a lot of insight from a candid self-assessment, you can learn even more from the honest feedback of your colleagues, friends, and family.

Remember, accountable people seek feedback and feedback creates accountable people.

THE BENEFITS OF EXERCISING THE MEANS TO *DO IT*®

We know from first-hand experience that it's a lot easier to preach accountability than to practice it. That's why it heartens us so much when we encounter that rare individual who, no matter how great the obstacle, refuses to get stuck *Below The Line.* Such people vigilantly and diligently strive to improve their circumstances and invariably create stunning results for themselves and others. Karsten Solheim deserves special recognition in this regard.

During the Great Depression of the 1930s, Karsten dropped out of college to earn enough money to survive, though he hoped he could return to school one day. He worked as a cobbler, then as an apprentice engineer at Ryan Aero-

Do It®
Self-Assessment

		Never	Seldom	Sometimes	Often	Always
ONE	You recognize the forces, when they present themselves, that could pull you back down *Below The Line*.	0	1	3	5	7
TWO	You are effective at avoiding additional excursions *Below The Line* as you work to *Do It*!	0	1	3	5	7
THREE	You report on your accountability no matter what the results are.	0	1	3	5	7
FOUR	You take the initiative to clarify your own responsibilities and accountabilities.	0	1	3	5	7
FIVE	You encourage others to clarify their own responsibilities and accountabilities.	0	1	3	5	7
SIX	You are willing to take risks in order to *Do It*.	0	1	3	5	7
SEVEN	You do not easily give up and are not easily overcome by obstacles, but continue to persist in seeking to make it happen.	0	1	3	5	7
EIGHT	Once personal or organizational goals have been set, you actively measure progress toward those goals.	0	1	3	5	7
NINE	As circumstances change, your commitment to getting the result does not vary—you remain determined to *Do It*!	0	1	3	5	7
TEN	You always keep yourself "seeing, owning, solving, and doing" until you achieve the desired results.	0	1	3	5	7

Do It®
Self-Assessment Scoring

TOTAL SCORE	EVALUATION GUIDELINES
55 to 70 points	Verifies a strong *Do It* attitude. However, you should avoid intolerance of those who feel less accountable lest you lose your ability to influence their journeys *Above The Line*.
40 to 54 points	Indicates fair to good *Do It* attitudes and behavior, but you can improve.
25 to 39 points	Suggests a problem with taking the risks associated with the *Do It* step.
0 to 24 points	Reveals serious *Below The Line* problems. You should go back to Chapter Four and start climbing the *Steps To Accountability* again.

nautical and Convair, gaining valuable on-the-job training but never quite saving enough money to continue his formal education.

Eventually, Karsten left Ryan for General Electric, where he helped develop the first portable television set. Shortly thereafter, on his own time, Karsten created the first "rabbit ears" antenna, but when GE executives dismissed the invention, he shared the idea and design with another company that went on to make a fortune with the device. Unfortunately, Karsten received no remuneration for his innovation except a set of gold-plated antennas after the company reached 2 million units in sales. Rather than give in to resentment, however, Karsten learned from his experience, faced the reality, owned his circumstances, and vowed, with a genuine *Solve It* attitude: "The next time I invent something, I'll make it myself." And that's exactly what he did.

While still employed by GE, Karsten spent his evenings and weekends developing innovative golf clubs in his garage. No one took him seriously in the beginning, as a *Sports Illustrated* article noted: "Karsten Solheim was considered a kook when he began showing up at tour events around 1960, but he was perceptive enough to head straight for the practice putting green. That is where the tour's sick and wounded pull in for repairs, and they always are looking for a miracle 'cure.'" Refining his inventions with the responses of professional golfers, Karsten finally developed a putter that provided a larger "sweet spot," facilitated lining up the ball with the hole, and worked beautifully on all kinds of grasses. Once he succeeded in convincing a few professionals to use the putter, he was delighted when they soon began winning tournaments. Word of the new Ping putter spread quickly, fueling demand not only for the putter but for other Ping irons and clubs as well.

Having learned from earlier experiences, Karsten knew that he himself must guide the future development of this new product. This meant he would have to take calculated risks, such as leaving his successful career at GE. But knowing that he could not realize the results he wanted unless he took such risks, he didn't think twice, he just did it. After leaving his job at GE, Karsten engineered a full-scale golf club manufacturing line, and, in just over two years, he grew his business from $50,000 to $800,000. By 1992 Karsten was leading the industry. Today, Karsten continues to stay *Above The Line*, even in the face of adversity. When he received some bad news not long ago from the United States Golf Association, which claimed that the distance between the grooves on Karsten's Ping "Eye 2" clubs did not conform to USGA standards, Karsten began contesting the allegations in court, all the while steadfastly developing more innovations at his plant. Karsten refused to abandon his commitment to *Do It*, and he refused to fall *Below The Line* the rest of his life. Solheim passed away in 2000 at the age of eighty-eight. His passing brought a wave of condolences, respect, and admiration from associates and leaders in the golf industry. "Perhaps no individual has had as profound an impact on the golf industry as Karsten Solheim," said Ken Lindsay, honorary president of the Professional Golfers Association of America. "In today's vast marketplace of golf equipment, one consistent message is the impact of technology as it relates to improving performance. All of us in golf can be thankful for the standards set by this former General Electric engineer in this area."

In another instance of impressive accountability, our client Guidant CRM faced a company-threatening situation: A supplier's factory burned down, leaving Guidant without access to a critical component used in its new cardiac resynchronization defibrillator (CRT-D) product. The CRT-D is a significant product for the treatment of heart failure and Guidant was first to market in the United States with the new technology. The company faced not only losing sales to a competitor—a competitor whose device was larger and used a less techno-logically advanced method of therapy delivery—but failing on its promise to customers to provide them with leading products to treat their patients with heart failure.

Despite the fact that product development cycles typically take months if not years, Guidant CRM's senior management charged the product engineer-ing group to take accountability for quickly bringing another device to market to support patients and customers relying on Guidant technology. Historically, product development did not take place in the product engineering group, so the thought process used to execute the project was slightly different than on a traditional R&D team. This device would be designed using a different plat-form to get around manufacturing issues, which had almost stopped produc-tion of the company's current CRT-D. A small group of cross-functional decision makers met on June 10, 2002, with ground rules set—one hour, one meeting, come out with a concept. With no time to waste, the team produced an approved concept document the next day and the clock started ticking.

This product had an impossible timeline—FDA submission was scheduled for August—and no resources assigned to support it. Kent Fox, project man-ager for the CONTAK CD 2, as the project was now called, put out a call to ded-icated team managers throughout the research and development organization asking them to give up critical talent. The loss of key personnel put other proj-ect deadlines at risk, but Fox was able to secure a high level of ownership for the CONTAK CD 2 CRT-D's success and staff the project quickly with the right skill set to achieve the objectives.

In the midst of this crisis, the company could have easily dropped *Below The Line*, hiding from the problem and its consequences, and waited for the next scheduled product launch. After all, Guidant CRM had never put out a product on such an aggressive timeline before. Why shouldn't the company just sit tight and hope that customers and patients could hold on until the next product, scheduled for a February launch? Instead, senior management opted for an *Above The Line* approach; an approach that they felt would enable Guidant to really remain a leader in providing heart failure technology to customers and patients. They charged a group to *Solve It*, moving from finger pointing, paral-ysis, and confusion to a level of organizational accountability that allowed the entire organization to own the company's circumstances.

The team worked tirelessly to *Do It*, with Fox reminding them that each day was equivalent to about 3 percent of the total project timeline. They were able to leverage existing hardware and software and even added a high-energy model—an industry first in the United States. The resulting CONTAK CD 2 was 38 percent smaller than the competitor's device and filled a crucial gap in the company's product offerings. The team not only met the deadline for FDA submission, but also managed to exceed it by a week. From the development of the concept to FDA approval took four and a half months: Under normal circumstances the FDA approval time alone is six months. The product was submitted to the FDA and, thanks to the thorough groundwork in place, a track record of *Above The Line* dealings with the agency, and the FDA's understanding of the critical nature of this product for customers, it was approved quickly. Guidant launched the device in December and immediately received a positive reception, providing lifesaving therapy to patients. This warm reception helped set the stage for the successful launch in February of the company's state-of-the-art CRT-D product, a product that had been in development for several years.

Without question, the CONTAK CD 2 project represented a difficult episode in Guidant's recent history, but to the credit of senior management and all the people who work at Guidant, they never wavered in their commitment to stay *Above The Line*. Undoubtedly, there were doubts and tension along the way. Guidant could have easily wasted time, energy, and resources denying the problem, deflecting blame to the component supplier and defending the status quo, but Guidant did what many organizations fail to do; it overcame the gravitational pull of the victim cycle and rose resolutely from solving it to doing it, despite the associated risks. Guidant's actions paid off, not only in terms of satisfied customers and healthy sales, but as a new paradigm for the development of inch-up products. In 2003 one entire product line was upgraded to include the fast-charge feature, developed during this project. This feature is highly valued by many of Guidant's physician customers and has contributed to market share gain. Since this project, the new inch-up development strategy has successfully brought other products to market in rapid succession. In addition, new safeguards were put in place to prevent future dependence on a single source for critical components.

The organization had learned that getting the right result, regardless of the challenge to the product development map, comes only when everyone takes ownership of the company's reputation as a leader. The entire company will face the future with greater confidence in the product development process and with a strengthened corporate culture, driven first and foremost by a sense of complete accountability.

We also witnessed the benefits of exercising the means to *Do It* when we observed a young business school graduate we will call Terry. Just out of graduate school with a shining new MBA, Terry was interviewed by the director of development of a midsized company for a position in product development. During the interviews, the director told Terry that his experience in graduate school was exactly what the company was looking for. In fact, he promised that if Terry came on board, he would lead a product development team with all the budget and time they would need to get the job done. Needless to say, Terry enthusiastically accepted the job with a great deal of confidence. He knew from interviews with people in the company that he possessed skills and knowledge far beyond anyone else in the organization.

Events unfolded precisely as the director had suggested they would. Upon beginning work, Terry received a budget, a time line, a project team, and all the freedom in the world to make decisions and put his knowledge to work. Although a keen ear might have heard some mumbling among the troops about why someone just out of school deserved such an opportunity, the director loudly expressed his confidence in Terry's ability to pull it off.

Over the next few months, Terry's team worked feverishly at developing the product. They found that co-locating (moving people from different functional areas in the company out of their respective departments and into the same working area) helped them focus and not get distracted by other daily issues facing the company. It was all going quite nicely, with Terry feeling fully empowered, even to the point that when people, including the president of the company, would ask him how it was going, he would respond, "Wait until you see what we're developing; it's everything you wanted and more."

To reach a key milestone set by the director, the team worked around the clock. They would even take turns sleeping on the couch in one of the conference rooms. Never had the individuals on the team worked so hard and with so much enthusiasm. Each of them believed that was what the company expected. As time passed, the need for the new product had become increasingly apparent, and everyone anxiously awaited its unveiling.

When the morning of the deadline came, the team stood ready to unveil its work. Having worked the previous two days straight, members of the team felt exhausted, but their enthusiasm and excitement about making the date and completing the project with an even better than expected outcome filled them with energy. They met with the director of development in his office. It was a busy morning, and the director was working with fierce concentration at his desk when the team entered his office. He looked up at the clock and asked what they needed. They eagerly replied that they had finished the project and had written a presentation full of impressive information. To the team's surprise, and to Terry's utter frustration, the director looked down and said, "Thank you, I will get to it as soon as I can. Do you need anything else?" Stunned, the team, confused by the director's response, marched dejectedly out of his office. Quickly, the confusion turned to frustration and then anger. Making matters even worse, the director uttered not another word about the project in the following days.

A week later, Terry asked the director what he thought of the work he and his team had done. The director replied that he had not found time to review the material because he had misplaced it. He needed another copy.

Terry could not believe his ears. Utterly dismayed, he went back to the team and told them what had happened. Their outrage quickly turned to mutiny. People began talking about updating their resumes and looking for better jobs. Terry himself felt he had been had, that he was a completely legitimate victim, but he hesitated telling other people the story. Who would believe it? However, it did not take long for word to get around the company that the director was displeased with the efforts of Terry and his team. Terry could not remember receiving such unfair treatment in his entire life. What's more, others in the company seemed to swallow what the director and others were saying hook, line, and sinker.

As with many MBAs fresh out of school, Terry began considering his options, talking to classmates about opportunities in their organizations and trying to get a feeling for the current job market. That's when a friend gave Terry a copy of *The Oz Principle* and he began thinking about the situation in a different light. If he walked away a victim, could he ever hold his head high again? Wisely, Terry resolved to move *Above The Line*.

As Terry took the *See It* step, he began talking to others in the company about what had happened. As he asked for candid feedback, he learned something interesting. First, he discovered that the company was on the verge of collapse as a result of the failure of some other product introductions. His team, having focused solely on their development efforts, remained blissfully un-aware of the severity of the situation. Smack in the middle of all the turmoil, the director of development, who remained responsible not only for the problem but also for coming up with the solution, had put Terry's project at the bottom of the list, something that surprised Terry because he had assumed the team's efforts would capture the attention of the company. After all, his team consid-ered the project central to the company's future. Everyone in development was working night and day on solving the urgent product problems, but Terry, hav-ing kept himself and his team fairly insulated, had never fully comprehended the magnitude of the company's difficulties.

To make matters worse, the day Terry's team made the presentation, he heard the rumor top management had given his boss, the director, six months to turn things around *or else!* The director had just bought a large new home near corporate headquarters, so the prospect of huge mortgage payments and losing his job had certainly been worrying him. Further, Terry heard from more than one person that many in the department actually resented his team for not sharing their work or asking for input. People disliked that secretiveness, espe-cially in light of the department's long history of teamwork.

After absorbing all the feedback, Terry regretted what he had done. Some-how, he had managed to alienate the entire department, which explained why no one expressed any sympathy for him or the team and why no one even questioned the unsubstantiated opinions of the director. While Terry saw that the director could have helped the team better understand what they should have done differently, he also accepted the fact that he and his team had been insular and shortsighted. Perhaps he wasn't such a total victim after all.

As he moved to the *Own It* step, Terry began to recount more fully in his mind all the things he could have done differently: understanding the team-work culture of the department, creating open communication with his peers, asking for feedback as he went along, and paying more attention to what else was happening in the department and in the company. As Terry came to realize that maybe he shared some accountability in all this, too, he came to feel more strongly that he wanted to stay and make things better. After meeting with his team and talking through his new insights, he was pleased to find that everyone could easily list things they could have been done to produce a better outcome. Solutions began to appear on the horizon.

As Terry moved to the *Solve It* mode, he resolved to prove to the department that he was a team player interested in more than just his own success. He knew this would take some time. It would also take courage for him to sit down with the director and discuss what had happened and what he had learned from the experience.

As he considered his circumstances, Terry knew that he had climbed *Above The Line* by taking the *See It, Own It,* and *Solve It Steps To Accountability.* While the feedback and perceptions of other people had made him uncomfortable and equally difficult to acknowledge, he took solace from the fact that although he had helped create this situation, he really could change how people felt about him and what he had to offer. All that awaited him now was to *Do It!,* the fourth and final step to accountability. Aware of the big difference between knowing what to do and actually doing it, he steeled his will to accept the risks involved in taking action.

And act he did. Having moved fully *Above The Line,* Terry took decisive steps to alter the way people viewed him. He grew along the way. By taking an accountable look at his experience, he was able to overcome the forces that might otherwise have dragged him *Below The Line* where he could keep feeling like a victim of his circumstances. Over time, Terry brought his new product knowledge and innovative ideas into proper focus and became an integral part of the larger team. Eventually he became director of development, a job he loves. These days he spends many an hour coaching new employees to *See It, Own It, Solve It,* and, most vitally, *Do It!*

PREPARING TO APPLY ACCOUNTABILITY THROUGHOUT YOUR ORGANIZATION

In the end, Dorothy exercised the means to *Do It.* Only when she recognized and utilized the skills she possessed all along could she cement her own accountability for her circumstances and for the result she wanted. With newfound determination, she finally clicked her heels and returned to Kansas. While Dorothy had worn the magic slippers throughout her journey, she had not tapped their power until she had learned *The Oz Principle:* People hold inside themselves the power to rise above their circumstances and get the results they want.

Accountable people have grasped this principle for centuries. For instance, the Bible stated over two thousand years ago in Ezra 10:4: "Arise, for this matter belongeth unto thee . . . be of good courage, and do it!"

W. E. Henley, the English poet, characterized it another way. During one of the most trying periods of his life, having lost his left leg to tuberculosis of the bone and now fighting to save his right leg at the Royal Infirmary, he composed what has become one of his most famous poems, "Invictus":

Out of the night that covers me,
Black as the Pit, from pole to pole,
I thank whatever gods may be
For my unconquerable soul.

In the fell clutch of circumstance
I have not winced nor cried aloud.
Under the bludgeonings of chance
My head is bloody, but unbowed.

Beyond this place of wrath and tears
Looms the horror of the shade,
And yet the menace of the years
Finds, and shall find me, unafraid.

It matters not how strait the gate,
How charged with punishments the scroll,
I am the master of my fate:
I am the captain of my soul.

Back home in Kansas, Dorothy would never be the same because she had learned, through her arduous journey, that she was the master of her own fate. Breathlessly, she told her family and friends about the marvelous things she had experienced and learned in the land of Oz, a sharing you can now commence yourself as you apply *The Oz Principle* throughout your organization, the subject of Part Three.

Part 3

Results Through Collective Accountability: Helping Your Organization Perform *Above The Line*®

*Getting your entire organization **Above The Line** requires every employee to accept both individual and joint accountability for results. The process of doing so demands effective **Above The Line** leadership. In Part Three, we draw upon a decade of experience working with **The Oz Principle** to show you how to incorporate it into your own leadership, install it in your own organization, and apply it to today's toughest business and management issues. In the end, we think you'll agree with us: Accountability for results rests at the core of every business success.*

Chapter 8

THE GOOD WITCH GLINDA: MASTERING *ABOVE THE LINE*® LEADERSHIP

Dorothy then gave her the Golden Cap, and the Witch said to the Scarecrow, "What will you do when Dorothy has left us?"

"I will return to the Emerald City," he replied, "for Oz has made me its ruler and the people like me. The only thing that worries me is how to cross the hill of the Hammer-Heads."

"By means of the Golden Cap I shall command the Winged Monkeys to carry you to the gates of the Emerald City," said Glinda, "for it would be a shame to deprive the people of so wonderful a ruler."

"Am I really wonderful?" asked the Scarecrow.

"You are unusual," replied Glinda.

—*The Wizard of Oz,*
L. Frank Baum

Once the four characters from Oz completed their journey *Above The Line*, they finally found the strength, wisdom, courage, and heart to help others get there as well. In their case, the good witch Glinda mentored the traveling companions, watching over them and helping them get on the right road to personal ownership, accountability, and results. Like any good leader, she did not do all the work. Rather, she pointed the group in the right direction and coached them along the way. With the right intervention at the right time, she stimulated the travelers to tap their resourcefulness, heart, courage, and wisdom that eventually propelled them safely to the land of Oz, and ultimately, home.

LEADING *ABOVE THE LINE*®

So far we've described how you can personally get *Above The Line*. Now, we'd like to discuss how you can help others discover the secret of *The Oz Principle*, move themselves *Above The Line*, and get the results they want. *Above The Line* leaders display a number of personal characteristics: While they may themselves fall *Below The Line* on occasion, they don't stay there for long; they actively seek and provide feedback; they hold themselves to the same accountability standard as everyone else; and they desire to help others follow their lead.

Organizations today demand the best from their leaders. You can't just hit the numbers anymore. You must do it ethically, honestly, and in a manner that proves your concern for everyone around you. In a survey of 726 corporate directors conducted by Korn-Ferry, the international executive recruiting and organizational consulting firm, respondents indicated they would be more likely to remove a chief executive officer for leadership flaws than for poor financial returns. This increasing emphasis on effective leadership at the top has been reinforced by the power shift taking place in most organizations in which senior executives seek to spread decision-making authority more widely to the lowest levels of the enterprise. As a result, *Above The Line* leadership will increasingly become a requirement, not merely an advantage, for most organizations.

In this chapter we want to share with you the experience we have gained over the last decade helping people become effective *Above The Line* leaders. First, of course, you must feel motivated to become such a leader. Assuming you have experienced the power and freedom that comes from rising *Above The*

Line, you must now decide whether or not you genuinely want to help others accomplish the same. If you want to browbeat them with your new-found knowledge, compete against them with your superior accountability, control them for your own personal gain, or ridicule their *Below The Line* behavior, then this chapter will not interest you. If, on the other hand, you want to help others escape their *Below The Line* patterns of behavior, then you can gain great benefits from it.

RECOGNIZING WHEN IT'S TIME TO INTERVENE

First and foremost, *Above The Line* leaders recognize when other people get stuck *Below The Line,* failing to obtain the results they want. By this point you should have developed an increased ability to identify *Below The Line* attitudes and behavior in yourself and others, and you should have come to appreciate how people can concoct elaborate explanations for everything that happens. Such victim stories, which can be quite convincing, make it difficult to discern the right time for intervention.

Media mogul Rupert Murdoch has long been praised, criticized, lampooned, and emulated for his unorthodox business strategies and practices. Worth over $7 billion himself, he has shaped his company News Corp into the most admired, most stable, and most profitable media giant on the planet. How does he do it? For one thing, he never accepts victim stories. *Fortune* magazine describes him as the media titan who "built his global empire of TV networks, newspapers, magazines, books, and movies by defying convention and taking risks. He gained a reputation as a gambler whose next move could never be anticipated, a pirate who played by his own rules, and an owner who cared little about short-term results." In reality, it appears that Murdoch has simply learned the art of *Above The Line* leadership, seizing opportunities and getting results no matter what the circumstances. When a situation demands a conservative and cautious approach, he chooses that option. When it requires aggressive risk-taking, he does that. As a leader, Murdoch never lets himself or his management team stay *Below The Line* for long. He recently referred to himself as a CEO who runs "a very conservative ship at the moment . . . keeping our heads down, running the businesses." But now he's beginning to take bold action again because he sees a shift in the balance of power taking place in the industry, away from programmers and toward gatekeepers such as Comcast and Time Warner (assuming they can avoid bankruptcy). That's why Murdoch wants to acquire a satellite platform such as DIRECTV or EchoStar. According to *Fortune,* "with a satellite platform, Murdoch would have a weapon to protect his prized array of fast-growing cable networks, which include Fox News, Fox Sports, National Geographic, and the Speed Channel, which carries motor sports. . . . The way the game is played, big cable operators won't give News Corp too tough a time about carrying its networks if they know that Murdoch controls distribution they want for their own programming services." Clearly, Rupert Murdoch never stops asking, "What else can we do to get the results we want?" No other questions will more consistently keep an organization *Above The Line.*

Above The Line leaders risk their own comfort and security by going beyond symptoms to the core problems that spring from a lack of accountability. When they see *Below The Line* behavior, they rip away the disguises worn by self-proclaimed victims to reveal the underlying reality. Unwilling to let themselves or others be fooled by the masks people fashion to hide the reality of a situation, they drive relentlessly to determine the real reasons why people aren't achieving results. Not even the most elaborate and creative victim stories fool them into thinking that if someone else would just do the right thing, all would be well in the world. They understand that symptomatic cures continue to hide and even exacerbate the problem, not *Solve It.* They do not fall prey to the excessive activity syndromes; they blow away the smoke screen of programmatic solutions offered by organizational special interest groups, desiring to mask their lack of results; they dismiss the chorus of voices trying to convince them that "if only we did this or that," everything would be fine. They understand that changes in structures and systems often only bury the real problems, problems they relentlessly work to uncover and solve.

When *Above The Line* leaders hear about a particular problem such as a lack of product quality, they don't bemoan that fact, but immediately try to figure out exactly how people at all levels of the organization, including themselves, have failed to shoulder responsibility for the quality of their own individual contributions. Such leaders know that whenever results fail to materialize, they must sweep away the curtain of excuses and finger pointing to reveal the real reason why people are operating *Below The Line.* When they detect *Below The Line* behavior, they begin coaching people out of the victim cycle, a process we will explore later in this chapter. By recognizing when it's time to intervene and helping others to rise above the victim cycle, *Above The Line* leaders can help people focus on the right issues in the right way. Then, and only then, can the group and the organization begin creating a better future.

LEARNING NOT TO TAKE ACCOUNTABILITY TO THE EXTREME

A word of caution: Like anything else in life, you can take your desire to seek out *Below The Line* behavior too far, turning an asset into a liability. Any virtue or strength taken to an extreme can eventually become a vice that actually gets in the way of achieving the performance and results you desire. One leader likened such an over-preoccupation to persistently pounding on a single piano key to the irritation and dismay of everyone present. In such a situation, the leader's effectiveness diminishes, and he or she loses the benefit and strength that comes from calling upon a broad range of resources, skills, and solutions. If you define everything that happens as an accountability problem, you may fail to see the complete picture. However, if you fail to discern the accountability factor in every problem, you will also make a mistake. Skillful intervention requires a delicate, yet decided, touch.

Over the years we have watched people take accountability to an extreme as they tried to force people to accept accountability for anything and everything that occurs in their lives. This may sound outlandish, but such extremists go so far as to argue that if a pedestrian walking down the sidewalk gets killed by a runaway car, the pedestrian can only blame herself because she chose to walk down that street at that particular time, instead of taking an alternate route. That's ridiculous! Nevertheless, we could argue that the pedestrian or the pedestrian's survivors will not get their lives back unless they accept responsibility for moving beyond the accident to a better future.

Additionally, some people go so far as to blame a person's illness on a lack of accountability when it comes to working out the emotional issues and stresses of life. While a certain level of physical illness may result from pent-up anxieties or unresolved issues, you make a big and potentially harmful mistake if you believe that all illness, tragedy, misfortune, and calamity occur as a result of something a person did or did not do. *The Oz Principle* teaches that people's circumstances result not just from what they do or did (although a person should always identify how his or her action or inaction has contributed to current circumstances) but also from variables they clearly can't control. Rather than continuing to suffer as victims of circumstance, people who practice *The Oz Principle* know how to overcome such circumstances and achieve the results they desire. Even in the most extreme cases, where people have been severely victimized, such individuals can take accountability for how they allow a traumatic experience to affect the rest of their lives.

People can also take accountability to the extreme by trying to control other people. Operating like self-appointed "thought police," controllers try to force others *Above The Line* into a world they themselves have created to suit their own beliefs and prejudices. A memorable *Time* magazine cover story labeled such overzealous extremists as *busybodies.* No one can or should try to force another person to be more effective, more righteous, more knowledgeable, more productive, friendlier, braver, more trustworthy, or in any other way more politically or socially correct. Coach them, encourage them, teach them, give them feedback, admonish them, love them, and lead them, but don't try to coerce them. In *Time*'s article, author John Elson tells the story of a Los Angeles security guard who was fired for being overweight: "Jesse Mercado was dismissed from his job as a security guard at the *Los Angeles Times* despite an excellent performance record." No one should be removed from or refused a job because they violate some whimsical, unprincipled standard of correctness. In Mercado's case, the courts upheld that view: "Overweight Mercado sued, won and got a judgment of more than $500,000, plus a return to his old post."

RECOGNIZING THAT YOU CANNOT CONTROL EVERYTHING

Wise *Above The Line* leaders apply a delicate touch in those situations where things lie completely or partially beyond their control, both in life and at work. Such situations occur all the time, caused by such events as severe weather, natural disasters, other people's choices, fluctuations in the global economy, physical limitations, a competitor's moves, accidents, and government intervention. And, of course, no one can control such functions as family, birth circumstances, inherited traits, and physical makeup. However, too many leaders today do worry about things over which they can exercise little control as discussed in a *Wall Street Journal* survey of chief executive officers, who revealed what keeps them up at night. The top five vote-getters in the "worry" survey received more than 50 percent of the votes: employees, the economy, competition, the political environment, and government regulation.

Wise leaders will separate those factors that remain beyond their control from those they can do something about. For example, since you cannot control nationwide economic conditions, why devote a lot of time to complaining about the economy? That will only squander your time and effort. Instead, you might spend your time developing strategies for addressing a variety of economic scenarios, an investment that might pay off handsomely.

Try to identify all the uncontrollable issues you face, separating them from the controllable ones. This way, you can avoid falling *Below The Line,* complaining or worrying about what you cannot affect. The separation also helps you resist trying to rise too zealously *Above The Line* in an attempt to refashion everything and everyone to your own liking.

Write down in the space below a few of the uncontrollables that currently receive too much of your attention at work or at home. Try to confine your list to characteristics, traits, situations, and events that are largely uncontrollable. Indicate the degree of control you have over the item listed by assigning to each item a 0 (no control), + (little to no influence), or ++ (some control). Creating such a list will help you isolate those aspects of your work and personal life that you can tackle effectively. As you ponder your list, consider how much time and energy you might save if you stopped getting stuck *Below The Line* worrying about what you cannot change.

My Uncontrollables

Uncontrollable	Degree of Control

At one of our *Accountability Training* workshops a woman told the group about her experience as a young girl listening to her father recount his workday at the dinner table. With great emotion, her father would often describe all the day's ills with particular emphasis on the "miscarriages of justice" that had been wrought against him. While the family ate, he bombarded his wife and children with tales of his boss treating him unfairly. His boss was always coming off as a completely unappreciative, unfeeling, and unrighteous man. As dessert arrived, everyone tried to make the father feel better by confirming his perceptions and agreeing that he had been dealt a bad hand. These expressions of sympathy and support helped the family progress to other nightly activities. Looking back, the woman realized that her mother and the rest of the family had not done her father any great favor by accepting his *Below The Line* complaints. Nor had they done themselves any favors. Her father's unhappiness and the resultant disruption in the family reinforced the notion that you can't alter what happens in life. You can only complain about it. Ironically, many studies have indicated that people cannot control over 90 percent of the things they worry about. That's a lot of misplaced worry! Imagine what additional good might have come into the life of the woman in our training session had her family's dinner discussions focused on what family members, including the father, could do to overcome whatever bad things happened to them.

Correctly understood and properly applied, accountability empowers people with a new sense of control and influence over their circumstances so they can achieve the results they desire. Basically, helping people get *Above The Line* involves assisting them to *See It, Own It, Solve It,* and *Do It,* in spite of all the variables in life they can't control.

PROVIDING A MODEL FOR OTHERS

If you hope to create accountability in your own organization, you must also provide a model others can emulate. You yourself must remain accountable for the consequences that flow from all your decisions and actions. If you offer a negative model, you will more than likely take not only yourself, but the entire organization *Below The Line.* For example, in a *Wall Street Journal* article entitled, "Bosses Who Deflect Blame Put Employees in a Tough Spot," Joann Lublin discusses one such negative role model: a boss who blames his or her personal blunders on subordinates. Lublin states, "Of all problem bosses, a 'blamer' is among the toughest to handle. Limiting damage from misplaced blame re-quires delicate judgments, sharp bureaucratic instincts and varying levels of risk tolerance. It's no wonder that many people end up doing nothing more than grinding their teeth." We have worked with thousands of individuals who would rate a boss who deflects blame as the worst boss in the world.

Bosses who lead from *Below The Line* may enjoy some short-term gains, but in the long run, their behavior will only destroy the trust, cooperation, and focus needed to maximize results. Such a model of leadership will ultimately give people permission to fall into a deliberate cover-your-tail mode. As Lublin observes, "A paper trail also can vindicate an unfairly accused subordinate, es-pecially if the mistake comes up later during a performance appraisal. Dr. Grothe, the Boston psychologist, proposes that you give yourself an account of an incident and verify its date by sending yourself a certified letter and keeping the envelope sealed. 'It's a little form of self-protection,' he says." What a waste of time, resources, and energy! How much better it would be for all concerned if the boss, first and foremost, put a stop to the blame game and concentrated instead on correcting the mistake or its consequences.

Successful *Above The Line* leaders model accountability for everyone within their sphere of influence, remaining accountable for everything they say and do that shapes the model. If a leader knows when to intervene and when to hold back, he or she will avoid particularly ugly situations in which others chafe under the leader's incessant follow-up on their activities in a misguided effort to make sure they are honoring their commitment to accountability. In such cases, the leader has forgotten to adhere to a well-tempered model of account-ability. Such behavior will often undermine people's confidence and sometimes even infuriate them. Again, good leadership demands a decided, yet delicate, touch.

Of all the books written about Jack Welch, including *Jack,* Welch's own au-tobiographical account of his tenure as CEO of General Electric, we found Noel Tichy and Stratford Sherman's *Control Your Destiny or Someone Else Will* the most enlightening. This book reveals how Jack Welch really transformed Gen-eral Electric. It struck a chord with us because its core message promoted ac-countability: "The remarkable story of GE's transformation teaches lessons essential for the well-being of managers and layperson alike. Control your des-tiny is more than a useful business idea. For every individual, corporation, and nation, it is the essence of responsibility and the most basic requirement for success. As the world endlessly changes, so must we. The greatest power we have is the ability to envision our own fate—and to change ourselves." That's *Above The Line* leadership. Welch set empowering his people as his overriding goal with the values of "self-confidence, candor, and an unflinching willingness to face reality, even when it's painful." Was it a cake walk? Not at all.

Here's how he himself described the difficulties: "I've made my share of mistakes—plenty of them—but my biggest mistake by far was not moving faster. Pulling off an old Band-Aid one hair at a time hurts a lot more than a sudden yank. Of course you want to avoid breaking things or stretching the organization too far—but generally, human nature holds you back. You want to be liked, to be thought of as reasonable. So you don't move as fast as you should. Besides hurting more, it costs you competitiveness."

He goes on to admit that he could have done most everything in half the time. "When you're running an institution like this you're always scared at first. You're afraid you'll break it. People don't think about leaders this way, but it's true. Everyone who's running something goes home at night and wrestles with the same fear: Am I going to be the one who blows this place up? In retrospect, I was too cautious and too timid."

Effective leaders like the legendary Jack Welch strive to keep themselves and their organizations climbing the *Steps To Accountability,* applying a delicate, and yet determined, touch whenever they or others momentarily fall *Below The Line.* The following list identifies ways in which you can apply the right touch in your organization:

- Constantly ask yourself the question, "What else can I do?" to achieve the result you desire.
- Always urge your people to ask the same question, "What else can I do?"
- Invite people to give you feedback on whether or not they perceive you operating *Above The Line* on a particular issue.
- Provide honest, yet encouraging, feedback to others when they drop *Below The Line.*
- Actively observe activities and offer coaching, rather than wait for others to report on their progress on any given project or assignment. Never delay reporting progress to your own superiors.

• Focus your discussions on things that you and others can control and do rather than on the uncontrollables. Acknowledge when you fall *Below The Line* and do not react defensively when others give you feedback.

Once you master these traits and personally exhibit and model *Above The Line* behavior yourself, you can begin successfully coaching others to do likewise.

COACHING PEOPLE *ABOVE THE LINE*®

The process of inspiring accountability in others takes time. It doesn't happen as a result of some singular event. Many leaders mistakenly think that once they have exposed their people to the concept of accountability and gotten them to understand it, no one will ever fall *Below The Line* again. This event approach to accountability, the notion that accountability happens at an identifiable moment, makes no sense to us.

Leaders who make this mistake often use accountability as a hammer, nailing people when they fall *Below The Line* in an unending game of "I gotcha." Such hammering will only propel people back into the victim cycle. Therefore, you must help people feel empowered by the concept of accountability, not trapped by it. While you don't want to let victim stories and behaviors go unchecked, you must bear in mind that the process of coaching people *Above The Line* requires patience, nurturing, and appropriate follow-up. Remember that the people you want to help climb the *Steps To Accountability* have developed ingrained perspectives and personalities they cannot quickly discard or consider from a new viewpoint, especially if they feel cornered by an ever-vigilant "Big Brother." Too heavy a hand tends to make people feel excluded from the process ("I'm right, you're wrong"), while a firm, delicate touch helps people feel included in the process ("We've got a problem, let's figure out how to *Solve It*").

A friend of ours, Jim, recently told us how betrayed he felt over a particular experience earlier in his career. Working as an accountant in a well-known regional accounting firm in Boston, he began looking, as so often happens in successful accounting firms, for opportunities to move over to the controllership of one of his firm's client organizations. Before long, an opportunity for just such a career move arose with a company he greatly respected. Eagerly, he started the interviewing process with the chief financial officer who was leaving the company, and then he continued interviewing with the new CFO, who would be joining the company from the outside in a few months. The interviews went well and Jim landed the job. Excited about his new responsibilities as controller of a $35 million company, he relished the initial autonomy he enjoyed. He was actually running the financial side of the house by himself while he awaited the arrival of the new CFO. Jim felt good about his future. The sky was the limit.

As Jim dug into his new job by thoroughly reviewing the company's financial statements, he discovered that a great deal of work lay ahead, especially with all the poorly organized financial statements he had found. When he approached Bob, the outgoing CFO, with a few questions concerning the statements, Bob dismissed his concerns with the wave of his hand, saying Jim's questions could wait until next week. "Hey, this is no big problem," he said. "Take some time to get into the swing of things."

The next Monday, Bob met with Jim again, quickly reviewing the company's books and asking Jim to sign his final check. Since the check only amounted to a few thousand dollars, and given his tenure as CFO, Jim didn't think twice about signing the check and wishing Bob well. To his alarm, as he dug further into the records over the next week, he found that Bob had persuaded three other people to sign his "last" paycheck. With continued scrutiny of the books over the next couple of months, Jim uncovered evidence that Bob had embezzled over $1 million through phony purchase requisitions.

As he gathered evidence of the former CFO's wrongdoing, Jim shared it with the new CFO, Steve, who had begun coming into the office one day a week while wrapping up his job with his former employer. Steve asked him to keep the situation to himself, and not even share it with the president of the company, until they had constructed an airtight case. Jim worked many fourteen-hour days and weekends trying to unravel the scheme and amass the necessary evidence against the former CFO and his collaborators.

When the president of the company stopped by one morning to speak with Jim, he casually mentioned that he suspected his former CFO of embezzlement but still couldn't believe the man could have actually done it. To Jim's utter disbelief, the president praised Steve, the new CFO, for uncovering the mess, and wondered why Jim had not seen it himself. Pointing an accusing finger at his new controller, he said, "You have been here three months, Jim. Why in the world didn't you find any of this?" Shocked by the revelation that Steve had taken credit for all his hard work, he vowed he would never trust another superior.

Does Jim's story sound familiar? Many people in organizations have found themselves victimized by someone in authority over them. As an *Above The Line* leader, you cannot assume that the people over whom you exercise responsibility will automatically trust your coaching efforts to get them *Above The Line.* Instead, your people may suspect you of harboring ulterior motives, particularly if you have participated with them in preparing victim stories in the past or if you have not previously established feedback as a pattern of communication in your relationship with them. Keep this in mind the next time you attempt to coach someone *Above The Line.*

Whenever you hear a victim story or a *Below The Line* excuse, try using the following five steps to coach that person away from reacting and toward learning:

1. Listen. Remain alert for instances of victim behavior, and when you engage someone in a discussion of their victim story (for the purpose of coaching them) or hear *Below The Line* excuses, listen sympathetically to what they have to say.

2. Acknowledge. Accept the victim facts and genuine obstacles that someone thinks have kept them from getting desired results. Show the person that you understand his feelings and know yourself how hard it is to overcome them. Agree that the challenges are real or that bad things do happen to good people.

3. Ask. If someone seems deeply attached to a victim story or a *Below The Line* excuse, gently edge the discussion toward the accountable version of the story. Continually pose the question: "What else can you do to achieve the result you desire or overcome the circumstance that plagues you?"

4. Coach. Use the *Steps To Accountability* to help a person identify where she currently stands and where that person needs to go to obtain desired results. Take a few minutes to explain *The Oz Principle* using this specific instance as an example, but also share an incident when you yourself got stuck *Below*

The Line. Emphasize that it's only natural to fall *Below The Line* on occasion, but staying there never yields results. Stress how rising *Above The Line* will produce positive outcomes. Walk through the *See It, Own It, Solve It,* and *Do It* steps. Then adapt each of the *Steps To Accountability* to this particular situation.

5. Commit. Dedicate yourself to helping a person create an *Above The Line* action plan and encourage him to report on his activities and progress. Don't end a coaching session without setting a specific time for follow-up, allowing sufficient time, but not too much time, to elapse. If the person does not approach you at the appointed time, take the initiative yourself. During these follow-up sessions, continue to look, listen, acknowledge, ask, coach, and recommit. Provide honest, caring feedback about progress, and express congratulations for every improvement.

Once you begin coaching others *Above The Line* you will quickly see the value of a person's accounting for her progress.

ACCOUNTING FOR PROGRESS

In an ideal world, it wouldn't be necessary for leaders to coach accountability because everyone would acknowledge his accountability in every situation. However, since this is not an ideal world, and since everyone is fallible, leaders must make coaching a daily habit. And while we have emphasized proactive coaching, which focuses on the present and the future, we have also come to appreciate the need to review the past, which we call *accounting for progress.* When handled properly, an after-the-fact accounting can provide a person with an opportunity to measure progress toward results, learn from previous experience, establish a sense of accomplishment, and determine what else she can do to get the desired results.

While most leaders intuitively know the value of urging people to account for their actions, many often fail to do it well. Too many leaders:

• Wait for their people to do the right thing. Rather than asking for regular reports, they let them go, hoping that people will automatically measure their own progress.

- Avoid unpleasant confrontation that might possibly result from an unacceptable report. They may fear that such a confrontation will damage their relationships with people.
- Allow skeletons to remain in the closet, rather than dragging them out and squarely facing troublesome issues that have gotten in the way of results. They assume that people simply cannot surmount some issues and therefore choose to ignore them.
- Tolerate excuses as true representations of reality when they know in their hearts that those excuses prevent people from accepting the true reality of a situation. They allow this to happen in the hope that the problem will simply fix itself over time.
- Let their other responsibilities consume all their time. They don't make regular accounting a top priority. They simply wait for the results to speak for themselves.
- Fail to convince people of the importance of reporting on progress. Their own low priority becomes their people's low priority.
- Insufficiently clarify their expectations or inadequately explain the purpose of accounting. They accept vague reports because they have set vague goals.
- Do not set a specific reporting timetable or schedule. They let people decide when and how they will account for progress.
- Fail to use accounting sessions to coach individuals toward desired outcomes. They simply applaud or criticize progress.
- Do not understand that holding people accountable need not be a negative, hand-wringing, knuckle-crunching, head-bashing, life-threatening experience for those involved. They make sessions so painful that people come to dread them.

If you can overcome these common mistakes, you will obtain the tremendous benefits of giving people the opportunity to account for their progress, which includes pinpointing what else people can do to achieve desired results, disseminating vital information people can use to break down barriers to results, identifying legitimate needs for the organization, and helping people look forward to their accounting sessions as a positive personal and organizational experience.

Above The Line leaders both give and require *Above The Line* accounting.

Note the differences between effective accounting and accounting that falls *Below The Line:*

From *Below The Line* People:
• report only when asked to do so.
• justify or explain their activities.
• run and hide when it's time to report.
• blame others for lack of results.
• react defensively to suggestions for improvement.

From *Above the Line* People:
• report regularly and thoroughly.
• analyze their activities in an effort to determine what more they can do to get results.
• stand and deliver when it's time to report.
• own their circumstances.
• welcome feedback.

If you account for progress from *Below The Line,* you give permission for everyone else in the organization to do likewise, but if you invariably account for your own progress from *Above The Line,* the organization will follow suit.

ABOVE THE LINE
LEADERSHIP CHECKLIST

1. *I Do* model accountability and set an example.

   I Don't hold others accountable without holding myself equally responsible.

2. *I Do* allow people to drop *Below The Line* from time to time to vent their frustrations.

   I Don't let victim stories and *Below The Line* excuses go unchecked or unresolved.

3. *I Do* recognize victim stories and *Below The Line* excuses when I hear them.

   I Don't avoid my responsibility to hold people accountable and to expect *Above The Line* behavior.

4. *I Do* use accountability as a way to empower people toward results.

   I Don't use accountability as a hammer to nail people when I catch them functioning *Below The Line.*

5. *I Do* expect people to coach me to get *Above The Line* when necessary.

   I Don't expect people to coach me if I am not seeking their feedback.

6. *I Do* practice what I preach.

   I Don't get caught thinking that accountability is something everyone else should work on.

7. *I Do* avoid focusing solely on accountability to the exclusion of everything else.

   I Don't hold everyone accountable for everything all the time—I do understand the uncontrollables.

8. *I Do* coach people *Above The Line* by listening, acknowledging, asking, coaching, and committing.

   I Don't view accountability as a principle that people ought to comprehend immediately.

LEADING FROM *ABOVE THE LINE*®

To help our clients master the art of accountable leadership, we have constructed the above checklist that covers the most important "do's" and "don't's" of *Above The Line* leadership behavior. Reviewing this list periodically should help you maintain a good model for your people.

With effective *Above The Line* leadership skills you can begin moving your entire organization to higher levels of accountability. Before you move on, however, take a moment to consider how long Dorothy and her companions took to come to the realization that they possessed the power within themselves to accomplish what they wanted. Glinda wisely provided the right kind of coaching and assistance throughout the journey. As an *Above The Line* leader, you should apply your leadership in ways that will help people and groups in your organization make progress. Serving as a model, recognizing when to intervene and when to step back, focusing on the controllables, coaching people *Above The Line*, and accounting for progress make anyone a better *Above The Line* leader.

Chapter 9

THE EMERALD CITY AND BEYOND: GETTING YOUR ENTIRE ORGANIZATION *ABOVE THE LINE*®

Turning to the Tin Woodsman, she [Glinda] asked: "What will become of you when Dorothy leaves this country?"

He leaned on his axe and thought a moment. Then he said, "The Winkies were very kind to me, and wanted me to rule over them after the Wicked Witch died. I am fond of the Winkies, and if I could get back again to the country of the West I should like nothing better than to rule over them forever."

"My second command to the Winged Monkeys," said Glinda, "will be that they carry you safely to the land of the Winkies . . . and I am sure you will rule the Winkies wisely and well."

—*The Wizard of Oz,*
L. Frank Baum

The Tin Woodsman chose to share his newfound power with others. Such a choice represents the ultimate application of accountability, helping others in your organization move *Above The Line*. Regardless of your current position in your organization, you can begin to promote *The Oz Principle* by encouraging people to climb out of the victim cycle and ascend the *Steps To Accountability*. The entire organization can benefit from what you've learned: your superiors, your subordinates, your peers, and all the stakeholders both inside and outside your organization.

In this chapter, we summarize five of the key activities that will substantially improve an organization's ability to create and sustain a culture of accountability. With these activities, you can build accountability into the very fabric of your organization:

1. Training everyone, at every level
2. Coaching accountability
3. Asking *Above The Line* questions
4. Rewarding accountability
5. Holding people accountable

These activities serve as the underpinnings to any successful organizational effort to create a culture of accountability. Throughout this chapter we will review some of the best practices that people have put into practice over the last decade that will accelerate your transition *Above The Line*.

TRAINING EVERYONE AT EVERY LEVEL

The first crucial challenge to creating greater accountability is training everyone from the boardroom to the mailroom to understand the crucial relationship between accountability and results. Quite likely, not everyone in your organization consciously appreciates that connection. However, once they do, they will much less often fall *Below The Line* into the victim cycle. To accomplish this shift in people's perspective, your training efforts must include three essential steps: Help people recognize *Below The Line* viewpoints; assist them in transitioning to a new view of accountability; and work to lock in the new *Above The Line* perspectives.

STEP ONE. UNDERSTANDING ACCOUNTABILITY
IN YOUR ORGANIZATION

Before you can implement an accountability program in your organization, you must determine how people currently define and practice accountability. You should acknowledge that people view accountability in different ways, and often not in the most helpful, positive ways. Some people fear it, hide from it, or think it applies to everyone but themselves. Whenever you hear someone ask the question, "Who's accountable for this?" that's usually a clue that someone has slipped *Below The Line.* Consider the results of an informal survey we conducted to find out how people define accountability:

"Accountability is something that happens to you when things go wrong!"

"Accountability is paying the piper."

"Accountability is reporting."

"Accountability is an explanation as to why you did what you did."

"Accountability is something management does to you: It's external, not internal."

"Accountability means reporting on actions, not results."

"Accountability is a negative concept to me."

"Accountability is burdensome."

"Accountability is a tool that management uses to pressure people to perform."

"Accountability is another word for punishing people for poor performance."

"Accountability is something that is put on you by your boss. It causes unnecessary pressure, fear, regret, guilt, and resentment."

"Accountability is something that nobody does around here."

From such descriptions, you might conclude that accountability is a disease to be avoided at all costs. Obviously, such a negative view of accountability, as something bad that happens to people when things go wrong, can do little to motivate people toward results. When such a view pervades an organization, creating greater accountability must begin at square one: becoming aware of their divergent, and often negative, views of what accountability is and showing them how much time and energy they waste operating *Below The Line.* The following Organizational Accountability Assessment can help you determine the current state of accountability within your organization. We suggest you quickly assess yourself before you evaluate your team or organization.

Recognizing *Below The Line* viewpoints requires an awareness of what accountability really means and a recognition of the extent to which people throughout your organization operate *Below The Line.* Only by achieving this awareness can you expect to abolish negative views of accountability. Since even the most accountable organizational culture can fall *Below The Line* from time to time, everyone must remain keenly alert for the appearance of any *Below The Line* behaviors and attitudes.

STEP TWO. INTRODUCING A NEW VIEW OF ACCOUNTABILITY

It can take time for people to change their perspectives and adopt new attitudes and behavior. Embracing a new view of accountability within the organization sets the stage for moving the entire organization *Above The Line.* Only when everyone embraces the same positive perspective of accountability can the entire organization maximize its effectiveness at getting results. Having achieved awareness and recognition in step one, you can begin building *Above The Line* attitudes that will improve performance throughout the entire organization. Without this consensus of perspective, however, *Below The Line* attitudes and behaviors will continue to form a resistive force to greater accountability and results.

Elements of the new view of accountability include:

- Understanding the victim cycle and its damaging effects
- Recognizing when they have fallen *Below The Line*
- Acknowledging when they have become trapped in the victim cycle
- Accepting *The Oz Principle's* definition of accountability and the need to climb the *Steps To Accountability*
- Tying increased accountability to achieving organization results
- Knowing what it means to *See It, Own It, Solve It,* and *Do It*
- Understanding what it means to work *Above The Line*
- Accepting accountability for results as an organizational expectation

ORGANIZATIONAL ACCOUNTABILITY
Assessment

Circle the response that best describes your situation.

ONE	Do you ever see people blaming others for what goes wrong in your organization?	Never	Seldom	Sometimes	Often	Always
TWO	Do you feel that people do not accept responsibility for what they do or how they do it?	Never	Seldom	Sometimes	Often	Always
THREE	Do you see people failing to take the initiative to report on their activities and their progress toward results?	Never	Seldom	Sometimes	Often	Always
FOUR	Do people fail to "dive for the ball" when it gets dropped?	Never	Seldom	Sometimes	Often	Always
FIVE	Do people "wait and see" if things will get better when serious problems engulf your organization?	Never	Seldom	Sometimes	Often	Always
SIX	Do you hear people saying they feel a situation is out of control and that they can do nothing to resolve it?	Never	Seldom	Sometimes	Often	Always
SEVEN	Do people spend their time "covering their tails" just in case things go wrong?	Never	Seldom	Sometimes	Often	Always
EIGHT	Do people seem to feel more responsible for their activity and effort than they do for their results?	Never	Seldom	Sometimes	Often	Always
NINE	Do you hear people say, "It's not my job or my department" and act as if they expect someone else to solve the problem?	Never	Seldom	Sometimes	Often	Always
TEN	Do you feel that people display a low level of personal ownership and involvement when problems arise?	Never	Seldom	Sometimes	Often	Always

Award the following points for each response: All the time—5, Often—4, Sometimes—3, Seldom—2, Never—1. Then total up your score and evaluate your organization using the scoring table that follows.

ORGANIZATIONAL ACCOUNTABILITY Assessment Scoring	
TOTAL SCORE	**EVALUATION GUIDELINES**
40 to 50 points	Your organizational culture operates *Below The Line*. It has adopted a self-reinforcing pattern that has become the way the organization does business. Altering this pattern will take a deliberate and conscious effort.
30 to 39 points	Your organization spends enough time *Below The Line* that it continues to compromise organizational results and personal fulfillment. Although a glimmer of understanding exists, it will take a focused effort to shift to a more positive pattern.
11 to 29 points	Your organizational culture typically operates *Above The Line*. Additional gains in productivity will come as you work to inculcate a positive definition of accountability throughout the organization.
0 to 10 points	Having mastered the art of living *Above The Line*, your organizational culture should continue to achieve outstanding results as long as people remain alert for occasional dips *Below The Line*.

Training everyone at every level of the organization to understand accountability will create the critical mass and necessary momentum to influence organizational results in a major way. It requires more than lip service and an intellectual acceptance; it also demands deep emotional and psychological commitment. If you doubt it, recall the last victim story you heard and consider the emotional and mental stress exhibited by the person telling the story. Before anyone can personally transition to a new view of accountability, he must experience, as well as intellectually understand, the difference between *Above The Line* and *Below The Line* behavior and attitudes. Training sessions designed to help people experience, and apply the concept of, accountability, not just learn about it, are extremely helpful. Daily experiences, incorporating the principle of account-ability into actual practice, will always provide the right reinforcement to the training, making implementation and execution a sure bet!

STEP THREE. MAKING THE NEW VIEW OF ACCOUNTABILITY A WAY OF LIFE

To accomplish this step, you must constantly encourage people to make an all-out effort to operate differently, replacing *Below The Line* attitudes with consistent *Above The Line* thinking. Such a commitment tends to come only after deep personal reflection and a lot of thorough feedback. The reflection and feedback should help a person clarify and plan the specific ways in which he or she can think and act differently.

Since feedback, more than anything else, will enable people in your organization to make the necessary commitment to stay *Above The Line,* you must learn to give and receive feedback in a timely and effective manner, a skill we will discuss in the next section on coaching. Before we explore that topic, however, we want to emphasize the importance of using the imagery and language of the victim cycle and the *Steps To Accountability* to enable people to reflect on the distinction between the two.

Most people find it harder to think about philosophical abstractions than about concrete images. Therefore, try using the concrete imagery and language of *The Oz Principle* to help people develop a common frame of reference everyone can easily understand. The mere mention of the phrase *Below The Line* can immediately communicate someone has fallen into the victim cycle, while the phrase *Above The Line* delivers the message that someone wants to focus on results. Terms such as *See It, Own It, Solve It,* and *Do It* quickly point to the attitudes and behaviors that produce results. *Above The Line* can become a rallying catch phrase that signals to everyone involved that it's time to take action and make it happen in spite of unpleasant circumstances.

With the concrete images of *The Oz Principle,* you can help every person in your organization search daily for ways to weave accountable attitudes into the very fabric of your organization's operations: performance appraisals, decision-making patterns, policy formulation, mentoring, verbal and written communications, standard operating procedures, and every other aspect of day-to-day organizational life.

Personal reflection and commitment, giving and receiving feedback, applying the language of accountability, and constantly looking for ways to inject accountability into every nook and cranny of your organization will ensure that people lock in new attitudes, beliefs, and behaviors. When that occurs, your organization will more likely achieve its goals and improve its overall performance.

COACHING ACCOUNTABILITY

In our experience, no organization can consistently function *Above The Line* without constant feedback. Continuous feedback must become a living, breathing part of the accountable organization's culture. Throughout this book we have emphasized the importance of feedback, but now we want to turn your attention to how you can and must incorporate it into an ongoing coaching program.

When you decide to build an organization-wide culture of accountability, you must first create an environment where people on the team agree to provide honest, respectful, and timely feedback to help everyone recognize when they fall *Below The Line* and to help them take steps to assume accountability and quickly get *Above The Line*. The feedback need not be elaborate, but it must be clear, concise, and constructive. Think about the subtle (or not so subtle) difference between accusing someone of descending *Below The Line* and helping them see the value of ascending *Above The Line*.

Take the case of Bill Hansen, a fictional manager who is representative of the typical manager we work with, who had experienced the accountability process and felt inspired to make accountability a core value in his organization. One morning he found himself in a management meeting where one of his peers, a fellow named Stan, was presenting a status report on one of his team's priority projects. As Bill listened, he concluded that Stan had gotten stuck *Below The Line* because many of his statements blamed others for his team's lack of progress on the project.

Bill shifted his attention from Stan's explanations to the others in the room because he wanted to see their reactions to the report. As he watched the audience, he was surprised to see that everyone else was buying Stan's explanations for the team's poor progress. In the past, he realized, he too would probably have accepted Stan's *Below The Line* excuses, but now he found them quite disconcerting. Should he reveal his feelings? If he didn't, would anyone else question Stan's report? But if he did, would the other managers take offense?

Pondering the personal risk associated with speaking up and attempting to pull the group *Above The Line,* Bill felt conflicting emotions: His own sense of accountability urged him to speak, while his sensitivity to the group cautioned him to hold his peace.

Suddenly, he caught himself. "I'm just as far *Below The Line* in my thinking as everyone else in this room. The company desperately needs me to speak up and accept accountability for moving us all *Above The Line.*" At that moment, Bill began considering exactly how to raise the issue. Should he simply tell Stan that he thought Stan was telling a victim story? Perhaps that made sense, but then he remembered the training that had taught him not to use accountability as a hammer. As he continued reflecting on his predicament, he wondered, again, whether anyone would see Stan's report the way he did. If so, a lively and productive discussion might ensue; if not, Bill might more wisely coach Stan away from the eyes and ears of the others in the room.

Just then, another colleague, Julie, raised her hand. "I hear what you're saying, Stan," she said, "and I know this project has been a bearcat, but I can't help wondering what else you and the rest of us can do to make it work." Julie's observations coincided precisely with what Bill had been thinking. He couldn't have put it better himself, and he immediately felt embarrassed for not speaking up earlier. Almost instantly the whole room began buzzing with suggestions. Far from attacking Stan, everyone began lending him a helping hand and offering creative suggestions. To Bill's relief and chagrin, it turned out that most everyone else had seen the same problem he had, but only Julie had mustered the courage to act on her belief.

Before the meeting adjourned, the president of the company singled Julie out for praise: "She's shown the kind of leadership we desperately need in this company."

Bill had learned a valuable lesson and would never hesitate to speak up again. Most people respond well to honest feedback, particularly when it comes from a coach and not an accuser, who offers it within the context of results, and accompanies it with an invitation to provide similarly candid feedback.

As you work on coaching others with prompt and candid feedback, make sure that you apply the *Steps To Accountability* to your own behavior. Good coaches always hold themselves to the same standards they apply to others.

ASKING *ABOVE THE LINE*® QUESTIONS

Throughout this book we have stressed the importance of constantly asking the question, "What else can I do?" Now we'd like to add several more vital questions that any employee, supervisor, manager, president, group, or team can ask themselves while inspiring their organization to greater levels of accountability.

Above The Line questions like these help flesh out the reality of a situation. You may want to refine these questions and add your own within the framework of the *Steps To Accountability,* incorporating our ten and your variations of them into your ongoing efforts to think, behave, and work *Above The Line.*

Use your customized list of *Above The Line* questions to review your progress and to help you break through persistent problems. By asking these questions, both individually and as a team, you will begin to talk yourself *Above The Line.*

Clint Lewis, a district sales manager for Pfizer working at the time in the Brooklyn district, found his team ranked last in the division out of fifty-seven districts. As he met with his sales reps, he heard comments like "I'm doing everything I possibly can" and "There must be something wrong with the numbers." Even Clint grew frustrated by an inability to turn the numbers around. He had picked up a copy of *The Oz Principle* at a local bookstore, and as he read it, he got to thinking, "Only if we can look at ourselves first will we have any chance of turning around these poor sales numbers." The book helped him to realize that by taking accountability for our own success, success will follow. Soon after, Clint began to use the concepts of accountability with his team at meetings and in one-on-one sessions. The team gradually began to change their mind-set and then their approach to the business. "What else can I do?" became their mantra.

A year later the district made marked improvement in their sales numbers and their outlook on the future! Meetings became more positive and the team more optimistic. Each successive year the team's performance dramatically improved, ultimately leading to the district's winning the top award in its division. Over the next several years that followed, the district never finished out of the top ten in the division. During that time, Clint was promoted to regional sales manager and eventually to vice president of sales. What has been even more special for Clint is the fact that many of the original district sales representatives have since been promoted to positions of greater responsibility and lead-

TEN MORE
ABOVE THE LINE QUESTIONS

1. What aspects of this situation will most likely pull us *Below The Line* in the future?

2. What can we control and what can't we control in this situation?

3. Have we fallen *Below The Line*?

4. What are we pretending not to know about our accountability?

5. Which areas of joint accountability may allow us to drop the ball?

6. If we really "owned it," what would we do differently?

7. Given recent decisions, what do we need to do to ensure the organization stays *Above The Line*?

8. Does anyone involved with this situation still fail to "own" the decisions we have already made?

9. Who is accountable for achieving the result and in what time frame?

10. What have we learned from our recent experience that we can apply as we move forward?

ership within the organization. "What else can I do?" still remains at the center of the culture of the Brooklyn District to this day.

REWARDING ACCOUNTABILITY

Winston Churchill once said, "First we shape our structures, and then our structures shape us." That's exactly how you create and sustain greater accountability! If you want accountability to become a lasting and important part of your own organization's culture, you must consciously foster accountability throughout the inner workings of every aspect of your organization.

Even in this age of downsized, dynamic organizations, it's not uncommon to hear people say, "You can't go against the system," "Don't rock the boat," or "You can't fight City Hall." Those comments reflect an assumption that bureaucracy is so strongly entrenched you can't do anything but go along with the status quo. However, creating greater accountability mandates that you change the system so that it reinforces accountability at every turn. That's more easily said than done, of course, because an organization's culture can exert a strong influence on people's behavior. If the culture in any way, either formally or informally, accepts *Below The Line* behavior, that behavior will continue unabated.

To get your accountability program off to the right start, you must begin to recognize and reward the *Above The Line* behaviors, attitudes, and practices you want to see perpetuated across the organization. While this sounds extremely basic, we've all too often seen organizations overlook the astonishing power of this management practice on shaping organizational culture.

You want to ensure that you align the performance appraisal and promotion practices of your organization with rewards for *Above The Line* behavior. Even more importantly, you should strive to recognize all the day-to-day steps people take to move and stay *Above The Line.*

One CEO we advised began devoting a half hour at every senior staff meeting to success stories from his vice presidents. He wanted to hear about his vice presidents' positive experiences coaching others to get *Above The Line.* The fact that he consistently spent time during important senior staff meetings to elicit these stories sent a message both to the staff and to everyone else who heard about the practice that the company really did value coaching and rewarding accountability. As a result, the senior staff improved its own coaching. This CEO had successfully spotted and seized an opportunity to reinforce and reward *Above The Line* behavior throughout the organization.

In another company where we have spent a good deal of time, the senior team chose the regular senior staff meetings as the right place for recognizing and rewarding accountability. Each Friday morning, the senior staff would invite selected people from throughout the organization to attend the meeting and report on their activities. Those invited would spend a lot of time preparing their presentations in the weeks before the meeting, and after the meeting they would engage their colleagues in a lot of discussion about how it went (who said what, who on the senior staff attacked the presenter, etc.). This turned out to be a very visible and dramatic way to prove to the entire organization that top executives really did value *Above The Line* thinking.

To their credit, the senior team knew that their own preparation for the meeting could make a world of difference. That required little effort, really, but it nevertheless represented a major shift in their thinking about their meetings. No longer would they just show up to hear and critique presentations, they would come fully prepared to use the *Steps To Accountability* as a tool to emphasize joint responsibility, detect *Below The Line* attitudes, coach the presenter, and most importantly recognize, praise, and reward *Above The Line* accomplishments.

Each meeting brought new opportunities to point out positive, proactive steps people were taking to achieve results, thus reinforcing the need for risk taking, effective cross-functional coordination, problem solving, and open and candid communication.

The meetings even offered real-time opportunities for the top executives to coach one another *Above The Line.* On one occasion, Joan, the presenter, brought several members of her project team along to help with the presentation because her last presentation had sparked a lot of heated debate. Since she knew that some members of the senior staff thought her project was in trouble, she organized the meeting around ways she and her team could improve the project. After Joan summarized the project's status with a lot of charts, graphs, and statistical analyses, she invited questions from the senior staff. Joan was surprised when one member, Anthony, immediately dropped *Below The Line* and began blaming three people on Joan's team for the lack of progress. However, she was relieved when other members of the senior team pointed out Anthony's slip *Below The Line,* and she was delighted when Anthony quickly brought himself back *Above The Line,* focusing on what else people could do to get results rather than on why they hadn't already done so. Throughout the ensuing discussion, the senior staff emphasized the importance of joint accountability and then used the *Steps To Accountability* to assess the status of the project and to coach Joan and her team on working through some of the problems that plagued their project. Anthony himself shared an example of how he, too, had once been stymied by a similar problem, and he offered to share his experience in more detail after the meeting.

In the wake of the meeting the usual company-wide, grapevine discussions continued to take place, and they took on an even more positive tone. No longer did anyone talk about what the presenter did wrong but only about what everyone had done to speed the organization toward results. Stories also circulated about how senior staff members themselves displayed accountability at meetings. A potentially eroding experience had become a rewarding one for all.

In addition to rewarding accountable behaviors, you can employ six additional culture-creating devices to instill greater levels of accountability in your organization:

SIX CULTURE-CREATING DEVICES

1. Use Trigger Words. Trigger words such as *Above The Line, Below The Line,* and *See It, Own It, Solve It, Do It,* can serve as behavioral cues for those who become familiar with the concepts of *The Oz Principle.* The language associated with the *Steps To Accountability* and the victim cycle can trigger the right response in another person. One client used the four main characters from Oz to develop employee awards called the Ozcars. Employees who best exemplified *See It* behaviors received miniature lions for their courage, those exemplifying *Own It* behavior took home miniature woodsmen for their heart, while miniature scarecrows went to those displaying *Solve It* behaviors, and little Dorothys went to those who best typified *Do It.* This became an annual event employees usually looked forward to, not to mention one that kept the *Oz* trigger words alive in everyone's mind.

2. Tell Inspiring Stories. Stories about falling *Below The Line* and then getting back *Above The Line* can stir people's imaginations. Such concrete examples and anecdotes can make the point much more memorably than any amount of philosophical abstraction. You can use storytelling to clarify what it means to get and stay *Above The Line* and to praise those who have done it. An engineering company organized brown bag lunches every two weeks to address the application of *Oz* principles into its daily work situations. Management started each brown bag lunch by asking the question, "What else can I do?"

During the lunches, leaders and employees discussed problems and told success stories about Seeing It, Owning It, Solving It, and Doing It.

3. Manage by Walking Around. Anyone with supervisory responsibilities can use "management by walking around" (MBWA) to seize opportunities for coaching people *Above The Line*. Another client organized Oz SWAT teams comprised of managers and supervisors who would randomly visit employees to ask them what key results they were working to achieve and how they were stepping *Above The Line* to do so. Depending on the employee's ability to articulate the organization's expected results and his or her own activities related to those results, they would receive awards, such as portable CD players, thirteen-inch color TVs, and DVDs.

4. Use the Framework. In meetings, conversations, written correspondence, contacts with customers, and most all other business activities, you can emphasize the need for people to include accountability in all their thoughts and actions. One client developed SOSD (*See It, Own It, Solve It, Do It*) plans to address pesky problems that the organization needed to tackle. The plans addressed issues of office morale, internal communications between competing departments, career path guidance, and other similar problems simmering below the surface and threatening to pull people *Below The Line*. Reinforcing the *Steps To Accountability*, these plans applied *The Oz Principle* in a highly positive way.

5. Create Role Models. As we have discussed earlier in the book, you want to model accountable behaviors and attitudes. Always set an example for others in your organization and praise those who do likewise. Find and celebrate role models at every level of the organization. One organization implemented the Pinnacle Award to recognize individuals who achieved results by operating on each of the steps *Above The Line*. Award recipients became acknowledged as accountability role models throughout the company.

6. Create *Above The Line* Experiences. Search for opportunities to give people new *Above The Line* experiences. Such experiences especially benefit people who anticipate *Below The Line* responses from you or others in the organization. Consistently creating such experiences will always move the culture

toward higher overall levels of accountability. One restaurant company constantly graded itself on how well people practiced the essential behaviors associated with each step *Above The Line*. General managers of the stores would anonymously submit their grades for both the store and the organization to the regional manager. Those managers, acting as discussion facilitators, would then review with their general managers, in a group setting, the obstacles the grades revealed. The group would thoroughly discuss how to overcome them. As a result of the program, this territory experienced large gains in productivity, and the program went from region to region until the company had established best practices across the board. By visibly and openly evaluating their performance, the management created the experience that accountability applied to everyone.

Used together, these culture-creating devices can make a big difference in speeding up your organization's progress toward higher levels of accountability and, of course, more satisfying results.

HOLDING PEOPLE ACCOUNTABLE

Think about *The Oz Principle* definition of accountability:

A personal choice to rise above one's circumstances and demonstrate the ownership necessary for achieving desired results—to *See It, Own It, Solve It,* and *Do It.*

Central to creating organizational accountability is the process of making, keeping, and accepting responsibility for personal commitments. In the end, personal accountability means that individuals choose to *See It,* decide to *Own It,* personally work to *Solve It,* and then individually commit to *Do It.*

In our work with organizations we hear so much about making and keeping personal commitments. Those who honor them win the admiration of their colleagues; those who shun or break them earn disapproval and anger. If too many fall into the latter category, that organization will suffer from disappointing results and endless rounds of the blame game. In the accountable organization, on the other hand, each and every individual honors his or her own personal commitments in a way that guarantees the best results.

Many organizations we've worked with maintain lists of active projects that continue to grow, while resources remain constant. While projects are added, nothing ever seems to drop from the list. In one instance, an organization found itself with such a bloated list of active new product projects that it was stripping the organization of the focus it needed to complete any of them. The unmanageable list of projects had unmistakably dragged the organization *Below The Line.* The very enormity of the task had sent people running for cover. Personal commitment? How can you commit to the impossible? Accountability looked more like suicide than a life preserver. As we recounted this story to the management team of another company, we were surprised to hear nervous laughter. They admitted with a chuckle that they could do our other client one better: They had 140 projects on their list! When we asked them why they let this happen, they observed that they just keep adding things to the list, expecting that people will figure out priorities on their own. The culture had developed an unspoken rule: "I will support your adding projects to the list as long as you support me by not confronting me when I do not follow through on my growing list." A newfound awareness of the relationship between list making and personal commitment enabled both of these organizations to replace the victim cycle with the *Steps To Accountability.*

As they began weaving accountability into the very fabric of their organizations, people began to follow through on their personal commitments and shrink those ballooning lists of unfinished projects.

It's important for people in the accountable organization to report on progress. As one leader observed: "When progress is measured, progress improves. When progress is measured and reported, improvement accelerates." But how do you do this positively and not punitively? We've developed three helpful guidelines for holding people accountable in a way that does not punish people, but motivates them to stay *Above The Line.* The chart on page 192 summarizes each of these guidelines.

GUIDELINE ONE: CLEARLY DEFINE THE DESIRED RESULT

As we have said before, you can't create accountability without clearly defining results. You can't score a goal if you can't see the goal line. At this stage, you want to talk in terms of results, not just activity. People can easily confuse work with results, particularly when it comes to challenging results. Clearly define desired outcomes by specifically stating what rings the bell. Ask the people you lead to send you a follow-up note to any results-oriented conversation summarizing the results they expect to get.

Holding People Accountable
The Oz Principle® Way

GUIDELINE TWO: DETERMINE A MUTUALLY AGREEABLE TIME FOR A PROGRESS REPORT

When we follow up on people, we lift some responsibility from their shoulders. All too often, a leader will take primary responsibility for the reporting system; i.e., it happens at his request and as a result of his effort. However, when a leader encourages people to suggest the timing of progress reports, the reporting is a function of the accountable person's efforts and actions.

In the typical cycle of making and keeping commitments, people think of the key report as the one they deliver after they've fulfilled the commitment. But such a late report obviously cannot positively affect results. It can only stimulate a reward or a punishment. Have you assigned someone a task, saying to yourself, "Let's see what they can do"? Then, if they succeed, you look smart; if they fail, they look dumb. That's why we much prefer setting people up to succeed by making sure they suggest and accept intermediate reports both you and they can use to influence their progress toward results. When they succeed, everyone wins.

GUIDELINE THREE: DELIVER PRAISE OR COACHING

This step is the perfect opportunity to praise people for progress made and results achieved with a robust, "Well done!" It is also the moment for coaching when results are falling below expectations. During such coaching sessions you might use the *Steps To Accountability* chart to make the discussion as concrete as possible. **Warning!** You must become an expert in asking the question, "What else can you do?" to make further progress toward the desired outcome. When leaders begin offering their own solutions or even solving the problem themselves, they remove accountability from those they're coaching. Avoid this temptation, providing, instead, the direction and coaching that will help people come up with what else *they* can do.

We'd like to share with you one final example of how the process of holding someone accountable worked wonders. It's a true story. Picture a hospital administrator in a busy hospital who oversees the work of a nurse supervisor notorious for her escapades *Below The Line*. After attending *The Oz Principle* training, the administrator challenged her to demonstrate a new attitude in her work. They agreed that she would report back at the end of her shift. This is an actual excerpt of her E-mail to her boss:

Instead of agreeing with the group and participating in negative thoughts, I determined to ask questions to redirect the focus.

A new employee on Saturday stated at 11 P.M. that she had had the worst night of her life and she felt she had no preceptor (i.e., supervisor) all shift. I wanted to go *Below The Line* and point out all the ways myself and the preceptor interacted with her. Instead I walked away for twenty minutes—got my head together and then sought her out. I asked her to talk about how she felt that night, why it was her worst night and why she felt she had no preceptor. We ended up having a twenty-minute discussion and both felt better.

Later, I asked a staff nurse, "How are you doing?" She replied she was sick of things and was ready to walk out very soon. She said this in front of people. I didn't want to know what happened. After avoiding her for a few hours, I went back and said, "You seem frustrated, would you like to tell me about it?" We proceeded to have a good conversation. She apparently had family issues and it truly wasn't related to work or me.

Yes, I find myself *Below The Line* a lot, now that I realize what I am doing. For example, I used to leave certain charting things for the next shift to do, but now I am taking accountability for those things and getting them done before I leave.

Assignments—I am able to direct others to talk to the "change nurse" if the assignment is difficult versus hearing them just complain about it.

I was in a conversation with an employee where the employee was attacking me and my actions. My first reaction was defensive. I then brought myself *Above The Line* by actively listening and finding what the problem was and acted on that. I acknowledged that a staff member was busy and that it was a busy day, however, I initially didn't offer assistance to the individual. I reflected and then brought myself *Above The Line* by giving permission to offer help.

The transforming power of accountability and *The Oz Principle* helps each of us discover within ourselves the ability to achieve the results we want. Accountability, properly administered, can lift individuals and whole organizations to unparalleled heights.

In every organization, opportunities abound for training, coaching, asking questions, rewarding behaviors, and holding people accountable. We suggest you pick one issue that currently beleaguers your organization. By selecting one key issue, you can more dramatically demonstrate the impact of greater accountability.

First, list all those issues facing your organization that have recently caused at least some people to slip or remain *Below The Line*. Possible candidates might include total quality management, product defects, new product development, production schedules, people development, customer satisfaction, customer complaints, budgets, sales quotas, and company reputation. Be sure to identify major issues that relate to you and the people with whom you work most closely.

Second, choose one of the issues from your list and then identify where on the *Steps To Accountability* or in the victim cycle you think you, your team, or your company currently stands. Begin discussing with your superiors, peers, and subordinates what realities everyone must acknowledge (*See It*), what ownership she must achieve (*Own It*), what possible solutions he can implement (*Solve It*), and what actions, exactly, everyone should take (*Do It*).

Third, once you have started to create some awareness of your organization's position relative to this specific issue, decide on the right sequencing and mix of the five culture-creating activities for addressing this particular issue.

Fourth, evaluate the success of your efforts both in terms of results and in terms of people's behavior and attitudes. After this experience, do you find more people in your organization more often thinking, behaving, and working *Above The Line*?

Once you have completed your evaluation, pick another issue or move to a more broad-based approach to getting your organization to live *Above The Line*. Regardless of your next steps, you should remain constantly on the lookout for opportunities to expand the pursuit of accountability in your organization.

Recall the journey along the yellow brick road. After the Scarecrow, the Tin Woodsman, and the Lion had mastered accountability for themselves, they found others eager to benefit from their personal gains. Likewise, as you work to keep yourself and others *Above The Line*, you will undoubtedly find more chances to apply *The Oz Principle* to your organization's toughest issues, the subject of our final chapter.

Chapter 10

SOMEWHERE OVER THE RAINBOW: APPLYING OZ PRINCIPLES TO THE TOUGHEST ISSUES IN BUSINESS TODAY

Then the Witch looked at the big, shaggy Lion and asked, "When Dorothy has returned to her own home, what will become of you?"

"Over the hill of the Hammer-Heads," he answered, "lies a grand old forest, and all the beasts that live there have made me their King. If I could only get back to this forest I would pass my life very happily there."

"My third command to the Winged Monkeys," said Glinda, "shall be to carry you to your forest. Then, having used up the powers of the Golden Cap, I shall give it to the King of the Monkeys, that he and his band may thereafter be free for evermore."

—*The Wizard of Oz,*
L. Frank Baum

The Lion symbolizes courage, and nothing tests your courage more than danger. To meet and conquer danger, of course, you must find the courage to take a risk, a calculated risk to be sure, but one that sets aside your natural desire for safety or comfort and your natural tendency to become a victim of the workplace. In his book *Technological Risk,* University of California professor and risk consultant Harold W. Lewis argues that we have come to fear risk, and that fear, more than anything else, impedes a nation's or a society's progress. "Are we over the peak in our willingness to take risks, which is the only reason we've evolved to the place we are now?" he asks. While Lewis offers his observation within the context of technology, we think his message applies equally well to the softer issues that beset business organizations today.

In our work with hundreds of organizations—from gutsy little start-ups to huge global corporations—we have observed that most of them will, from time to time, shun the risk associated with resolving a number of perennial and costly issues. Consider for a moment the top, unresolved issues in your own organization. What would your list of issues include? How long have they bothered you? What specific steps have you taken to deal with them?

The Latin phrase, *est factum vitae,* means "it's a fact of life." In other words, "It's just the way it is, and since you can't change it, you might as well accept it." *Est factum vitae:* the enemy of change, the number one foe of accountability. Unfortunately, many organizations have made *est factum vitae* an organizational mantra and apply it to those big problems that never seem to go away. Only by tackling and resolving these issues can you hope to increase profits, improve performance, and accelerate growth, not to mention make your company a vibrant and joyful place to work.

Here's our own list of today's top ten most threatening unresolved organizational issues:

1. Poor Communication
2. People Development
3. Empowerment
4. Misalignment
5. Entitlement
6. Work and Personal Life Imbalance
7. Poor Performance

   8. Senior Management Development
   9. Cross-functional Strife
  10. Programitis

These unresolved issues plague the full spectrum of organizations, be they nuclear power plants, financial institutions, retail outlets, insurance companies,
health care providers, fashion designers, construction contractors, computer
manufacturers, fine jewelers, schools, as well as the offices of doctors, lawyers,
and accountants. In some cases, individuals perceive these issues as part of the
inescapable reality of contemporary organizational life. Others dismiss the cost
of remaining *Below The Line* on these issues as inconsequential. In our opinion,
however, these problems are hampering organizations in their quest to become
more competitive, more profitable, and more successful at fulfilling the dreams
of their people, and more capable of achieving world-class results.

   In this chapter we will take a hard look at these issues within the context of
accountability and *The Oz Principle.* While we can shed some light on them,
only you can muster the courage to solve them in your own organization.

ISSUE ONE: POOR COMMUNICATION

Poor communication always stands in the way of results. It has appeared at or
near the top of every list of "what's not working" in all the major organizations
with which we have worked over the last two decades. Every day we hear people
describe the lack of communication between employee and manager, between
one function and another, between one division and another, between team
members, between senior management and middle management, as an ongoing problem that impedes progress. According to Patricia McLagan, author
of *On-the-Level: Performance Communication That Works,* an emphasis on accountability places even more importance on effective communication in the
organization. As McLagan says, "When you are accountable for the work you
and your team are producing, you need to keep all the channels of communication open. You need information constantly on what is working and
what isn't." Conversely, without good communication, accountability cannot
flourish.

   From skyscrapers in any major city, where people talk about the communication problem between the second floor and the eleventh floor, to the geo-
graphically separated sites of headquarters and manufacturing, where people

just don't seem to connect, communication issues abound. We have heard people attribute their communication problems to such physical conditions as different floors, opposite sides of the same building, and even a single wall, but behind these physical barriers we hear the hum of the victim cycle. The more people talk about their communication problems, the clearer it becomes that most of them feel victimized by them. They say they feel unheard, unlistened to, unacknowledged, and uninvolved, choosing to play the blame game, and that others don't understand them, allowing them to duck responsibility. "I am not responsible because I did not know," or "they did not listen."

Ironically, in this so-called information age, with all its high-speed Internet connections, sophisticated telecommunication systems, and video-conferencing capabilities, many people accept poor communication as an organizational reality they feel powerless to correct. Yet, as we hear those same people reflect on the price they pay for poor communication, it becomes painfully clear that they must risk something to change the situation. Otherwise, their organizations will continue to suffer the consequences of missed schedules, delayed products, wrong shipments, incorrect designs, and missed sales. While consulting with one particularly well-known high-fashion apparel company, we couldn't quite get this point across. Rather than face the danger directly, people preferred to wait and see if things would improve over time. Finally, however, when we asked a group of key people to quantify what poor communications with the management group had actually cost them, they concluded that better communication could have saved the company at least $3 million over the past six months. This number drove the message home. Now that the group could *See It,* they could begin working on the problem.

To its credit, this group took action, but in most groups it's surprising how much talk and how little action surrounds a communication problem. One client CEO grew so exasperated hearing his management team talk about a vague communication problem that he issued an edict that no one ever again utter the phrase. Of course, that didn't work, because silence would not make the problem go away, either. He would have been much wiser to stimulate people to go beyond talking about it to doing something about it. Communication problems may be inherent in contemporary organizations, but that does not mean you can't tackle and solve them. In fact, if you leave communication problems unsolved, they will create habitual *Below The Line* behavior, employees who feel victimized, and a granite roadblock to accountability.

What's the value in getting *Above The Line* and solving this problem? When Pfizer bought out Warner Lambert, the company wrestled with the problem of merging the operations of the two companies. In the sales organization, a multitude of questions arose: What should I do about E-mail and voice mail, who does my expense reports, how do I get my money back, and what about sales reports? The post-merger environment was a breeding ground for *Below The Line* behavior. Common complaints included, "We should have had this all ready," "This should have been thought through beforehand," "This isn't working," and "My new manager doesn't know what is going on!" Every level—reps, district managers, regional managers—found themselves thrust onto a communications battlefield. Having adopted *The Oz Principle,* the Pfizer team determined that only an *Above The Line* approach would help everyone take accountability for communication. When people asked post-merger questions, they were urged to ask another set of questions: "What else can I do about it?" and "Who else can I contact to obtain the information I need?" By placing accountability with the person who asked the questions, managers created an organization full of people working to solve the problem, rather than merely complaining about it. Increased dialogue about how to operate post-merger actually helped reduce the amount of change forced on people because they came up with their own systems. When the Pfizer sales organization adopted several of the Warner Lambert approaches, and vice versa, both groups felt comfortable with the resultant mix of best practices. All this came about because Pfizer management demanded a healthy robust dialogue at a time when communication and confusion could have paralyzed everyone. By creating accountability around communication, Pfizer estimated that they kept more than 25 percent more people than they would have kept had the problem persisted. The company reaped huge savings from reduced turnover and greater consistency in its sales territories.

Moving *Above The Line* with respect to communication problems means that you become accountable for how you communicate with other people. First, you must *See It,* acknowledging the cause of a communication breakdown; second, you must *Own It,* determining what you are doing or not doing to cause the problem; third, you must *Solve It,* defining what else you can do to improve communications; and fourth, you must *Do It,* committing yourself to action. While this approach may appear simplistic, we have seen it work. It's not magic, but we guarantee that it will set off a spark that can ignite a chain reaction as others join you *Above The Line.*

ISSUE TWO: PEOPLE DEVELOPMENT

Most executives will agree that people are their organization's most important asset. However, it would astonish those same executives to hear that their people don't believe it. If communication problems rank number one on the list of impediments to organizational progress, then allocating the resources and taking the time to develop people comes in a close second. And if poor communication rankles people, poor personnel development enrages them.

Rather than looking inside themselves for personal accountability in this area, people often blame their lack of advancement on the organization for not creating the requisite systems and programs. Quite often, the blame includes a lack of timely and comprehensive performance appraisals. Just as often, people find fault with their supervisors' inaccessibility, believing that it prevents them from getting and receiving the feedback they need to grow and improve. Inconsistent and unfair job posting practices and ineffective human resource support add to the long list of obstacles to personal development and advancement. Paralyzed by feelings of powerlessness, many people simply wait for future opportunities and hope that someone, someday will ultimately award them with the promised promotions they think they deserve.

On the other hand, we have also seen many individuals, in a variety of companies, climb *Above The Line* with respect to their development. One such individual, a highly qualified and effective industrial engineer we'll call Stuart, received accolades from management for his contributions. However, Stuart never could find a way to play a bigger management role at the manufacturing site he knew so well. After years of waiting for an invitation to move up, and feeling somewhat victimized when it didn't materialize, Stuart decided to step *Above The Line* and actively pursue the opportunity. He made it clear to upper management that he wanted more management responsibility and that he had come up with ideas for what supervisors could do differently to heighten quality, increase efficiency, and improve their own management skills. After sharing that vision with his current production manager, he set about implementing it. Later that same year, when the current production manager accepted a transfer, management gave Stuart the job he had so long desired but only recently pursued. Management later claimed that they had never known Stuart's desires.

While every organization shoulders responsibility for people development and always benefits from understanding the career aspirations of its people, individual employees who allow themselves to feel victimized by a faulty process will seldom move forward an inch. For such individuals, getting stuck *Below The Line* when it comes to their personal development invariably results in missed opportunities for growth, progress, and career advancement. Even in organizations that manage people development poorly, talented and account-able people can still grow, develop, and win promotions if they assume personal accountability for their own progress.

Without question, we agree that joint accountability for people develop-ment should exist between employees and their organizations, but we also be-lieve that individuals at all levels of an organization should take charge of their own development. By functioning *Above The Line,* they will actively look for what more they can do to create their own opportunities for growth. They will pursue classes and training that will prepare them for advancement or in-creased effectiveness in their current jobs, find an appropriate mentor to advise them on a longer-term career path, continually seek feedback on their perfor-mance to measure their overall progress, and constantly ask themselves what else they can do to get the results they want for their careers. Looking at the big-ger picture, they may also work to make sure the organization installs the right systems so the company can improve its ability to develop people. If that sort of attitude grows from the grass roots, it becomes so pervasive that it helps the en-tire organization rise *Above The Line* and own the responsibility to overcome any lethargy or inertia that impedes its investment in developing its most im-portant asset.

ISSUE THREE: EMPOWERMENT

The concept of employee empowerment has received a lot of attention in recent years. Although much has been written and spoken on the subject, we con-stantly hear people throughout organizations blame poor results on a lack of empowerment. For example, two of the questions we hear senior management ask most frequently are: "Why are the directors not directing?" and "Why don't they make decisions, own their areas, and get results?" On the other hand, we often hear directors, managers, and employees question why senior manage-ment does not listen to their input, trust them to make decisions, and empower them to get results; they talk about having the responsibility to accomplish cer-tain goals but not having the necessary authority to get there. At the center of the debate over empowerment lies a great deal of continuing confusion. "Just exactly what does it mean to be empowered?" asks one CEO. "I am so tired of hearing people say that they are not empowered. What more do they want? Everybody wants it, no one seems to know what it means, and nobody feels like they have it. If they don't feel they have what they need to get the job done, then why don't they go out and make it happen? If you have to wait for someone to empower you, then how in the world can you ever be empowered?" Many contemporary managers and leaders echo this frustration.

On the other hand, employees resent what they perceive as management's lofty and dismissive attitude and feel that management should realize that it often withholds from them the authority to direct resources, which, at the root, prevents people from becoming empowered. The confusion mounts as organizations debate whether empowerment requires an invitation or accrues through initiative. While the argument rages, organizations remain stuck *Below The Line,* employees allow themselves to feel like victims of managers, management behaves accordingly, and results get held hostage by indecision and inaction.

The director of a midsized, high-tech company, whom we'll call Mark, found himself in charge of the development of a key new product. Mark got the job because management prized his ability to make things happen, and that's exactly what the development of this new product demanded. Most people in the company saw this move as an incredible career opportunity for Mark, and everyone assumed that Mark would soon become vice president.

However, as Mark launched into the task, one that required a great deal of functional cooperation, he became frustrated with his inability to move ahead as quickly as he had hoped. Over a short period of time, his reputation among teammates suffered as others began to perceive him as a person who demanded that people do things his way. In Mark's mind, empowerment meant doing whatever he felt needed to be done no matter what. He turned into a dictator. Since the organization had given Mark more authority, resources, and autonomy than it had to any other project team leader in its history, Mark felt entitled to say, "If you don't do this by Friday, I will not be responsible for the result." But the empowered dictator let himself off the hook. In essence, Mark relieved himself of accountability whenever he assigned it to someone else. With this attitude, he held the company hostage to his own limited definition of empowerment. Ultimately, Mark left the organization in frustration, and the product he left behind came onto the market two years late.

In our way of thinking, *empowered* to get results and *accountable* for results are two sides of the same coin, but confusion over the meaning of empowerment sometimes blocks the path to getting *Above The Line*. Empowerment has come to be seen as something that someone does to you. We see accountability as something you do to yourself. Why not simply drop empowerment from your vocabulary and replace it with "What else can I do to get the result?" Yes, management should own the responsibility for empowering people throughout the organization, but at some point everyone must realize that, ultimately, you must empower yourself. Rather than focusing on what someone else *should* do for you, focus more on what you *must* do yourself. Rather than shouting, "Empower me!" just ask yourself the question "What else can I do to achieve the result?" and then take the steps to *See It, Own It, Solve It,* and *Do It*.

These steps, if replicated throughout the organization, will yield tremendous benefits in terms of improved results; and, in the end, they will deliver to the company an empowered organization and workplace. Like happiness, empowerment is more of an outcome than it is an activity. It stems from accountable people. You can either get lost in the debate over what it means, or you can take accountability and act to make it happen.

ISSUE FOUR: MISALIGNMENT

Every organization needs a clear focus, a strategy that drives its actions in the marketplace. However, in virtually every company with which we've worked over the past two decades, we have found that different people, and particularly the senior staff, hold quite different views of the organization's overall direction, a misalignment of visions that can permeate every level of the company. Many organizations spend countless hours discussing such strategic questions as "What business are we in?" and "Where are we going?" without forging a clear answer. Without answering such questions, key people and their teams march to the tunes of their own favorite drummers, unaligned on a playing field where ultimate success hinges on everyone marching in the same direction. As a result, teams work tentatively and never forge the full-fledged ownership necessary to bring projects to successful conclusions. Eventually, as more and more projects fail, misalignment flourishes and thrusts a great many people *Below The Line*.

The mid-Atlantic area of Johnson Controls suffered such misalignment before the company decided to implement *The Oz Principle*. Although each function and department had been focusing on meeting its own objectives, that wasn't achieving overall business results. When the company put together proposals and bid on major climate control projects for large buildings, the same problems kept cropping up: Each department and function prepared its piece of the proposal, they combined them all together and submitted them promptly, but the company kept losing out to competitors. According to area manager Allen Martin, "We were so process oriented that we fell into a sort of default mode, just doing the same thing over and over. But the different parts of the organization did not want to change." Market share declined, growth stagnated, morale plunged, and customers grew more and more dissatisfied with the company's performance. As Martin recalled, "People in the different departments were so concerned about covering their tails and documenting the things they'd done to prove their value that it really impeded the organization's ability to be innovative and strategic, and no one was working together to build the business." That's when *The Oz Principle* came aboard. After several months spent building greater accountability around the three strategic thrusts of the organization—grow 15 percent, become number one in the market, and change the business's value proposition—everything started to improve. "15, 1, and change" became the mantra of every department in the organization. Sales, operations, installation, and services all began working together in harmony. "People began rethinking their roles and responsibilities, they started communicating with each other and they got aligned," Martin recounted. "Once everyone had been through the training, they began saying things like 'okay, we need to do something different.'" A jumbled box of puzzle pieces now fit together beautifully as people became more operationally flexible and began building greater trust between departments. The emphasis changed from the tired old excuses and finger pointing to "What else can we do to get the results we want?" "We had to actualize everything that we'd gone through in the *Oz* training," Martin told us in a recent interview. "First we had to *See It*, see what the issues were, what was impeding our ability to *Do It*. We had to look at our situation from each of the *Oz* steps—*See It, Own It, Solve It, Do It*. That's when the accountability plan started to take hold. Everyone seemed to recognize that this was the only way we were going to turn things around—by getting our business *Above The Line* together." In the three years after Johnson Controls implemented the *Oz* training, Allen Martin's mid-Atlantic area sales more than doubled, profitability tripled, customer satisfaction soared, and employee turnover dropped to its lowest level in years. Now the business is chanting, "25, 1, and change!"

While everyone benefits from tightly focused direction and concerted effort in pursuit of a common goal, creating alignment should not fall solely on the shoulders of the top brass. These challenges extend to every facet of an operation. The directors and managers beneath the senior management team can usually see the effects of misalignment quite clearly. They often complain that they seem to be working at odds with their peers throughout the organization, and they cite numerous examples of mixed messages flowing from their superiors about the direction they should pursue in a given situation. The confusion caused by misalignment then trickles all the way down to the mailroom. Such confusion always signals a *Below The Line* attitude. As role models, misaligned managers give license to everyone beneath them to do the same. By allowing confusion to dictate company direction, they breed lack of respect for senior company leadership, not to mention a need for people to be told what to do every step of the way. Eventually, they create victims. Post-evaluations of bankruptcies almost always point to an alignment problem at the top that eventually infested every part of the organization. A close friend of ours worked for International Harvester before it went bankrupt. He still remembers how the misalignment among the company's senior team grew in the years before the bankruptcy from a seed of half-hearted support and whispered criticism of corporate policies into a towering oak of dissatisfaction that eventually gridlocked the entire organization, forcing it into Chapter 11.

Even when management creates alignment, many team leaders fail to communicate the message to their people, somehow assuming that team members will intuitively understand and buy into important decisions they have made. Thus, even when alignment does exist, managers sometimes wait to see if effective and consistent implementation of the desired direction will occur.

Everyone must accept accountability for creating and maintaining alignment within their organization by first acknowledging that failing to do so will keep their organizations *Below The Line,* creating inefficiencies, low morale, stress, finger pointing, and confusion. To get *Above The Line* you should consider the ramifications of every decision and then involve everyone affected in discussion before finalizing the decision. By welcoming a diversity of opinions, suggestions, and perspectives, by utilizing an open decision-making process to determine your course of action, by communicating the aligned message clearly to the rest of the organization, by actively promoting the decision as a collective effort, and by coaching away any misalignments, you can ensure more coherent and cohesive action throughout your organization.

ISSUE FIVE: ENTITLEMENT

Over time, and quite naturally, some people become accustomed to an organization's systems of rewards, benefits, and traditions. From the yearly bonus to periodic celebrations of success, people tend to expect certain events to continue, an expectation that can transform events from meaningful occasions to rights or entitlements the people feel they deserve, no matter what.

As companies seek to become more competitive by changing the way they do business, and as they strive to get closer to their customers, become more efficient, more productive, and more profitable, they find that certain cultural entitlements can do more harm than good. The right to an annual bonus, a routine annual increase in compensation, an eight-to-five workday, regular recognition events, lifetime job security regardless of performance, and other long-established traditions and practices may have served their purposes in the past, but they may undermine the future if people expect them to continue regardless of their level of performance or ability to get results. In time, every organization reaches a point where it must reconsider its entitlements. Unfortunately, when they do so, employees tend to drop *Below The Line*, feeling victimized by the company to such an extent that morale evaporates and people begin questioning their very association with the organization.

Not long ago, we observed a relatively new, fast-growing company as it encountered predictable competitive pressures that slowed its growth rate and weakened its profit picture. In its early years, the company, let's call it Nu Tech, Inc., had soared. Its product had grabbed the number one position in the market, and its profit margins outshone everyone else's in the industry. For employees, Nu Tech seemed like paradise. It operated the best equipment, ran the best computers (one on each desk), offered the best benefits, threw the best parties, and generally promoted a first-class image. When executives traveled, they stayed in luxury hotels and dined at the most exclusive restaurants. Throughout the industry stories of the good life at Nu Tech prompted the best and the brightest in the industry to seek jobs there.

However, when a tough new competitive environment hit Nu Tech, and the company began to implement far-reaching changes that reversed much of what people had come to expect as entitlements, the organization quickly fell *Below The Line*. Each time management questioned or abandoned an entitlement, new victims emerged, each disgruntled that management had taken away something they deserved. No one had ever bothered linking benefits to performance when performance came so easily, so the new emphasis on performance shocked the culture to its roots. Eventually, the people at Nu Tech faced up to the reality that they did not deserve anything they could not produce, but not until after a massive layoff and a precipitous decline in market share forced them to do so.

Every day in the business press you can find an example of a company once known for its lifetime-employment policies, an Eastman Kodak, IBM, or AT&T, that has resorted to laying off people because the company's performance has fallen. To employees conditioned to think of their jobs as a lifelong guaranteed right, the idea that their jobs depend on their company's ability to fund them does not come easily. To help people make that shift, more and more companies are attempting to build employee ownership into their cultures. If employees own their circumstances, they will more readily work to solve problems and guarantee their own continued employment. In today's unforgiving environment, companies must learn how to manage organizational processes in a way that does not disconnect individual accountability from organizational results. They must understand that almost everything they give to employees at any level (with the exception of fundamental values such as fairness, honesty, and respect) flows from individual and organizational performance.

Individual employees can avoid the feelings of victimization that attend the loss of entitlements by viewing all the practices, rewards, and benefits the organization offers as privileges that come by virtue of excellent performance, rather than rights that automatically begin accruing the day you're hired. By striving to ensure that your performance will earn you the rewards you want, and by working to make your organization as productive as possible to create such rewards, you will move yourself *Above The Line*. To paraphrase the Smith Barney commercial, "I get my rewards the old-fashioned way. I earn them."

ISSUE SIX: WORK AND PERSONAL LIFE IMBALANCE

Our work in hundreds of organizations convinced us that most every company struggles with conflicting priorities. These conflicts include: focusing on quantity while at the same time delivering a high degree of quality; hitting short-term target numbers and at the same time thinking long-term strategy; and sacrificing all your time and energy to succeed in business, while spending the time you need to nurture family relationships. We think success in the future will come to those who learn to master such conflicting priorities. To do so, people must view these apparent conflicts not as mixed messages, but as challenges of balance, accomplishment, and growth. Perhaps the most difficult of them all is that of creating a balance between work and personal life.

The World Health Organization recently called job stress a worldwide epidemic. Work-life balance has become a hot topic in most organizations and the rising generation, those hitting the job market today, clearly prefers better balance to more salary. Still, most everyone deals with the threat of burning out in their job because of personal work life imbalance. From the Monster.com and MSN Careers Web site, Bill Delano, founder of an Internet service that provides confidential, individualized advice via E-mail to those experiencing job stress, provides some suggestions, a few of which align perfectly with *The Oz Principle.*

See It. What, exactly, is stressing you out? Is it your job? Your home life? Your relationships? Without knowing the root of the problem, you cannot hope to resolve it. If you find it difficult to pinpoint the source of your stress, seek professional help from your Employee Assistance Program or a mental health professional.

Own It. Try not to personalize any criticism you receive. Look at negative comments as constructive help that allows you to improve your work. If, however, the criticism is verbally abusive; e.g., your boss yells at you or uses vulgar language, discuss this problem with your manager or human resources department.

Solve It. Recognize the difference between elements at work and at home that you can control and ones you cannot. Make a list of these two categories. Starting today, promise yourself to stop stressing about uncontrollable aspects of your job. Delegate or share work whenever possible. Don't fall into the trap of thinking you are the only person who can do the job right. Your coworkers and boss might start to buy into that concept as well.

Do It. Take note of all the good work you do and give yourself credit for it. Set short-term goals, rewarding yourself when you achieve them. Although you do want to learn how to manage a stressful job, sometimes it makes more sense to leave it. How can you determine when it's time to throw in the towel? When:

- You've tried all the appropriate channels and methods for resolving your situation to no avail (or the appropriate channels don't even exist).
- Your boss treats you in ways that you find intimidating, disrespectful, or demeaning.
- You feel so bored on the job that you come home exhausted at the end of the day. If you cannot see an upwardly mobile career path that challenges you to grow professionally, you should probably look for a more interesting position.

As more and more companies embark on programs of downsizing, delayering, and parallel pathing in an effort to enhance productivity and profitability, employees who survive the organizational reengineering find themselves under even more pressure to do more with less. In most cases, more with less equals stress. During our consulting engagement with scores of such organizations, we have heard a lot of talk about the tremendous stress that major changes can cause, with most of the concern centering on the dilemma of balancing a successful career with a fulfilling personal life. John Sculley, former CEO of Apple Computer, told *USA Today,* "A good night's sleep is a remnant of agrarian and industrial ages. The information age, with easy communication around the globe and constant access to changing data, is making a night's sleep a thing of the past. It's a 24-hour day, not an 8-to-5 day." *USA Today* reporter Kevin Maney went on to say, "A few executives share Sculley's wide-eyed approach. President Clinton often gets by on a couple hours of sleep. David Johnson, CEO of Campbell Soup, works throughout a twenty-four-hour day so he can keep track of worldwide operations." In this same article, Maney asks, "Is Sculley's routine the model for The New Millennium executive, or is it just weird? While John Sculley may be an extreme example, there is a trend toward longer hours and less free time. If your company has downsized or flattened itself to save resources, you may expect to work longer hours, extend your average workweek, and find all too little time for family, friends and recreation."

Organizational life can disrupt your family and personal life so much that you can easily start feeling taken advantage of and betrayed by the company to which you have pledged your heart and soul. And increasingly in corporate America organizations are expecting people to give more and more of their time to work, leaving less time for home and loved ones. Learning to balance the two will take just as much time and effort as solving any major business problem.

One of our clients dealt head on with a similar kind of problem. The company's senior management team understood the added pressures their employees faced as they worked to bring several new products to market. But rather than just wait for the situation to change, they decided to do something about it. Aware that their people were sacrificing the quality of their personal lives for the company, the management team invited candid feedback so they could understand exactly how people felt about the situation. Then the management team met and talked at length about the increased pressures on employees. After some tough deliberation, they agreed to make balancing personal and professional life one of the six corporate beliefs that would guide their organizational culture. As a result, any employee could say no to a late-night meeting without fear of retribution. If someone seemed to feel that saying no would evidence disloyalty, a manager would quickly send that person home with a pat on the back. In effect, the company promised to support its people if they assumed their own accountability for what they chose to do and not to do. We admired their handling of the issue. Full of young, aspiring, professional people who want to make a difference and succeed, the company has turned in incredible growth and profits, all the while nurturing a culture imbued with accountability for both corporate and personal goals.

Resource constraints will continue to rule business life. Few organizations can escape the reality of a world where you must do more with less. To avoid falling *Below The Line* on this issue, management must acknowledge the personal price it asks its employees to pay and then work to find ways to help them correct any imbalance.

By the same token, employees must get *Above The Line* and own their own circumstances. The storm of change will not abate. The average workweek will grow longer. More will be required of everyone. Understanding this reality will help you adjust to it, making the personal and professional trade-offs that work best for you.

ISSUE SEVEN: POOR PERFORMANCE

Throughout this book we have talked about the pivotal role feedback plays in creating high levels of accountability within an organization. Yet it continually amazes us that few organizations establish an environment that fosters the free flow of feedback. In such cases, obviously, you cannot expect to confront poor performance skillfully or coach performance effectively. By failing to confront poor performance, organizations unwittingly foster feelings of victimization among people who do perform poorly, but don't know it and thus can't affect improvements, as well as among people who must pick up the slack because of the poor performance of others. Poor performance leads to poor results, and poor results keep entire organizations *Below The Line*.

When we urge executives, managers, and supervisors to confront this problem, they tend to cite several reasons for failing to deal with performance issues: the specter of lawsuits by poor performers who claim wrongful dismissal, a reluctance to hurt people's feelings, the difficulty of establishing a fair but effective review process, a tendency to shy away from time-consuming documentation, and a general fear of the risk involved in confronting poor performance. Others cite loyalty to coworkers as a transcendent cultural code—a twisted application of the golden rule (be nice to them, and others will be nice to you), while still others cite a lack of training on how to handle such situations, especially when they themselves hate confrontation. A few organizations even claim that they enjoy sufficient resources to carry nonperformers whose efforts neither hurt nor help much, but even those companies end up paying a price eventually.

Everyone has heard about a person who suffered great trauma when fired from one job, but after grueling months of searching, found another, even more suitable job. One such case occurred with a young MBA, whom we'll call Ted. Ted was very aggressive and had set his eyes on a marketing management position that he hoped to attain in relatively short order. He accepted any and every project with great enthusiasm and worked nights and weekends to do everything better and faster than it had ever been done before. To get things done quickly, Ted applied a great deal of pressure to coworkers and soon developed an abrasive style that seemed to get results. In particular, he insulated his own project teams from the demands and needs of other parts of the organization to fulfill his own fast-track objectives. Ted's projects received a great deal of praise within the company as they came in on time and under budget, and Ted's apparent ability to get results won him distinction as the best marketing project leader in the company's history.

However, in the midst of all this glory, Ted's boss, along with several other senior managers, grew deeply concerned about Ted's actual performance. The way he ran roughshod over people and destroyed relationships would, management felt, eventually undermine his effectiveness, but rather than confront Ted over these issues, they decided to let Ted learn his lesson the hard way (besides, rocking the boat might undermine the results he was turning in). Shunning the uncomfortable prospect of confronting Ted over his style and coaching him beyond it, they let him run loose, hoping he'd end up learning the error of his ways all on his own.

Over time, however, Ted's behavior grew worse, not better, as he continued to burn bridges and force outcomes. Eventually, the head of the department began privately approaching Ted's boss demanding that she do something about Ted's abrasiveness. When Ted's boss did finally sit Ted down to offer him specific feedback on the problem, Ted blew up: "I thought results were the only thing that mattered around here!" Now he felt betrayed and confused. "Why didn't you say something earlier?" he demanded. As it turned out, the feedback came too late, as Ted concluded that he could never be happy in this organization. He left, but to his credit, he took a greater awareness of himself to his next job, where, after a few short years, he forged a reputation not only as a guy who gets results, but as one who get results as a respectful team player. Ted eventually won. But his original organization paid a price by losing their investment in all the learning and experience they had given Ted. Had they dealt with performance issues in a proper and timely way, they would have saved themselves more than just money.

We strongly believe management must learn how to confront poor performance in a precise, constructive, and supportive way. By dealing head on with this universal issue, you can move more surely *Above The Line*, improving results while at the same time making people happier. Very simply, you must learn to tackle poor performance when you see it and accept constructive feedback when you receive it, and you must develop a culture that encourages this behavior in others. If you pretend the issue doesn't exist, or wait to see if it will solve itself, stop right now. Make confronting performance a daily habit. Don't let the problems build and get handed down from one generation of managers to the next.

ISSUE EIGHT: SENIOR MANAGEMENT DEVELOPMENT

Who will tell the emperor that he has no clothes? Many of the CEOs and senior managers we know lament the loneliness of leadership, and most would agree that they receive too little feedback on their effectiveness, style, or overall impact on their organizations. However, if a senior manager thinks he or she cannot affect the flow of feedback, that opinion reflects a true *Below The Line* attitude. We have heard leaders in all types of organizations say, "No matter how much I ask my people for feedback, I just cannot get them to muster up the courage to give it to me straight." Given the fact that employees also tend to function *Below The Line* on this issue, believing that coaching senior management can spell career suicide, senior managers would do well to take the first step by opening themselves up to such coaching. If they don't learn to do so in these perilous times, they stand to lose everything they have worked so hard to achieve. It's happening to Steven Jobs, for the second time. Several years ago, *The Wall Street Journal* reported, "His computer company, NeXT Inc., stopped making computers. In March (of 1993), his president and his chief financial officer quit. Then, several big computer makers—some of which he had hoped would use his software—formed a software alliance that excluded NeXT." Just as happened at Apple Computer, the company he founded and eventually lost to John Sculley, Steven Jobs's unwillingness to receive feedback may have destroyed any opportunity for him to attain stardom once again. "His insistence on complete control over a project with IBM, for example, doomed a 1989 agreement that would have lent Big Blue's backing to NeXT's software. And, he lost valuable time last year when he ignored advisors' repeated warnings that NeXT couldn't compete in hardware and should become a software company." The result of Steven Jobs's inability to welcome coaching "amounts to a steep fall from a very lofty perch." According to the same article, "His NeXT workstation seems destined to become a high-tech museum relic. He himself is fighting to show he still matters in the computer industry." According to Richard Shaffer, editor of *Computer Letter*, "People have stopped paying attention to him; it's sad."

But that wasn't the end of the story. Alan Deutschman sets the record straight in his book, *The Second Coming of Steven Jobs*. Two years after his premature postmortem in *The Wall Street Journal*, Steven Jobs rose "triumphant, vindicated and far richer than before." He had learned how to take the criticism and grow from it. "His stunning redemption came from an unexpected source: It turned out that he owned another company, Pixar, which struggled quietly for a decade. In November 1995, Pixar released the first full-length computer-animated feature film, *Toy Story*." His stake in the company was valued at over a billion dollars. A year later he returned to Apple. Then, "in the summer of 1997 he took the title of interim chief executive officer and became the company's unexpected savior. He propelled Apple's stock price from $13 a share to $118 a share." Steven Jobs's experience should convince anyone of the value of candid feedback for everyone, especially those at the top.

Both employees and senior management must accept the fact that feedback creates accountability. Every action by a member of senior management affects the organization, and, being human, every senior manager possesses both strengths and weaknesses. No company can grow unless the senior managers grow. And the CEO is not immune; he or she must also grow. If they do not, either the organization will falter or it will outgrow them. The best senior managers not only search for ways they can improve their performance, they encourage those around them to tell them the truth, no matter how painful.

Most leaders really do want feedback from their people. Consider a case in point, Ginger Graham, then president and CEO of Advanced Cardiovascular Systems, who began her tenure as president of the company by soliciting candid feedback from all levels of the organization on how both she and the company could grow in the future. People who would have otherwise ducked the danger inherent in offering a new CEO honest feedback eagerly accepted the risk. Graham went out of her way to follow up on all feedback, letting people know how much she valued it and describing exactly how she was going to use it to improve herself and ACS. And she did. In fact, in an article Ginger wrote in the *Harvard Business Review* entitled, "If you want Honesty, Break Some of the Rules," she described the feedback process we helped her take her team through. One by one, each member of the team would sit on a tall stool and receive both appreciative and constructive feedback on their performance. The person in the hot seat could only listen. As Ginger recounts, "The stool exercise sounds cruel, but it is just the opposite. It is probably the most powerful tool for building mutual accountability and honest communication I've ever seen . . . and when I sat on it, I found out how much my managers cared about me and wanted me to succeed." Ginger gets feedback because she holds herself accountable to ask for it and to provide it.

We urge CEOs to follow Ginger's lead and assume personal accountability for obtaining feedback by making it widely known that they want it and value it. Openly thanking those who give them "tough" feedback will cause others to do likewise. For their part, employees must overcome the fear of risk and tell inquiring senior managers what they really need to hear.

ISSUE NINE: CROSS-FUNCTIONAL STRIFE

Marketing versus manufacturing, manufacturing versus research and development, R & D versus sales, and sales versus the world. Sound familiar? We see it everywhere we go: cross-functional strife. In fact, these battles have become something of a tradition in organizational life, even though they represent one of the most shortsighted *Below The Line* occurrences in business today. Why can't corporate functions rise *Above The Line* and finally recognize, to misquote Pogo, that "we have met the enemy, and the enemy is *not* us"?

One organization we worked with came to a virtual standstill as the research and development department and the marketing department waged a feud that would have made the Hatfields and the McCoys look like kids quarrelling in a sandbox. Each of the combatants consistently worked as if the other were its nemesis. The vice presidents literally hated each other and openly discussed their disdain for one another's style and competence with their respective management teams. As a result, this company, which once led its industry in product innovation, failed to turn out any breakthrough products for an entire year. Furthermore, the products that did make it to market came in way over budget and far behind schedule. We could clearly see that the future of the entire organization depended on the two departments getting *Above The Line* and bringing the blame game to a screeching halt. It took a year, but vigorous application of *The Oz Principle* resulted (after more than a little stress and strain) in a renewed sense of cooperation and camaraderie. "We were nuts," one vice president told us later. "We were both in the same boat, but were doing our level best to sink each other. We still get into tussles over priorities, but now we're at least rowing in the same direction."

This scenario repeats itself every minute of every working day in thousands of organizations. However, you can eliminate cross-functional strife more easily than you think. All it takes is a constant reminder that your organization's real enemy is not Joe or Sally down the hall, but your mistaken assumption that Joe or Sally is not on your team. *Above The Line* leadership requires people and functions across the organization to acknowledge the reality that the market will not forgive the damage caused by cross-functional strife. People and functions must give each other the benefit of the doubt and the feedback essential to making appropriate and necessary performance improvements. They must step out of their functional "silos" and create a correlated effort between departments based on a productive give-and-take attitude that can drive a concerted focus on producing the greatest good for the company. As Pogo might have put it, "We have met the enemy, and the enemy is our own divisiveness."

Remember ALARIS Medical Systems and their incredible turnaround? It was carrying a backlog of nine thousand instruments, with five thousand spare parts on order, and disposable fill rates below 85 percent, all in the face of declining revenues. Key to turning around their poor performance, eliminating backorders, achieving dramatically improved product quality, and maintaining a twenty-four-hour delivery rate of 99.8 percent, were a series of cross-functional feedback sessions held between operations, sales, customer care, quality and service, where individuals confronted the group with hard facts that many did not want to hear. These sessions helped everyone to *See It* and build greater cooperation. Sally Grigoriev, a vice president with ALARIS, said, "The sessions were the equivalent of 'walk a mile in my shoes' in both directions!" The prior adversarial relationship between operations and customer care disappeared. Sally describes, "Now when there is an issue, people pick up the phone. Before, people didn't pick up the phone because they did not know each other. Since that meeting, we've had customer care down to tour the plant, something they had never done before. Now, they understand our processes, have a feel for how things work, and have put faces with names." The organization began measuring order fulfillment on a daily basis, a measurement the entire organization received daily by E-mail. This measurement showed performance during the last twenty-four hours. People saw it. In the past, hundreds of late orders on a daily basis came to no one's attention. Since beginning the candid and open cross-functional meetings, just one late order will send people scurrying to coordinate resolution of the problem between all the different functions. On this point Sally said, "It is just the most amazing transformation you have ever seen."

When people hurdle the natural barriers of functional expertise and preferences and align themselves for the common good, powerful forces go to work, forces that can affect performance in dramatic ways. Getting *Above The Line* to capture these advantages should preoccupy every leader and team.

ISSUE TEN: PROGRAMITIS

A disease has spread throughout corporate America, a disease we call *programitis*. Its symptoms include every new program or fad that comes down the road. A complete list of all the management fads that have come down the road in the last twenty years would look like the Manhattan telephone directory. A short list of the most popular ones might include: strategic planning, total quality management, just-in-time manufacturing, breakthrough innovation, total customer satisfaction, learning organizations, core competencies, business reengineering, zero-based budgeting, flat organizations, self-management, team-driven leadership, humble leadership, and creative destruction. In a classic *Sloan Management Review* article entitled, "Consulting: Has the Solution Become Part of the Problem?" authors Shapiro, Eccles, and Soske make this observation: "Fad surfing—riding the crest of the newest panacea and then paddling out just in time to ride the crest of the next one—has been big business over the past twenty years. . . . Each of these concepts comes with a prepackaged set of tools, many of which existed previously and which have been repackaged and marketed as 'The Answer' to competitiveness." Over the years we've watched many fads come and go, leaving little more than a ripple in their wake. AT&T, for example, laid off one thousand out of sixty-six hundred employees at a factory that won the Malcolm Baldrige National Quality Award. The factory, which makes transmission systems equipment, including hardware used by phone and cable TV companies, blamed the layoffs on slow sales and technological advances. The Wallace Company, another winner of the same award, filed for Chapter 11 just two years later! No matter how you look at this situation, it's obvious that total quality management alone does not prevent a thousand people from losing their jobs, check a factory's sales decline, or deal with the human side of technological advancement.

Back when American companies were emulating the Japanese, *The Wall Street Journal* reported that "Some American manufacturers are discarding billions of dollars of investment they made in the 1980s to adopt Japanese manufacturing ideas. They haven't decided that the Japanese systems don't work. Rather, they realize that some of those systems, however useful in lifting productivity in Japan, haven't achieved much in their own plants." So, if the Japanese fad did not produce lasting value for most American manufacturers, where do we turn next? The *Journal* article continues, "Federal-Mogul Corp., deciding that its automation had gone too far, has removed much of the fancy equipment at an auto-parts plant, and General Motors Corp. is now relying more heavily on 'people power.' Whirlpool Corp. has soured on Japanese-style 'quality circles' as a means of tapping employees' ideas, and General Electric Co. and Corning Inc. have turned to other ways of tapping employee ideas. Losing favor at some companies is the Japanese 'just-in-time' system of minimizing inventory by having suppliers deliver parts only as needed."

In the field of computer technology, where changes come at lightning speed, downsizing has become the latest fad. According to William Zachman, the columnist and industry watcher credited with coining the term *downsizing* in an earlier *Wall Street Journal* article, "People have gone overboard on the concept. It's like people, upon first hearing about electricity, stuck their finger in the light socket to check it out. It's become a mindless fad." Even companies with a lot of experience in managing technology have made silly mistakes by pursuing downsizing and rightsizing programs that produce more confusion than results. The problem, as we see it, is that any number of management philosophies and techniques can and do produce results, but too many organizations look for the wizard's magic in the latest one, when, in fact, results will only come through a unified sense of accountability for results throughout the organization. We feel strongly that organizations must find a cure for programitis, part of which involves paying attention to the basic fact that most anything will work if you get *Above The Line* and use your head. Act with courage, maintain a stout heart, and keep your eye on the main objective, whether you want to "get back to Kansas," bring products to market faster, or fulfill the true needs of customers. The benefits will more than please you.

REAPING BENEFITS *ABOVE THE LINE*®

As we conclude this journey, we'd like to show some final examples of clients that have benefited greatly from getting *Above The Line* and staying there. Precor, one of the largest fitness manufacturers in the United States, has built a global reputation for innovation and excellence in fitness equipment quality and customer service. Despite a clear history of entrepreneurial success, they never felt satisfied merely staying in place. Rather, they strove constantly to step up to the next level and achieve even greater results by transforming their entire culture into one of accountability and focusing even more tightly on innovation, results, and product development. In Precor's 2003 All-Employee Kick-Off, President Paul J. Byrne stated, "The world's a mess, the economy is slow and the weather is bad (the company is in Seattle). We're simply not going to accept any of these old excuses anymore."

After fifteen months of focused, concerted effort to transform their culture, imbue accountability in everyone, and improve business operations, Precor recorded their best year ever: increasing revenues by 13 percent, and profitability by 66 percent, while substantially increasing their service measures. These performance improvements did not come because the company has slumped. To the contrary, the improvements came because a highly effective organization knew that it could always accomplish more by rigorously applying *The Oz Principle.*

Indiana-based Eli Lilly & Company struggled with the public perception that they were not supporting minority owned business in their home state. For years, company officials would say: "We try to get minority business, we've sent out proposals, we've waited here with the paperwork and have been willing and would be pleased to work with anyone who came in and took the job." Then, dedicating itself to getting *Above The Line* on this issue, the company decided to stop waiting for something to happen, and, instead, go out and make it happen. Members of Lilly's capital project engineering group sat down with a long-time supplier, Jacobs Engineering, to plan how they could actually help create a minority owned business. They concluded that a start-up business could quickly grow into a full-line firm that would not only work for Lilly but for other companies as well. The CEO of Jacobs Engineering gave Lilly's capital projects engineers total support, stating that they would provide work process and procedures and help line up needed investors in Indianapolis to start this firm from scratch. For its part, Lilly committed that it would pay the new firm within fifteen days instead of the thirty-five days afforded to other vendors. In a short period of time, they lined up the needed investors to start a small minority-owned engineering firm. During the first year, this firm billed over $3.5 million worth of engineering service fees in the Indianapolis area. Again, we see a high performing organization benefit from greater accountability by driving beyond the expected to deliver unexpected results. Operating *Above The Line* opens doors that cause things to happen, things that would never, ever happen *Below The Line.*

One last example comes from AmerisourceBergen, a wholesale pharmaceutical and health care supply and service company. Not long ago the company faced a situation not uncommon in the business world, the loss of a significant national account. People in the organization found themselves wrestling with the dilemma that every reader of this book encounters most every day in one form or another: Do you fall *Below The Line* and justify a setback by ignoring, denying, blaming, and finger pointing; or do you go *Above The Line,* acknowledging the reality, and find a way to get the result in spite of the setback. Rallying the company with a sense of ownership and accountability, AmerisourceBergen's management team helped to inspire a *Solve It* mentality within the organization. People at every level, however remote from sales their job may have seemed, began asking what else they could do to ensure results. With that mind-set, some people came up with ways to cut costs, while others found ways to increase revenue.

Impressively, this organization set out to replace the business they knew they were going to lose *before* they actually lost it. With their focus on "What else can we do?" they added, in just the three months prior to the anticipated loss of business, sixty-seven new accounts and replaced approximately 70 percent of the projected loss. Accountability begins with clearly defined results, people committed to operating *Above The Line* and leaders who relentlessly reinforce that culture. While each of these three stories reflects a variety of results and circumstances, they all share one common moral: accountable people working together can achieve almost anything.

THE UNENDING JOURNEY

So, we arrive at the end of the book. The Lion has found his courage, the Tin Woodsman his heart, the Scarecrow his brain, and Dorothy has awakened safely at home with Auntie Em. And, if we've accomplished our own mission in these pages, you're well on the road to accountability, applying *The Oz Principle* to every aspect of your life and work.

Remember, only when you assume full accountability for your thoughts, feelings, actions, and results can you direct your own destiny; otherwise someone or something else will.

As a final note, just inside the cover of one of the many sequels to *The Wiz-*

ard of Oz, the publisher, Del Rey Books, printed the following message to readers: "When we mention Oz to people who haven't grown up with the books, they nod, mention Judy Garland and think they know all there is to know about Oz. How wrong they are!" We echo that sentiment as we write the end of our own book. There's a lot to learn in Oz. Enjoy the lifelong journey.

THE BEGINNING . . .

OVERVIEW OF *JOURNEY TO THE EMERALD CITY*

In addition to the best-selling book *The Oz Principle,* Roger Connors and Tom Smith are also the authors of *Journey to the Emerald City: Implement the Oz Principle to Achieve a Competitive Edge Through a Culture of Accountability.*

Journey to the Emerald City builds upon the principles introduced in *The Oz Principle* and guides the reader through the shifts that must occur in order to successfully create a culture of accountability. Connors and Smith establish a direct link between a company's culture and the results it produces, and provide a clear road map for accelerating the move to a *Culture of Accountability*®. *Journey to the Emerald City* gives the reader tools they can use to accelerate the transition, and provides impactful and motivating accounts of the success that other companies have achieved by implementing the principles described in the book.

Connors and Smith, who are also cofounders of *Partners In Leadership,* LLC, commented, "We have seen companies achieve extraordinary results, and they attribute their success to implementing the concepts found in the book. *Journey to the Emerald City* provides useful tools and methodologies to help leaders, in any industry, create the organizational culture they need to achieve results."

One client that has had substantial success in creating a *Culture of Accountability* is Eli Lilly and Company. Sidney Taurel, Chairman and CEO, said of *Journey to the Emerald City:*

> The transformation of corporate culture—perhaps the most important single leadership challenge facing organizations today—has largely eluded the recent wave of performance improvement innovations. In *Journey to the Emerald City,* Connors and Smith fill this gap by taking another impressive step in outlining how their processes for cultural change work not only in theory but also in practice. This volume provides hands-on, concrete tools for helping organizations fulfill their potential.

Partners In Leadership offers *Cultural Transition Process* services based on the concepts presented in *Journey to the Emerald City*. To learn more about *Partners In Leadership's Cultural Transition Process*, or to purchase copies of *Journey to the Emerald City*, please contact *Partners In Leadership* at:

phone: 800-504-6070
Web: www.ozprinciple.com
E-mail: pil@ozprinciple.com

THE OZ PRINCIPLE®
Accountability Training

THE FIRST STEP TO
CREATING A *CULTURE OF ACCOUNTABILITY*®

Partners In Leadership, LLC, is the world-wide leader in *Accountability Training®* services and technologies. We have helped hundreds of companies experience phenomenal results directly attributable to the training. *Partners In Leadership's Accountability Training* services are available in a wide variety of formats, ranging from one-day workshops to keynote speaking engagements to national sales meetings.

The Oz Principle Accountability Training derives from the best-selling book, *The Oz Principle;* however, the training provides important skills and essential methodologies not presented in the book.

OBJECTIVES OF THE TRAINING

1. Create greater accountability and ownership for key organizational results.
2. Use the *Steps To Accountability®* to assist people in operating *Above The Line®*.
3. Learn critical skills for operationalizing a positive approach to accountability.
4. Develop *Team* and *Individual Accountability Plans* that ensure commitment and follow-up to achieving desired organizational results.

Partners In Leadership has worked with organizations of all sizes in many different industries. Our client list includes hundreds of companies such as Pfizer, ADP, Microsoft, Eli Lilly & Company, LensCrafters, Office Depot, BP Amoco, Paine Webber, Nestle Purina, Marriott, Johnson Controls, AT&T Wireless and numerous departments of the U.S. Government. *Partners In Leadership* has helped these organizations, and many others, achieve extraordinary results, some of which you have read about in this book.

For more information, or to begin *The Oz Principle Accountability Training* at your organization, please contact *Partners In Leadership* at:

Phone: 800-504-6070
Web: www.ozprinciple.com
E-mail: pil@ozprinciple.com

INDEX

ABOUT THE AUTHORS

Roger Connors and Thomas Smith are the principals and founders of *Partners In Leadership*, LLC, a leadership training and management consulting firm that has implemented *The Oz Principle®* over the last decade within hundreds of organizations in nearly every major industry. The universal appeal of *The Oz Principle* has been recognized throughout the world and has been implemented at every conceivable level of the organization, including wide application to the senior executive team.

After receiving their MBAs from Brigham Young University, the authors have spent the last two decades pioneering and perfecting the implementation of the principles embodied in *The Oz Principle*. Through their internationally acclaimed *The Oz Principle® Accountability Training*, their organization has assisted tens of thousands of leaders in their quest to achieve specific and often extraordinary results. Their experience in assisting senior management teams in creating greater accountability throughout their organizations has made them leaders in the arduous struggle to achieve results through empowerment, employee involvement, continuous improvement, and a *Culture of Accountability*. An overview of *The Oz Principle Accountability Training Workshop*, offered by *Partners In Leadership*, appears on page 225. Roger and Tom have also written *Journey to the Emerald City: Implement the Oz Principle to Achieve a Competitive Edge Through a Culture of Accountability*.

Craig Hickman is the author or coauthor of a dozen books, among them such best-sellers as *Creating Excellence; Mind of a Manager, Soul of a Leader; The Strategy Game*, and *The Organization Game*. He founded the Management Perspectives Group, whose clients included some of the largest domestic and international companies. Currently, he is CEO of Headwaters Technology Innovation Group, a subsidiary of Headwaters Incorporated (Nasdaq: HDWR). He earned his MBA with honors from the Harvard Business School.